Fodor's InFocus

CHARLESTON

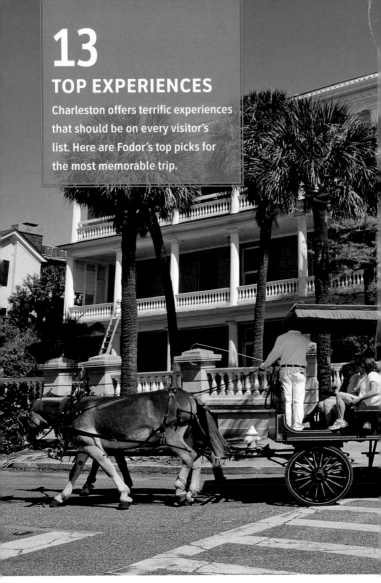

13
TOP EXPERIENCES

Charleston offers terrific experiences that should be on every visitor's list. Here are Fodor's top picks for the most memorable trip.

1 Carriage Ride

Get your bearings the fun way with a carriage ride through the historic district. You'll soak up history, lore, and architectural tidbits all while enjoying amazing views. *(Ch. 1)*

2 White Point Gardens and the Battery

The tip of Charleston's peninsula has been home to everything from strolling ladies in hoopskirts to booming Civil War cannons. Today the stunning view of the harbor remains, along with a regal oak allée. *(Ch. 2)*

3 Old Slave Mart Museum

Charleston was the main point of entry into America for enslaved people in the 18th and 19th centuries. Visit this museum (and one-time slave auction house) for a detailed telling of their journey. *(Ch. 2)*

4 Sullivan's Island

Drive 20 minutes north of town to this slow-paced island. Family friendly and mellow, the beaches are edged in dunes and maritime forests. *(Ch. 6)*

5 Sweetgrass Baskets

"Sewn" from sweet-smelling plants that line the Lowcountry's marshes, these baskets were first made to winnow rice. The designs can be traced to West African countries. *(Ch. 7)*

6 USS *Yorktown*

Charleston's naval history is long, and Patriot's Point on the Charleston Harbor offers three amazing (and retired) ships for tours: the aircraft carrier USS *Yorktown*, the destroyer USS *Laffey*, and the submarine USS *Clamagore*. *(Ch. 2)*

7 King Street

Shop for antiques, artisan candy, fashion, jewelry, and home goods at hip local boutiques and superior national chains on King Street. The two-mile mecca is Charleston's hottest shopping and dining area. *(Ch. 7)*

8 The Wreck of the Richard and Charlene

Named after an old shrimp boat, this seafood dive on Shem Creek is home to famed fried grits, red rice, okra, and fresh-off-the-docks crab, shrimp, and fish. *(Ch. 3)*

9 Drayton Hall

Head 40 minutes out of town to explore this rare, still-standing pre-Revolutionary plantation home on the banks of the Ashley River. *(Ch. 2)*

10 Fort Sumter National Monument

Take the boat tour to this fort in the harbor to see where the first shots of the Civil War were fired in 1861. You can also learn about the lives of the Federal and Confederate troops who occupied it. *(Ch. 2)*

11 Regional Cuisine

A national culinary destination, Charleston has talented chefs who offer innovative twists on traditional Lowcountry cuisine. Pull up a chair at Husk, where James Beard Award-winning Sean Brock wows diners. *(Ch. 3)*

12 Spoleto Festival USA

Visit in late May and early June for Spoleto Festival USA's flood of indoor and outdoor performances by international luminaries in opera, music, dance, and theater. *(Ch. 5)*

13 Nathaniel Russell House Museum

Go behind closed doors at this mansion-turned-museum to wander around grand parlors and drawing rooms, and learn about antebellum life in Charleston. *(Ch. 2)*

CONTENTS

ABOUT THIS GUIDE

Fodor's Ratings

Everything in this guide is worth doing—we don't cover what isn't—but exceptional sights, hotels, and restaurants are recognized with additional accolades. Fodor'sChoice ★ indicates our top recommendations. Care to nominate a new place? Visit Fodors.com/contact-us.

Trip Costs

We list prices wherever possible to help you budget well. Hotel and restaurant price categories from $ to $$$$ are noted alongside each recommendation. For hotels, we include the lowest cost of a standard double room in high season. For restaurants, we cite the average price of a main course at dinner or, if dinner isn't served, at lunch. For attractions, we always list adult admission fees; discounts are usually available for children, students, and senior citizens.

Hotels

Our local writers vet every hotel to recommend the best overnights in each price category, from budget to expensive. Unless otherwise specified, you can expect private bath, phone, and TV in your room. For expanded hotel reviews visit Fodors.com.

Restaurants

Unless we state otherwise, restaurants are open for lunch and dinner daily. We mention dress code only when there's a specific requirement and reservations only when they're essential or not accepted.

Credit Cards

The hotels and restaurants in this guide typically accept credit cards. If not, we'll say so.

Top Picks
★ Fodor'sChoice

Listings
⊠ Address
⊠ Branch address
🕮 Mailing address
☎ Telephone
🖷 Fax
⊕ Website
✎ E-mail

🎫 Admission fee
☉ Open/closed times
Ⓜ Subway
⊹ Directions or Map coordinates

Hotels & Restaurants
🏨 Hotel
🛏 Number of rooms
🍴 Meal plans

✕ Restaurant
🍷 Reservations
👔 Dress code
🚫 No credit cards
$ Price

Other
⇨ See also
☞ Take note
⛳ Golf facilities

EXPERIENCE CHARLESTON

WHAT'S WHERE

1 North of Broad. The main part of the downtown peninsula, where you'll find most hotels, shops, and restaurants, is divided into distinct neighborhoods like the French Quarter and Cannonborough/Elliotborough. King Street, Charleston's main shopping artery, bisects the peninsula.

2 South of Broad. The southern tip of the peninsula is home to the Battery and many of the city's most historic, grand mansions but lacking in restaurants and amenities.

3 Mount Pleasant. East of Charleston, across the Cooper River, is Mount Pleasant, an affluent suburb with interesting sites like Boone Hall Plantation and the USS *Yorktown*. There are several good hotels in Mount Pleasant, and a quickly growing restaurant scene. It's also the access point to beaches at Sullivan's Island and the Isle of Palms.

4 West Ashley and James Island. Across the Ashley River lies the West Ashley suburb, beckoning visitors with its three major historic plantations on Ashley River Road. Just south is James Island, with views of the Stono River at James Island County Park, and access to Folly Beach.

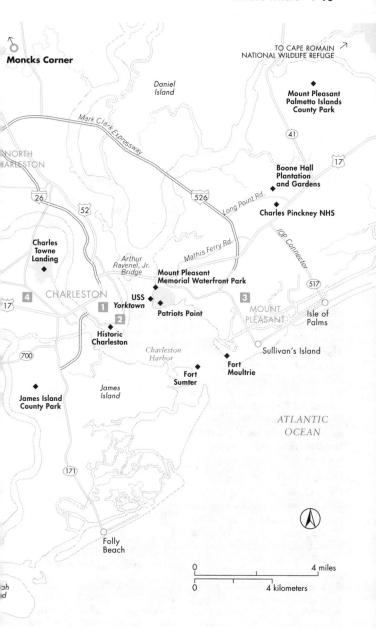

Moncks Corner

TO CAPE ROMAIN
NATIONAL WILDLIFE REFUGE

Daniel
Island

Mount Pleasant
Palmetto Islands
County Park

Mark Clark Expressway

41

NORTH
CHARLESTON

17

526

Boone Hall
Plantation
and Gardens

Long Point Rd.

Charles Pinckney NHS

26

52

IOP Connector

Charles
Towne
Landing

Arthur
Ravenel, Jr.
Bridge

Mathis Ferry Rd.

Mount Pleasant
Memorial Waterfront Park

517

4

CHARLESTON

3

1

USS
Yorktown

MOUNT
PLEASANT

17

2

Patriots Point

Isle of
Palms

Historic
Charleston

Sullivan's Island

700

Charleston
Harbor

Fort
Moultrie

Fort
Sumter

James Island
County Park

James
Island

ATLANTIC
OCEAN

171

Folly
Beach

0 ——————————— 4 miles

0 ——————————— 4 kilometers

CHARLESTON PLANNER

Visitor Resources

The **Charleston Area Convention & Visitors Bureau** (⊕ *www.charleston-cvb.com*) is the best place to begin your trip, whether in person or via their website. Other great resources include *Charleston City Paper* (⊕ *www.charlestoncitypaper.com*), a free weekly with events galore, and *Charleston* magazine (⊕ *www.charlestonmag.com*); check out both publications for their extensive online calendars. To plan your menu for Restaurant Week in this food-driven city (held each January and September), look at the website for the **Charleston Restaurant Association** (⊕ *www.charleston-restaurantassociation.com*). And to browse options for both home and garden tours, head to the websites of the **Preservation Society of Charleston** (⊕ *www.preservation-society.org*) and **Historic Charleston Foundation** (⊕ *www.historiccharleston.org*).

Getting Here and Around

Fly to Charleston: Flying into the Charleston International Airport is a straightforward affair. Alaska, American Airlines, Delta, JetBlue, Southwest, and United all offer flights. Another option is the inexpensive (read: no-frills) Spirit Airlines, which flies into Myrtle Beach International Airport, 90 miles north of Charleston. Once you land, you'll have to take a taxi, Uber, or shuttle into the city, about 15 minutes to downtown, unless you rent a car.

Hop a Train: Amtrak pulls into Charleston thanks to the Silver Service / *Palmetto* trains, which span New York City to Miami, with stops that include Washington, D.C., Savannah, and Orlando.

Drive In: Two main highways feed into Charleston—Highway 17 and Interstate 26.

To gauge driving distance, the city is 299 miles from Atlanta, 209 miles from Charlotte, and 108 miles from Savannah.

In the City: A car isn't a must in this walkable city, but for those who prefer not to hoof it, there are bikes, pedicabs, tour buses, taxis, water taxis, and trolleys, plus buses that go to the suburbs. Street parking is irksome, as meter readers are among the city's most efficient public servants. If you purchase a SmartCard from the Division of Motor Vehicles downtown, you can "deposit" meter money and credit it back to your card when you leave a metered spot. Parking garages, both privately and publicly owned, charge approximately $2 an hour.

Planning Your Time

You can get acquainted with downtown Charleston's historic districts at your leisure, especially if you can devote at least three days to the city, which will also allow time to explore some of the plantations west of the Ashley River. With another day, you can explore Mount Pleasant, and if you have even more time, head out to the coastal islands.

Savings

You can bank on "high season" running year-round, with minor dips in the heat of late July through early September, and mid-January to Valentine's Day. But if you're motivated, there are deals to be found. Always look online to book hotel packages. Restaurant Week, where multicourse meals are offered at discounted prix fixe, hits twice, in January and September. Year-round, the city-run trolley service offers free hop-on, hop-off service along routes throughout downtown. If you must drive, know that metered parking is free from 6 pm to 9 am. And for those looking to hop on a carriage tour, be sure to raid your hotel's lobby rack cards for coupons offering a few dollars off. Freebie events include the City Farmers' Market, where food vendors, farmers, and artisans offer their wares; Piccolo Spoleto (late May to mid-June), where artists sell their work and musicians give gratis performances; *Charleston City Paper* 's Movies in

Marion Square in April and May; Artwalk in the French Quarter, where galleries offer evening viewing, cocktail nibbles, and drinks on the first Fridays in March, May, October, and December; and Second Sundays on King, when King Street closes to traffic from Calhoun to Broad streets and sales hit the sidewalks along with restaurants offering Sunday specials.

Reservations

Reservations are always a good idea at upscale restaurants and a must for downtown hotels. Although you can call around a few days ahead for most tables, top-tier eateries often require several weeks or more advanced booking for Friday or Saturday nights. Holidays (Thanksgiving, Christmas, New Year's Eve and Day, Valentine's Day, Mother's Day, or Easter brunch) demand reservations made a month or more prior. For those willing to fly by the seat of their schedules, deeply discounted same-day hotel reservations are available through the Lowcountry Reservation Service, operated at the Charleston Area Convention & Visitors Bureau, the Isle of Palms Visitor Center, and the North Charleston Visitors Center.

WHEN TO GO

Spring and fall are the most popular times to visit Charleston. The former sees courtyard gardens exploding in blooms and warm temperatures coaxing sundresses and seersucker suits out of local closets. The latter finds residents and tourists alike returning to the sidewalks to stroll, now that summer's most intense heat (and hair-curling humidity) is mellowing out. There are truly only two slightly slower times for tourism in Charleston (July to mid-September and January to mid-February), so those loath to brave crowds or vie for dinner reservations are best advised to visit during those months. Airfare is reasonable year-round. Book money-saving hotel packages online or make day-of reservations through Lowcountry Reservations Service at the Charleston Convention & Visitors Bureau.

Climate

Aside from the dog days of summer, where temperatures range from 80°F to 100°F and the humidity nears a stifling 100%, Charleston boasts mild temperatures and a semitropical climate. Expect afternoon rainstorms to blow in and out during summer months, but know that an umbrella is more than enough to keep you happily exploring outside. Come fall, pack light sweaters, and when winter rolls in from December to early February with low 50°F temps, pull on a coat if you're thin-blooded. There are four seasons here, but summer and spring stretch out the longest.

Festivals and Events

The **Southeastern Wildlife Exhibition** in mid-February marks the first big annual event on Charleston's busy social calendar. Dog trials, birds-of-prey exhibits, and wildlife-art sales make it quite testosterone fueled, but it's fun for kids, too. Next up in March comes the **Charleston Wine + Food** festival in Marion Square, where cook-offs, sampling, and special dinners reign. Spring home and garden tours hit in late March, and the catwalks are crawling with fashionistas for **Charleston Fashion Week.** The **Cooper River Bridge Run** welcomes some 44,000 runners and walkers for the 10K on the first weekend in April, and some 30,000 attendees catch the tennis matches at the **Volvo Car Open** in early April. **Spoleto Festival USA** and **Piccolo Spoleto** both offer live performances and art exhibitions (combined, they total more than 700 options) from late May to mid-June. Charleston's African American and Caribbean heritage is celebrated with the **MOJA Arts Festival** in September and October, and fall home and garden tours rev up then as well.

PERFECT DAYS IN CHARLESTON

Here are a few ideas to make the most out of a day in Charleston.

Tour Waterfront Park, South of Broad neighborhood, the Battery, and City Market. To soak up Charleston's best, you've either got to walk it, pedal it (via bike or pedicab), or cover it by carriage. The common thread: move slowly to see the intricate details in the gardens and architecture and to discover the hidden alleys. Start at Waterfront Park, and read the history markers there. Wander down to the Battery along East Bay Street and sit in White Point Gardens, taking in the view across Charleston Harbor. Head up King or Church to gawk at the amazing antebellum residences, and then head over to the old City Market to shop for everything from sweets to sweetgrass baskets. Lunch at Husk is a good bet.

Shop King Street. King Street is Charleston's version of the Miracle Mile. On King Street, this amounts to beautifully renovated storefronts that look much like they have for centuries. Start at Broad and King streets and work your way north for the most comprehensive experience. Try breakfast at Kitchen 208, and then wander from Broad to Market streets, checking out antiques shops and fancy clothing boutiques. Continue shopping in central King, where you'll find chic chains as well as locally born shops like Hampden Clothing. Get lunch at 39 Rue de Jean while heading into the Upper King Area. North of Calhoun, things get funkier. Here's where you'll find Blue Bicycle Books. Dinner at The Macintosh and drinks at The Belmont make for a lovely end to the day.

Explore the Plantations. Charleston started as a port city in the late 1600s and later dominated in the rice and indigo trades until the Civil War. Many of the large plantations still exist outside the city. Whether you opt to visit Boone Hall Plantation in Mount Pleasant or Middleton Place and Magnolia Plantation along Ashley River Road in West Ashley, you will get a better understanding of what built Charleston and helped the colonies break away from England so long ago.

Play at the Beach. Hit the shore at Folly Beach if you like waves that you can surf, a hopping bar scene, and natural parks to wander. Head east from downtown to Sullivan's Island for kiteboarding and family-friendly beaches. Volleyball aficionados aim for Isle of Palms, where the sporting life and beach bars rule the surfside.

IF YOU LIKE

Exploring Living History

Time-travel to the 18th century with Charleston's wealth of markets, historic homes, and churches, and explore the agrarian side to the city via its outlying former plantations. Taken together, the sum tells the story of wars, wealth, collapse, and rebirth.

Aiken-Rhett House. This downtown estate includes slave quarters, a stable, and a remarkable mansion with original furniture and historic art.

Boone Hall Plantation and Gardens. This still-working plantation was founded in 1681 and is famous for its "Avenue of Oaks."

City Market. See where locals shopped for produce, seafood, and meat from the late 1700s to the early 1900s. Shop the souvenir stalls that now thrive there.

Drayton Hall. One of the few remaining plantation homes in the Lowcountry, Drayton Hall was completed in 1752 and lived in by descendants of the original family until the 1970s.

Magnolia Plantation and Gardens. The gardens and trolley tour of rice paddies, slave quarters, and the swamp is the main draw at this popular destination.

Middleton Place. After viewing the house (once torched during the Civil War, its "gentlemen's wing" has been restored to its former glory), be sure to visit the estate's rolling green spaces, lively stable yard, and Butterfly Lakes.

Nathaniel Russell House Museum. Built in 1808, this remains one of the nation's finest surviving examples of Adam-style architecture.

Old Slave Mart Museum. Learn about the city's part in the slave trade, which was responsible for Charleston's grandeur and the eventual death of the Confederacy.

St. Philip's Church. The namesake of famous Church Street, this graceful late-Georgian structure dates from 1838.

Playing Outside

Water plays a major part in the recreation here, with the Atlantic Ocean and the Ashley, Cooper, Stono, and Wando rivers, as well as myriad tidal creeks and estuaries explorable by stand-up paddleboard and kayak. Charters are available to fish or just sightsee and dolphin-watch. On land, tennis and golf are the top tickets.

Beaches. Head to Sullivan's Island for family-friendly beaches and a view of Charleston from Fort Moultrie.

Bike. Rent a bike from various outfitters downtown and beyond, and explore Charleston on two wheels. Consider biking the **Cooper River Bridge**; the trails at **James Island County Park** or **Palmetto Islands County Park**; **Charles Towne Landing**; or **Magnolia Plantation and Gardens**. Those looking to log miles downtown can loop **Hampton Park** with its mile-long bike and pedestrian lane.

Golf. Golfers rave about the links on **Kiawah Island** (the 2012 PGA Championship was played on the Ocean Course there) and at **Wild Dunes** on Isle of Palms.

Run. Although all of downtown makes a great track, the **Cooper River Bridge** and Hampton Park's mile-long asphalt parcourse, half-mile garden circle, and mile-long bike-pedestrian lane are where the locals go.

Tennis. Wild Dunes Resort on Isle of Palms reigns for the best tennis camps in the area, and the **Volvo Car Open** takes place each spring on Daniel Island.

Learning Gullah and African American History

"Gullah" is the uniquely African American culture that sprang from Lowcountry plantations and persists on the coastal islands. The term can refer to the people themselves, to their language, or to their culture, now regarded as one of the most distinctive regional cultures of African American history.

Avery Research Center for African American History and Culture. Part museum and part archive, this center began in 1865 as a school that trained freed slaves and people of color to be teachers. Artifacts and documentation of the slave era are on display here.

Boone Hall Plantation and Gardens. Take a self-guided tour through the *Black History in America* exhibition on view in eight original brick slave cabins, or attend a performance at the estate's outdoor Gullah Theater.

Gullah Tours. These tours cover Charleston, Beaufort, and Hilton Head, and give you a glimpse into the authentic history of the Gullah.

Middleton Place. Eliza's House, built in the 1870s for the freed slaves who stayed on at this plantation, has a fascinating *Beyond the Fields* exhibition that reveals how reliant this estate was on its former slaves.

MOJA Arts Festival. During the last week of September and first week of October, African heritage and Caribbean influences on Lowcountry culture are celebrated.

Mount Pleasant Memorial Waterfront Park. You can chat with Gullah locals selling their traditional baskets in the Sweetgrass Cultural Arts Pavilion at this beautiful park.

Shopping

Charleston has evolved into a shopper's haven. Most of the action happens on King Street, and Upper King has an evolving Design District, with a new wave of antiques, furniture, and home-fashion stores. Add to this more than two dozen art galleries, predominantly in the French Quarter, and there's plenty to browse and buy.

Ben Silver. A Charleston institution, this provider of preppie blazers and polo shirts keeps locals looking snappy.

Blue Bicycle Books. While away a rainy afternoon at this deceivingly large store that sells used, rare, and new books with local ties.

City Market. Sweetgrass baskets, candies, T-shirts, bags, spices, and much, much more are for sale from the vendors here.

Copper Penny. Designers like Ella Moss, Trina Turk, and Milly are well represented on these racks.

Croghan's Jewel Box. This family-owned gem has sold wedding silver, engagement rings, anniversary presents, and jewelry galore to Charlestonians for more than 100 years.

George C. Birlant & Co. Silver, silver, and more silver.

Hampden Clothing. Find out why New York fashion editors consider this high-end women's clothing paradise a must-see.

Ibu. This unique women's clothing store works with artisans in over 30 countries to design and create handmade items.

Getting Away from It All

Charleston itself is a little step off the beaten path, but for those looking to isolate and unwind further, there are options.

The Inn at Middleton Place. A super-mod-style hotel in the woodlands adjacent to Middleton Place, this inn affords private access to the plantation grounds.

The Sanctuary at Kiawah Island. Luxury knows no bounds at this hotel with its acclaimed restaurant, spa, and nearby golf courses.

Wentworth Mansion. When celebrities want to stay downtown but out of the limelight, they head to this 1886 mansion with its spa, restaurant, and quiet neighborhood a few blocks from King Street.

Eating Out

You can't toss a plate without hitting a James Beard Award nominee or winner in Charleston these days. Take advantage of this and try some of these spots for fresh cuisine from Lowcountry farms and artisan purveyors.

Basil. Don't fret over the line at this downtown Asian eatery. It's always worth the wait.

Charleston Grill. Chef Michelle Weaver runs one of the city's most popular eateries, known through the region for its groundbreaking New South cuisine.

Chez Nous. Head to the tiny outdoor patio at this hard-to-find local eatery, the perfect place for a romantic dinner.

Cupcake DownSouth. If you're in the mood for sweets, this darling little shop features more than 50 kinds of cupcakes. Peanut butter banana fluff, anyone?

FIG. Chef Jason Stanhope's impeccable Lowcountry-accented dishes are born of perfectly sourced and perfectly prepared ingredients.

Husk and **McCrady's.** Chef Sean Brock brought the Southern locavore movement into the mainstream with the former, and treats you to a multicourse prix-fixe experience with the latter.

Macaroon Boutique. Sweet treats that make for great gifts are the order of the day here.

Market Street Sweets. Hit this confectionery to sample cinnamon-and-sugar-crusted pecans or benne wafers—a Charleston original.

Martha Lou's Kitchen. This palace of soul food is one of the best places to go for traditional fare.

The Ordinary. For raw oysters and exquisite seafood, this converted bank building from Chef Mike Lata is second to none.

Peninsula Grill. Break out the fancy clothes for supreme service and gourmet decadence at this Charleston institution. Don't leave without trying the coconut cake.

The Tattooed Moose. Homey eats like house-smoked barbecue brisket, jumbo chicken wings, and fried turkey breast are on offer at this unpretentious hangout.

Ted's Butcherblock. One-stop shopping for gourmet picnic provisions, Ted's is also a great place to hit for wine tastings.

Trattoria Lucca. Italian food never tasted so fine as it does at Chef Ken Vedrinski's friendly neighborhood kitchen.

KIDS AND FAMILIES

What kid wouldn't delight in a town that looks like a fairy tale? With its cobblestone streets, secret alleyways, horses pulling carriages, real-life pirate stories, and candy shops with free samples, Charleston is made for kids, and exploring it is a great (and painless) way to get them to learn history.

Activities

As for entertainment, **carriage tours** (and the stables at Pinckney and Anson streets) captivate, as do rides on the **water taxis** and **pedicabs.** Rainy days are best passed in the **Children's Museum of the Lowcountry** (the interactive gravity and water exhibits and model shrimp boat are favorites), the **South Carolina Aquarium,** or at **Patriots Point Naval & Maritime Museum** with its decommissioned aircraft carrier and destroyer. Sunny days call for a visit to the blacksmith's shop and stable yard at **Middleton Place,** the petting zoo at **Magnolia Plantation and Gardens,** or a **RiverDogs** baseball game at "The Joe" ballpark. If you're looking to cool off, head to any beach, or to the fountains at **Waterfront Park.** For shopping, try **Market Street Sweets** for goodies and **City Market** for souvenirs.

Dining

Kids are welcome at most restaurants—but they are expected to mind their manners. Kids of all ages are especially welcome at **Taco Boy, Mellow Mushroom,** and **Hominy Grill** (especially for weekend brunch).

Resorts

Kiawah Island Golf Resort and **Wild Dunes Resort** on Isle of Palms offer the most activities for kids. From tennis and golf lessons to swimming and crabbing and more, there are scores of ways to keep the junior set entertained. In town, **Embassy Suites** on Marion Square enchants with its castlelike appearance, and sits in a prime location for all the events held on the square: the Saturday Farmers' Market with its jump castle and pony rides; the Southeastern Wildlife Exposition which has dog trials; and Piccolo Spoleto which holds arts activities for children.

EXPLORING
CHARLESTON

Updated
by Stratton
Lawrence

WANDERING THROUGH THE CITY'S FAMOUS downtown peninsula, it's obvious why filmmakers look to Charleston as a backdrop for historic movies. Dozens of church steeples punctuate the low skyline, and horse-drawn carriages pass centuries-old mansions, their stately salons offering a crystal-laden and parquet-floored version of Southern comfort. Outside, magnolia-filled gardens overflow with carefully tended heirloom plants. At first glance, the city may resemble a 19th-century etching come to life—but look closer and you'll see that block after block of old structures have been restored. Happily, after three centuries of wars, epidemics, fires, and hurricanes, Charleston has prevailed and is now one of the South's best-preserved cities.

Although it's home to Fort Sumter, where the bloodiest war in the nation's history began, Charleston is also famed for its elegant houses. These handsome mansions are showcases for the "Charleston style," a distinctive look that is reminiscent of the West Indies. Before coming to the Carolinas in the late 17th century, many early British colonists first settled on Barbados and other Caribbean islands. In that warm and humid climate they built homes with high ceilings and rooms opening onto broad "piazzas" (porches) at each level to catch sea breezes. As a result, to quote the words of the Duc de La Rochefoucauld, who visited in 1796, "One does not boast in Charleston of having the most beautiful house, but the coolest."

Preserved through the hard times that followed the Civil War, the earthquake of 1886, and an array of fires, many of Charleston's earliest public and private buildings still stand. Thanks to a rigorous preservation movement and strict architectural guidelines, the city's new structures often blend in with the old. In many cases, recycling is the name of the game—antique handmade bricks literally lay the foundation for new homes. But although locals do dwell—on certain literal levels—in the past, the city is very much a town of today. A rush of new hotel and apartment development is transforming the city into a modern metropolis, spurred by an influx of national attention to Charleston's culture and dining scene.

Take, for instance, the internationally heralded Spoleto Festival USA. For 17 days every spring, arts patrons from around the world come to enjoy international concerts, dance performances, operas, and plays at various venues citywide. Day in and day out, diners can feast at upscale restaurants, shoppers can look for museum-quality paintings and antiques, and lovers of the outdoors can explore Charleston's outlying beaches, parks, and waterways. But as cosmopolitan as the city has become, it's still the South, and just beyond the city limits are farm stands cooking up boiled peanuts, the state's official snack.

EXPLORING CHARLESTON

Bounded by the Ashley River to the west, the Cooper River to the east, the Battery to the south, and Calhoun Street to the north, the city's historic heart is a fairly compact area of 800 acres that contains nearly 2,000 historic homes and buildings. The peninsula is divided up into several neighborhoods, starting from the south and moving north, including the Battery, South of Broad, the Market area, and Upper King Street, ending near the "Crosstown," where U.S. 17 connects downtown to Mount Pleasant and West Ashley.

You'll see no skyscrapers in the downtown area, because building heights are strictly regulated to maintain the city's historic setting. In the 1970s, most department stores decamped for suburban malls, turning King Street buildings into rows of (architecturally significant) empty shells. Soon, preservation-conscious groups began to save these beauties, and by the mid-1980s the shopping district was revived with the addition of the Omni Hotel (now Belmond Charleston Place). Big-name retailers quickly saw the opportunity in this attractive city and settled in as well. Lower King thrives and Upper King is booming, with many new businesses—hip bars and restaurants in particular—targeting the city's young, socially active population. Look up at the old-timey tile work at the entrances; inevitably it will have the names of the original businesses.

Beyond downtown, the Ashley River hugs the west side of the peninsula; the region on the far shore is called West Ashley. The Cooper River runs along the east side of the peninsula, with Mount Pleasant on the opposite side and Charleston Harbor in between. Lastly, there are outlying sea islands: James Island with its Folly Beach, Johns Island, Wadmalaw Island, Kiawah Island, Seabrook Island, Isle of Palms, and Sullivan's Island. Each has its own appealing attractions, though Johns and Wadmalaw have farms instead of beaches. Everything that entails crossing the bridges is best explored by car or bus.

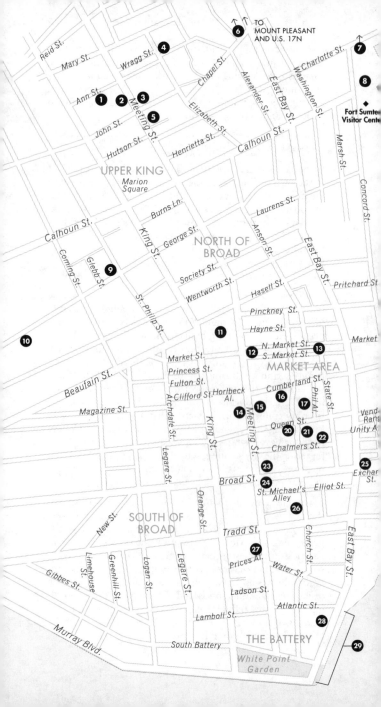

Charleston
Maritime Center

Downtown Charleston

Cooper River

30

Aiken-Rhett House Museum, **4**	Fort Sumter National Monument, **30**
Avery Research Center for African American History and Culture, **10**	French Protestant (Huguenot) Church, **21**
	Gibbes Museum of Art, **14**
The Battery, **29**	Heyward-Washington House, **26**
Belmond Charleston Place, **11**	The *Hunley*, **7**
Charleston Museum, **3**	Joseph Manigault House, **5**
Charleston Visitor Center, **2**	Magnolia Cemetery, **6**
Children's Museum of the Lowcountry, **1**	Market Hall, **12**
Circular Congregational Church, **15**	Nathaniel Russell House Museum, **27**
City Gallery at Joseph P. Riley, Jr. Waterfront Park, **19**	Old Exchange Building & Provost Dungeon, **25**
	Old Slave Mart Museum, **22**
City Hall, **23**	Powder Magazine, **16**
City Market, **13**	St. Michael's Church, **24**
College of Charleston, **9**	St. Philip's Church, **17**
Dock Street Theatre, **20**	South Carolina Aquarium, **8**
Edmondston-Alston House, **28**	Waterfront Park, **18**

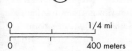

0	1/4 mi
0	400 meters

NORTH OF BROAD

During the early 1800s, large tracts of land were available North of Broad—as it was outside the bounds of the original walled city—making it ideal for suburban plantations. A century later the peninsula had been built out, and today the resulting area is a vibrant mix of residential neighborhoods and commercial clusters, with verdant parks scattered throughout. The district between Broad Street and the Crosstown comprises three primary neighborhoods: Upper King, the Market area, and the College of Charleston. Though there are a number of majestic homes and pre-Revolutionary buildings in this area (including the Powder Magazine, the oldest public building in the state), the main draw is the rich variety of stores, museums, restaurants, and historic churches.

As you explore, note that the farther north you travel (up King Street in particular), the newer and more commercial development becomes. Although pretty much anywhere on the peninsula is considered prime real estate these days, the farther south you go, the more expensive the homes become. In times past, Broad Street was considered the cutoff point for a coveted address. Those living in the area Slightly North of Broad were referred to as SNOBs, and, conversely, their wealthier neighbors South of Broad were nicknamed SOBs.

TOP ATTRACTIONS

Belmond Charleston Place. The city's most renowned hotel is flanked by upscale boutiques and specialty shops, as well as several restaurants. Stop in for cocktails, appetizers, and live tunes at the classy Thoroughbred Club. The city's finest publicly accessible restrooms are downstairs near the shoeshine station. ⊠ *205 Meeting St., Market* ☎ *843/722–4900* ⊕ *www.charlestonplace.com.*

FAMILY **Charleston Museum.** Although housed in a modern-day brick complex, this institution was founded in 1773 and is the country's oldest museum. The collection is especially strong in South Carolina decorative arts, from silver to snuffboxes. There's also a large gallery devoted to natural history (don't miss the giant polar bear). Children love the permanent Civil War exhibition and the interactive "Kidstory" area, where they can try on reproduction clothing in a miniature historic house. The Historic Textiles Gallery features rotating displays that showcase everything from uniforms and flags to couture gowns to antique quilts and needlework.

Combination tickets that include the Joseph Manigault House and the Heyward-Washington House are a bargain at $25. ⌂ *360 Meeting St., Upper King* ☎ *843/722–2996* ⊕ *www.charlestonmuseum.org* ⌁ *$12; $18 combination ticket with Heyward-Washington House or Joseph Manigault House; $25 combination ticket all 3 sites.*

Charleston Visitor Center. Exhibits about Lowcountry culture and a 36-minute film called *Forever Charleston* make a fine introduction to the city. ■ TIP→ **The first 30 minutes are free at the center's parking lot, making it a real bargain.** ⌂ *375 Meeting St., Upper King* ☎ *800/774–0006* ⊕ *www.charlestoncvb.com* ⌁ *Free.*

FAMILY **Children's Museum of the Lowcountry.** Hands-on interactive exhibits at this top-notch museum will keep kids—from infants to 10-year-old children—occupied for hours. They can climb aboard a Lowcountry pirate ship, drive an antique fire truck, race golf balls down a roller coaster, and create masterpieces in the art center. ⌂ *25 Ann St., Upper King* ☎ *843/853–8962* ⊕ *www.explorecml.org* ⌁ *$10 SC residents; $12 non-SC residents* ⊘ *Closed Mon.*

Circular Congregational Church. The first church building erected on this site in the 1680s gave bustling Meeting Street its name. The present-day Romanesque structure, dating from 1890, is configured on a Greek-cross plan and has a breathtaking vaulted ceiling. While the sanctuary is not open to visitors except during Sunday morning service, you are welcome to explore the graveyard, which is the oldest English burial ground in the city, with records dating back to 1695. ⌂ *150 Meeting St., Market* ☎ *843/577–6400* ⊕ *www.circularchurch.org* ⊘ *Graveyard closed Sat.*

★ Fodor'sChoice **City Gallery at Joseph P. Riley, Jr. Waterfront Park.** This city-owned, admission-free art gallery, with handsome contemporary architecture and a delightful location within Waterfront Park, rotates paintings, photography, and sculpture exhibits, showcasing predominately Charleston and South Carolina artists. Young and emerging talents exhibit, and residents and visitors alike love the many opening receptions and artist lectures. The second floor offers a privileged riverfront view. ⌂ *34 Prioleau St., Market* ☎ *843/958–6484* ⊕ *www.citygalleryatwaterfrontpark.com* ⌁ *Free* ⊘ *Closed Mon.*

FAMILY **City Market.** Most of the buildings that make up this popular attraction were constructed between 1804 and the 1830s to serve as the city's meat, fish, and produce market.

These days you'll find the open-air portion packed with stalls selling handmade jewelry, crafts, clothing, jams and jellies, and regional souvenirs. A major renovation transformed the market's indoor section, creating a beautiful backdrop for 20 stores and eateries. Local craftspeople are on hand, weaving sweetgrass baskets—a skill passed down through generations from their African ancestors. From April through December, a night market on Friday and Saturday hosts local artists and food vendors. This shopping mecca's perimeters (North and South Market streets) are lined with restaurants and shops. ⊠ *N. and S. Market Sts. between Meeting and E. Bay Sts., Market* ⊕ *www.thecharlestoncitymarket.com.*

College of Charleston. A majestic Greek revival portico, Randolph Hall—an 1828 building designed by Philadelphia architect William Strickland—presides over the college's central Cistern Yard. Draping oaks envelop the lush green quad, where graduation ceremonies and concerts, notably during Spoleto Festival USA, take place. Scenes from films like *Cold Mountain* and *The Notebook* have been filmed on the historic campus of this liberal arts college, founded in 1770. ⊠ *Cistern Yard, 66 George St., College of Charleston Campus* ☎ *843/805–5507* ⊕ *www.cofc.edu.*

Dock Street Theatre. The original Dock Street, built in 1736, was the first theater building in America. The current structure, reopened in 1935 and renovated in 2010, incorporates the remains of the old Planter's Hotel (circa 1809). Green velvet curtains and wonderful woodwork give it a New Orleans French Quarter feel. Charleston Stage Company performs full seasons of family-friendly fare, and the Spoleto Festival USA uses the stage for productions in May and June. ⊠ *135 Church St., Broad Street* ☎ *843/577–7183* ⊕ *www.charlestonstage.com/dock-street-theatre.html.*

NEED A BREAK?✕ **Bakehouse.** Bakery. Delicious seasonal desserts—heavenly sweet 'n' salty brownies, cheesecake bars, and whoopie pies—are baked at this popular spot. Soft as a pillow, the homemade marshmallows make great take-away treats. ⊠ 160 E. Bay St., Market ☎ 843/577–2180 ⊕ www.bakehousecharleston.com.

★ Fodor'sChoice **Fort Sumter National Monument.** Set on a manFAMILY made island in Charleston's harbor, this is the hallowed spot where the Civil War began. On April 12, 1861, the first shot of the war was fired at the fort from Fort Johnson across the way. After a 34-hour battle, Union forces surrendered and Confederate troops occupied Fort Sumter, which became a symbol of Southern resistance. The Confederacy managed to hold it, despite almost continual bombardment from August 1863 to February of 1865. When it was finally evacuated, the fort was a heap of rubble. Today, the National Park Service oversees it, and rangers give interpretive talks.

To reach the fort, take a private boat or one of the ferries that depart from Patriots Point in Mount Pleasant and downtown's Fort Sumter Visitor Education Center, which includes exhibits on the antebellum period and the Civil War. There are seven trips daily to the Fort between mid-March and mid-August, fewer the rest of the year. ✉ *Charleston* ☎ *843/883–3123* ⊕ *www.nps.gov/fosu* ✍ *Fort free; ferry $21.*

HISTORY LESSON. A ferry ride to Fort Sumter is a great way to sneak in a history lesson for the kids. During the 30-minute ride, you get a narrated journey that points out the historic sites and explains how the Civil War began.

French Protestant (Huguenot) Church. The circa-1845 Gothic-style church is home to the nation's only practicing Huguenot congregation. English-language services are held Sunday at 10:30, with a tour given to any visitors afterward at 11:15. ✉ *136 Church St., Market* ☎ *843/722–4385* ⊕ *www.huguenot-church.org.*

★ Fodor'sChoice **Gibbes Museum of Art.** Housed in a beautiful Beaux-Arts building, this museum boasts a collection of 10,000 works, principally American with a local connection. An $11.5 million renovation was completed in 2016, expanding on-site studios, rotating exhibit spaces, and visiting artist programs. Different objects from the museum's permanent collection are on view in "The Charleston Story," offering a nice overview of the region's history. ✉ *135 Meeting St., Market* ☎ *843/722–2706* ⊕ *www.gibbesmuseum.org* ✍ *$15* ⊘ *Closed Mon.*

WHAT'S IN A NAME. The Manigaults are descendants of the French Huguenots who fled Europe because of persecution, and are a golden example of the American dream fulfilled. They became a wealthy rice-planting family and are still prominent in Charleston; Manigaults own the daily newspaper, among other businesses.

Joseph Manigault House. An extraordinary example of Federal architecture, this 1803 residence and National Historic Landmark reflects the urban lifestyle of a well-to-do rice-planting family and the Africans they enslaved. Engaging guided tours reveal a stunning spiral staircase, rooms that have been preserved in period style, and American, English, and French furniture from the early 19th century. Outside, stroll through the artfully maintained period garden with a classical Gate Temple and interpretive signs that note where historic buildings once stood. ⊠ *350 Meeting St., Upper King* ☎ *843/723–2926* ⊕ *www.charlestonmuseum.org* ⌸ *$12; $18 combination ticket with Heyward-Washington House or Charleston Museum; $25 combination ticket all 3 sites.*

FARMERS' MARKET. Set in Marion Square, at the intersection of King and Calhoun streets, the market runs from 8 am to 2 pm every Saturday from mid-April through mid-December. Here you can find organic produce, homemade jams, and handcrafted everything—from jewelry to decor and dog collars. Breakfast and lunch options are plentiful, too.

Old Slave Mart Museum. This is thought to be the state's only existing building that was used for slave auctioning, a practice that ended here in 1863. It was once part of a complex called Ryan's Mart, which also contained a slave jail, kitchen, and morgue. The structure is now a museum that shares the history of Charleston's role in the slave trade, a horrific part of the city's history, but one that is important to understand. Charleston was a commercial center for the South's plantation economy, and slaves were the primary source of labor both within the city as well as on the surrounding plantations. Galleries are outfitted with interactive exhibits, including push buttons that allow you to hear voices relating stories from the age of slavery. The museum sits on one of the few remaining cobblestone streets in town. ⊠ *6 Chalmers St., Market* ☎ *843/958–6467* ⊕ *www.charleston-sc.gov* ⌸ *$8* ⊙ *Closed Sun.*

St. Philip's Church. Founded around 1680, St. Philip's didn't move to its current site until the 1720s, becoming one of the three churches that gave Church Street its name. The first building in this location (where George Washington worshipped in 1791) burned down in 1835 and was replaced with the Corinthian-style structure seen today. A shell that exploded in the churchyard while services were

2

JOHN JAKES'S BEST BETS

Renowned historical novelist John Jakes achieved the rare distinction of having 16 consecutive novels on the *New York Times* list of best sellers. Considered the contemporary master of the family saga, Jakes is best loved locally for his trilogy *North and South,* which was made into three miniseries for ABC in the 1980s and '90s. They focused on Charleston before and during the Civil War, with much of the filming done in the city. Less famous but equally entertaining and educational are his books and audiotapes, *Charleston* and *Savannah,* or a *Gift for Mr. Lincoln.* Jakes shared some suggestions for experiencing Charleston's historical sites with us:

"**Fort Sumter.** A boat ride to the famous Civil War fort is an attraction that shouldn't be missed by any visitor who appreciates history. Close your eyes just a bit and you can imagine Sumter's cannon blasting from the ramparts— maybe even spot a sleek, gray blockade-runner from Liverpool sneaking into the harbor at dusk.

Carriage Rides. We lived in the Lowcountry for years before I took one of the carriage rides that originate next to the outdoor market. I had a misguided scorn for such tours until I jumped impulsively into a vacant carriage one day. I found the young guide enormously informative, and learned a lot, even some years after writing the *North and South* trilogy.

Boone Hall Plantation. This finely preserved property just a few miles north of the city stood in for Mont Royal, Patrick Swayze's home in the David L. Wolper miniseries *North and South.* The avenue of live oaks leading to the house is well worth the visit."
—John Jakes

being held during the Civil War didn't deter the minister from finishing his sermon (the congregation gathered elsewhere for the remainder of the war). Amble through the churchyards, where notable South Carolinians such as John C. Calhoun are buried. If you want to tour the church, call ahead, as open hours depend upon volunteer availability. ⊠ *142 Church St., Market* ☎ *843/722–7734* ⊕ *www.stphilipschurchsc.org.*

★ Fodor'sChoice **South Carolina Aquarium.** Get up close and personal with more than 5,000 creatures at this waterfront attraction, where exhibits invite you to journey through distinctive habitats. Step into the Mountain Forest and
FAMILY

find water splashing over a rocky gorge as river otters play. Enter the open-air Saltmarsh Aviary to feed stingrays and view herons, diamondback terrapins, and puffer fish; gaze in awe at the two-story, 385,000-gallon Great Ocean Tank, home to sharks, jellyfish, and a loggerhead sea turtle. Kids love the Touch Tank, and the newly expanded Sea Turtle Recovery exhibit makes the celebrated sea turtle rehabilitation hospital accessible to all visitors. ⊠ *100 Aquarium Wharf, Ansonborough* ☎ *800/722–6455, 843/577–3474* ⊕ *www.scaquarium.org* ⊠ *$30.*

FAMILY **Waterfront Park.** Enjoy the fishing pier's "front-porch" swings, stroll along the waterside path, or relax in the gardens overlooking Charleston Harbor. The expansive lawn is perfect for picnics and family playtime. Two fountains can be found here: the oft-photographed Pineapple Fountain and the Vendue Fountain, which children love to run through on hot days. ⊠ *Vendue Range at Concord St., Market* ⊠ *Free.*

ON THE CHEAP. A $52.95 Charleston Heritage Passport, sold at the Charleston, North Charleston, and Mount Pleasant visitor centers, gets you into the Charleston Museum, the Gibbes Museum of Art, Drayton Hall, Middleton Place, and five historic houses for two consecutive days. Three- and seven-day passes are also available.

WORTH NOTING

★ Fodor's Choice **Aiken-Rhett House Museum.** One of Charleston's most stately mansions, built in 1820 and virtually unaltered since 1858, has been preserved rather than restored, meaning visitors can see its original wallpaper, paint, and some furnishings. Two of the former owners, Governor Aiken and his wife, Harriet—lovers of all things foreign and beautiful—bought many of the chandeliers, sculptures, and paintings in Europe. The carriage house remains out back, along with a building that contained the kitchen, laundry, and slave quarters, making this the most intact property to showcase urban life in antebellum Charleston. Take the audio tour, as it vividly describes both the ornate family rooms and the slave quarters, giving historical and family details throughout. ⊠ *48 Elizabeth St., Upper King* ☎ *843/723–1159* ⊕ *www. historiccharleston.org/house-museums* ⊠ *$12; $18 with admission to Nathaniel Russell House.*

Avery Research Center for African American History and Culture.
Part of the College of Charleston, this museum and archive
was once a school for African Americans, training students
for professional careers from approximately 1865 to 1954.
The collections here focus on the civil rights movement,
but also include slavery artifacts such as badges, manacles,
and bills of sale, as well as other materials from throughout
African American history. The free guided tours begin with
a brief film. ⊠ *125 Bull St., College of Charleston Campus*
☎ *843/953–7609* ⊕ *avery.cofc.edu* ⊠ *Free.*

The *Hunley*. In 1864, the Confederacy's H. L. *Hunley* sank
the Union warship USS *Housatonic,* becoming the world's
first successful combat submarine. But moments after the
attack, it disappeared mysteriously into the depths of the
sea. Lost for more than a century, it was found in 1995 off
the coast of Sullivan's Island, and raised in 2000. The *Hunley*
is now preserved in a 90,000-gallon tank, which you
can see during an informative guided tour. An exhibit area
includes artifacts excavated from the sub and interactive
displays. In downtown Charleston, there's also a full-size
replica of the *Hunley* outside the Charleston Museum.
⊠ *1250 Supply St., Old Charleston Naval Base, North
Charleston* ☎ *843/743–4865* ⊕ *www.hunley.org* ⊠ *$16*
⊙ *Closed weekdays.*

Magnolia Cemetery. Ancient oak trees drip Spanish moss over
funerary sculptures and magnificent mausoleums in this
cemetery on the Cooper River. It opened in 1850, beautifully
landscaped (thanks to the rural cemetery movement of
the era) with paths, ponds, and lush lawns. The people of
Charleston came not only to pay respects to the deceased,
but also for picnicking and family outings. Similarly, visitors
still find joy in the natural surroundings—and intrigue
in the elaborate structures marking the graves of many
prominent South Carolinians. All three crews of mariners
who died aboard the Civil War sub the H.L. *Hunley* are
buried here, and more than 850 Confederate servicemen
rest in the Soldiers' Ground. Walking maps are available
in the front office. ⊠ *70 Cunnington Ave., North Morrison*
☎ *843/722–8638* ⊕ *www.magnoliacemetery.net* ⊠ *Free.*

Market Hall. Built in 1841, this imposing landmark was
modeled after the Temple of Wingless Victory in Athens.
While City Market vendors occupy the ground floor, the
second story contains the **Confederate Museum**, in which
the United Daughters of the Confederacy mount displays

of flags, uniforms, swords, and other Civil War memorabilia. ✉ *188 Meeting St., Market* ☎ *843/723–1541* ⊕ *www. thecharlestoncitymarket.com* 💲 *$5 (cash only).*

Powder Magazine. Completed in 1713, the oldest public building in South Carolina is one of few that remain from the time of the Lords Proprietors. The city's volatile—and precious—gunpowder was kept here during the Revolutionary War, and the building's thick walls were designed to contain an explosion if its stores were detonated. Today, it's a small museum with a permanent exhibit on colonial and Revolutionary warfare. ✉ *79 Cumberland St., Market* ☎ *843/722–9350* ⊕ *www.powdermag.org* 💲 *$6.*

BUILDING BOOM. Charleston grew apace with the plantation economy in the mid-1700s, thanks to the booming trade in South Carolina's rice, indigo, and cotton crops. Seeking a social and cultural lifestyle to match its financial success, the plantocracy entertained itself in style by using the talents of the local goldsmiths, silversmiths, gunsmiths, and cabinetmakers. More than 300 private residences were built between 1760 and 1770 alone, a surge reflective of Charleston's position as the wealthiest city in British North America at that time.

SOUTH OF BROAD

Locals jokingly claim that just off the Battery (at Battery Street and Murray Boulevard), the Ashley and Cooper rivers join to form the Atlantic Ocean. Such a lofty proclamation speaks volumes about the area's rakish flair. To observe their pride and joy, head to the point of the downtown peninsula. Here, handsome mansions and a large oak-shaded park greet incoming boats and charm passersby.

The heavily residential area south of Broad Street brims with beautiful private homes, many of which have plaques bearing brief descriptions of the property's history. Be respectful, but feel free to peek through iron gates and fences at the verdant displays in elaborate gardens. Although an open gate once signified that guests were welcome to venture inside, that time has mostly passed—residents tell stories of how they came home to find tourists sitting in their front-porch rockers. But you never know when an invitation to have a look-see might come from a friendly owner-gardener. Several of the city's lavish house museums call this famously affluent neighborhood home.

TOP ATTRACTIONS

★ Fodor's Choice **The Battery.** During the Civil War, the Confederate
FAMILY army mounted cannons in the Battery, at the southernmost
point of Charleston's peninsula, to fortify the city against
Union attack. Cannons and piles of cannonballs still line the
oak-shaded park known as White Point Garden—kids can't
resist climbing them. Where pirates once hung from the gal-
lows, walkers now take in the serene setting from Charleston
benches (small wood-slat benches with cast-iron sides). Stroll
the waterside promenades along East Battery and Murray
Boulevard to enjoy views of Charleston Harbor, the Ravenel
Bridge, and Fort Sumter on one side, with some of the city's
most photographed mansions on the other. You'll find locals
dangling their fishing lines, waiting for a bite. ⌂ *E. Battery
St., at Murray Blvd., South of Broad* 🖅 *Free.*

OLD-FASHIONED WALK. In spring and early summer, Charleston's
gardens are in full glory. In fall and early winter, the homes are
dressed in their holiday finest. Twilight strolls are a Dickensian
experience, with houses lighted from within showing off one
cozy scene after another.

Heyward-Washington House. This Georgian-style double
house was the town home of Thomas Heyward, patriot
leader and signer of the Declaration of Independence.
The city rented the residence for George Washington's
use during the president's weeklong stay in Charleston in
1791. Inside, visitors find historic Charleston-made furniture, notably the withdrawing room's Holmes Bookcase,
considered to be one of the most exceptional examples of
American colonial furniture. Also significant is the 1740s
kitchen building, as it's the only one of its kind open to
the public in Charleston. Don't miss the formal gardens,
which contain plants commonly used in the area in the late
18th century. ⌂ *87 Church St., South of Broad* 🖀 *843/722–
0354* ⊕ *www.charlestonmuseum.org/historic-houses/hey-
ward-washington-house* 🖅 *$12; $18 combination ticket
with Joseph Manigault or Charleston Museum; $25 com-
bination ticket all 3 sites.*

IF THE SHOE FITS. Wear good walking shoes, because the sidewalks,
brick streets, and even Battery Promenade are very uneven. Take
a bottle of water, or stop to sip from the fountains in White Point
Garden, as there are practically no shops south of Broad Street.
The area also lacks public restrooms.

★ Fodor's Choice **Nathaniel Russell House Museum.** One of the nation's finest examples of Federal-style architecture, the Nathaniel Russell House was built in 1808 and is restored to a 19th-century aesthetic. Its grand beauty is proof of the immense wealth Russell accumulated as one of the city's leading merchants. In addition to the famous "free-flying" staircase that spirals up three stories with no visible support, the ornate interior is distinguished by Charleston-made furniture as well as paintings and works on paper by well-known American and European artists, including Henry Benbridge, Samuel F. B. Morse, and George Romney. The extensive formal garden is worth a leisurely stroll. ⊠ *51 Meeting St., South of Broad* ☎ *843/724–8481* ⊕ *www. historiccharleston.org/house-museums* ⊠ *$12; $18 with admission to Aiken-Rhett House Museum.*

St. Michael's Church. Topped by a 186-foot steeple, St. Michael's is the city's oldest surviving church building. The first cornerstone was set in place in 1752 and, through the years, other elements were added: the steeple clock and bells (1764); the organ (1768); the font (1771); and the altar (1892). A claim to fame: George Washington worshipped in pew number 43 in 1791. Listen for the bell ringers on Sunday morning before worship services. ⊠ *78 Meeting St., corner of Meeting and Broad Sts., South of Broad* ☎ *843/723–0603* ⊕ *www.stmichaelschurch.net.*

WORTH NOTING

City Hall. The intersection of Meeting and Broad streets is known as the Four Corners of Law, representing the laws of nation, state, city, and church. On the northeast corner is the Adamesque-style City Hall, built in 1801. Highlights of the historic portraits that hang in the second-floor council chamber (the second-oldest continuously used council chamber in the country), include John Trumbull's 1791 portrait of George Washington and Samuel F. B. Morse's likeness of James Monroe. ⊠ *80 Broad St., North of Broad* ☎ *843/577–6970* ⊠ *Free.*

Edmondston-Alston House. In 1825, Charles Edmondston built this house in the Federal style on Charleston's High Battery. About 13 years later, second owner Charles Alston began transforming it into the Greek revival structure seen today. The home is furnished with family antiques, portraits, silver, and fine china. ⊠ *21 E. Battery, South of Broad* ☎ *843/722–7171* ⊕ *www.edmondstonalston.com* ⊠ *$12.*

FAMILY **Old Exchange Building & Provost Dungeon.** Built as a customs house in 1771, this building once served as the commercial and social center of Charleston. It was the site of many historic events, including the state's ratification of the Constitution in 1788 and two grand celebrations hosted for George Washington. However, the place was also used by the British to house prisoners during the Revolutionary War, an ordeal detailed in one of the exhibits. Costumed interpreters bring history to life on guided tours, and kids are fascinated by the period mannequins on display in the dungeon. ⊠ *122 E. Bay St., South of Broad* ☎ *843/727–2165* ⊕ *www.oldexchange.org* ⊴ *$10.*

MOUNT PLEASANT AND VICINITY

East of Charleston, across the beautiful Arthur Ravenel Jr. Bridge, is the town of Mount Pleasant, named not for a mountain but for a plantation founded there in the early 18th century. In its Old Village neighborhood are antebellum homes and a sleepy, old-time town center with a drugstore where patrons still amble up to the soda fountain and lunch counter for egg-salad sandwiches and floats. Along Shem Creek, where a dwindling shrimping fleet still brings in the daily catch, several seafood restaurants serve some of the area's freshest (and most deftly fried) seafood. Other attractions in the area include military and maritime museums, a plantation, and, farther north, the Cape Romain National Wildlife Refuge.

TOP ATTRACTIONS

★ Fodor's Choice **Boone Hall Plantation & Gardens.** A drive through
FAMILY a ½-mile-long live-oak alley draped in Spanish moss introduces you to this still-functioning plantation, the oldest of its kind. Tours take you through the 1936 mansion, the butterfly pavilion, and the heirloom rose garden. Eight slave cabins on the property have been transformed into the Black History in America exhibit, displaying life-size figures, recorded narratives, audiovisual presentations, photos, and historical relics. Seasonal Gullah cultural performances are perennial crowd favorites. Stroll along the winding river, or pluck in-season fruits (like strawberries, peaches, and pumpkins) from the fields. Across the highway is Boone Hall's Farm Market, with fresh local produce, a café, and a gift shop. The miniseries *North and South* was filmed here, as was the movie adaptation of Nicholas Spark's *The Notebook*. ■ TIP→ **Plan your visit to coincide with annual events like the Lowcountry Oyster Festival in January**

PAT CONROY'S CHARLESTON

South Carolina's most celebrated modern writer Pat Conroy passed away in 2016, but his prose about the Lowcountry will live on for generations. He described Charleston in his 2009 novel, *South of Broad*: "I carry the delicate porcelain beauty of Charleston like the hinged-shell of some soft-tissued mollusk. . . . In its shadows you can find metal work as delicate as lace . . . it's not a high-kicking, glossy lipstick city."

"I know of no more magical place in America than Charleston's South of Broad," Conroy told Fodor's. "I remember seeing this area near the Battery when I was a kid and I was stunned as to how beautiful it was. In meeting with my Doubleday publisher about writing [*South of Broad*], which is set there, she wanted to understand the big draw of this neighborhood. I said, 'It is the most beautiful area of this gorgeous city. It is what the Upper East Side is to Manhattan, what Pacific Heights is to San Francisco, or what Beverly Hills is to Los Angeles.' SOB is mysterious. It keeps drawing you back like a magnetic force. I am fortunate that my writer friend Anne Rivers Siddons lets me stay in her carriage house there when I come to town. As a cadet at The Citadel, I would walk along the Battery and watch the ships come in and out of port. They looked so close you thought you could touch them."

Conroy's other Charleston favorites: "When my children come to town, I go to the aquarium with my grandchildren. It is small enough to take in. Aquariums always make me believe in God. Why? You see the incredible shapes of things and the myriad capacity for different forms of animals. And there is that wonderful outdoor area where you can look at the fish tanks and then look out to the river and see porpoises playing.

"Thanks to Mayor Riley [the city's mayor from 1975 to 2016], who [was] like Pericles for Charleston, there are so many parks and open spaces. Waterfront Park is a great example.

"And one of the true joys of Charleston in these last decades is its restaurant renaissance."

or the Scottish Games and Highland Gathering in September. ✉ *1235 Long Point Rd., off U.S. 17 N, Mount Pleasant* ☎ *843/884–4371* ⊕ *www.boonehallplantation.com* 🖃 *$24.*

FAMILY **Fort Moultrie.** A part of the Fort Sumter National Monument, this is the site where Colonel William Moultrie's South

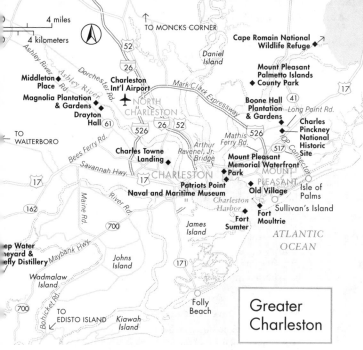

Ashley River Rd.
Ashley River

↑ TO MONCKS CORNER

Dorchester Rd.

52

26

Charleston
Int'l Airport

Mark Clark Expressway

NORTH
CHARLESTON

Daniel
Island

Cape Romain National ↗
Wildlife Refuge ◆

Mount Pleasant
Palmetto Islands
◆ County Park

17

Middleton ◆
Place

Magnolia Plantation
& Gardens ◆

Drayton
Hall   61

Boone Hall
Plantation   41
& Gardens ◆   Long Point Rd.

◆ Charles
Pinckney
National
Historic
Site

TO
WALTERBORO

526

26 52

Bees Ferry Rd.

Savannah Hwy.

Charles Towne
Landing ◆

Mathis
Ferry Rd.

Arthur
Ravenel, Jr.
Bridge

526

517

Connector

Mount Pleasant
Memorial Waterfront
◆ Park

MOUNT
PLEASANT

17

CHARLESTON

17

River Rd.

Maine Rd.

700

162

Patriots Point
Naval and Maritime Museum

Charleston
Harbor

Old Village ◆

James
Island

Fort
Sumter ◆

Fort
Moultrie

Isle of
Palms

Sullivan's Island

ATLANTIC
OCEAN

ep Water
neyard &
efly Distillery

Maybank Hwy.

Johns
Island

171

Wadmalaw
Island

700

Bohicket Rd.

TO
EDISTO ISLAND   Kiawah
Island

Folly
Beach

Greater Charleston

Carolinians repelled a British assault in one of the first patriot victories of the Revolutionary War. Completed in 1809, the fort is the third fortress on this site on Sullivan's Island, 10 miles southeast of Charleston. Set across the street, the companion museum is an unsung hero. Although much is made of Fort Sumter, this smaller historical site is creatively designed, with figurines in various uniforms that make military history come alive. A 20-minute educational film that spans several major wars tells the colorful history of the fort. There's also an exhibit focusing on the slave trade and Sullivan's Island's role in it. ■TIP→ **Plan to spend the day bicycling through Sullivan's Island, where you'll find a cluster of century-old beach houses.** ⊠ *1214 Middle St., Sullivan's Island* ☎ *843/883–3123* ⊕ *www.nps.gov/fosu* ☜ *$3.*

★ **Fodor'sChoice** **Mount Pleasant Memorial Waterfront Park.** Sprawl-
FAMILY ing beneath the Ravenel Bridge, this beautifully landscaped green space invites lounging on the grass with views of Charleston Harbor. You can also take a path up to the bridge for a stroll. Find helpful info in the visitor center, chat with Gullah locals selling traditional baskets in the Sweetgrass Cultural Arts Pavilion, and spend a quiet moment listening to the waterfall fountain in the Mount

Pleasant War Memorial. Kids love the playground modeled after the Ravenel Bridge, and parents appreciate that it's fenced, with benches galore. A 1,250-foot-long pier stretches into the water—grab a milk shake from the River Watch Cafe and a seat on one of the double-sided swings to watch folks fishing for their supper. Better yet, rent a rod and bait for $10 from the pier's tackle shop and cast your own. ⊠ *71 Harry Hallman Blvd., Mount Pleasant* ☎ *843/762–9946* ⊕ *www.ccprc.com.*

★ Fodor'sChoice **Patriots Point Naval and Maritime Museum.** Climb
FAMILY aboard the USS *Yorktown* aircraft carrier—which contains the Congressional Medal of Honor Museum—as well as the destroyer USS *Laffey*. The flight deck features stunning views of the harbor and city skyline, and up-close views of 25 airplanes and helicopters from throughout the last century of American warfare. A life-size replica of a Vietnam support base camp showcases naval air and watercraft used in that military action. ⊠ *40 Patriots Point Rd., Mount Pleasant* ☎ *843/884–2727* ⊕ *www.patriotspoint.org* ⛴ *$22.*

BASKET MAKERS. **Drive along U.S. 17 North, through and beyond Mount Pleasant, to find the "basket makers" set up at roadside stands, weaving the traditional sweetgrass, pine-straw, and palmetto-leaf baskets for which the area is known. Be braced for high prices, although baskets typically cost less on this stretch than in downtown Charleston. Each purchase supports the artisans, whose numbers are dwindling year by year.**

WORTH NOTING

FAMILY **Cape Romain National Wildlife Refuge.** Maritime forests, barrier islands, salt marshes, beaches, and coastal waterways make up this 66,287-acre refuge established in 1932 as a migratory bird haven. The **Sewee Visitor & Environmental Education Center** has information and exhibits on the property and its trails, as well as an outdoor enclosure housing endangered red wolves (feedings are Thursday at 3 pm and Saturday at 11 am). The refuge is aiding the recovery of the threatened loggerhead sea turtle, and a video details the work. ■TIP→ **From the mainland refuge, you can take a $40 ferry ride to remote and wild Bulls Island to explore its boneyard beach and freshwater ponds teeming with alligators.** ⊠ *Sewee Center, 5821 U.S. 17 N, Awendaw* ☎ *843/928–3368* ⊕ *www.fws. gov/caperomain* ⛴ *Free* ☉ *Closed Sun.–Tues.*

Charles Pinckney National Historic Site. This site includes the last 28 acres of the plantation owned by Charles Pinckney, a drafter and signer of the U.S. Constitution. You can tour an 1820s coastal cottage, constructed after Pinckney's death, that features interpretive exhibits about the man, the Constitution, and slave life. A nature trail leads to the archaeological foundations of three slave houses. ⊠ *1254 Long Point Rd., off U.S. 17 N, Mount Pleasant* ☎ *843/881–5516* ⊕ *www.nps.gov/chpi* ☑ *Free.*

FAMILY **Mount Pleasant Palmetto Islands County Park.** With an observation tower, paved nature trails, and boardwalks extending over the marshes, this 943-acre park offers a day full of family fun. You can rent bicycles and pedal boats, set the kids loose in the playground, or pay an extra fee ($6.99) for entrance to the small Splash Island water park (open daily June through mid-August and weekends in May and mid-August through Labor Day). ⊠ *444 Needlerush Pkwy., Mount Pleasant* ☎ *843/884–0832, 843/795–4386* ⊕ *www.ccprc.com* ☑ *$2.*

FAMILY **Old Village.** The historic center of Mount Pleasant, this neighborhood is distinguished by white picket fences, storybook cottages, antebellum homes with wide porches, tiny churches, and lavish waterfront homes. It's a lovely area for a stroll or bike ride, and Pitt Street offers a couple of locally loved eateries and boutiques. Head south along Pitt Street to the Otis M. Pickett Bridge & Park, popular for picnicking, fishing, and sunset views. ⊠ *Pitt St. and Venning St., Mount Pleasant.*

WEST ASHLEY

Ashley River Road (Route 61) begins a few miles northwest of downtown Charleston, over the Ashley River Bridge. Sights are spread out along the way, and those who love history, old homes, and gardens may need several days to explore places like Drayton Hall, Middleton Place, and Magnolia Plantation and Gardens. Spring is a peak time for the flowers, although many of them are in bloom throughout the year.

TOP ATTRACTIONS

★ Fodor's Choice **Magnolia Plantation & Gardens.** Sprawling, beau-
FAMILY tiful Magnolia Plantation was established in the 1670s by Thomas Drayton after he moved from Barbados. The extensive garden—the oldest public one in the country—was begun in the late 17th century to be an "earthly par-

adise," and has evolved into a Romantic-style green space overflowing with plants, including a vast array of azaleas and camellias, and a topiary maze. Take a train or boat to tour the grounds, or traverse more than 500 acres of trails by foot or bike (bring your own). The adjacent Audubon Swamp Garden invites a long stroll on its network of boardwalks and bridges. There's also a petting zoo, a nature center, and a reptile house. Five pre- and post-Emancipation cabins have been restored and serve as the focal point of an interpreter-led tour called From Slavery to Freedom. Also be sure to visit the 19th-century plantation house, which originally stood near Summerville. The home was taken apart, floated down the Ashley River, and reassembled here. Leashed dogs are allowed at Magnolia, including on the train and guided tours. ⊠ *3550 Ashley River Rd., West Ashley* ☎ *843/571–1266* ⊕ *www.magnoliaplantation.com* ☜ *Grounds $20; house tour $8; train $8; boat $8; From Slavery to Freedom exhibit $8; Audubon Swamp $8.*

★ Fodor'sChoice **Middleton Place.** Established in the 1730s, Middleton Place was at the center of the Middleton family's empire of rice plantations, which consisted of 63,000 acres and 3,500 slaves on properties throughout the South Carolina Lowcountry. With its massive three-story brick manor home and prized gardens, begun in 1741 by Henry Middleton, second president of the First Continental Congress, Middleton Place was a grand statement of wealth.

FAMILY

The original manor home was destroyed in the Civil War, but one of its flanking buildings, which served as the gentlemen's guest quarters, was salvaged and transformed into the family's postbellum residence. It now serves as a house museum, displaying impressive English silver, furniture, original paintings, and historic documents, including an early silk copy of the Declaration of Independence. In the stable yards, historic interpreters use authentic tools to demonstrate spinning, weaving, blacksmithing, and other skills from the plantation era. Heritage-breed farm animals, such as water buffalo and cashmere goats, are housed here, along with peacocks.

To get the complete picture of life on a rice plantation, allow time for the Beyond the Fields tour and film, focused on the lives of African Americans at Middleton. The tour begins at Eliza's House, a restored 1870s sharecropper's home.

Restored in the 1920s, the breathtakingly beautiful gardens include camellias, roses, and blooms of all seasons that form

Cruises from Charleston

For almost 300 years, this queen of port cities has been primarily known for its commercial activity, but it recently became a port of embarkation for cruises. Charleston's most frequent visitor is the *Carnival Ecstasy,* which departs from the city on 4- to 12-day cruises to Bermuda and the Bahamas.

City officials have gone to great lengths to accommodate the needs of cruise-line passengers, with plans in place for a grand new cruise terminal. Everyone should consider a pre- or post-cruise stay in Charleston, considered by many to be one of the most romantic cities in the United States. Several hotels around the area offer free parking for the duration of their guests' cruise. For complete information on cruising from Charleston, visit ⊕ *www.scspa.com.*

floral *allées* (alleys) along terraced lawns and around a pair of ornamental lakes, which are shaped like butterfly wings. Wear comfortable walking shoes to explore Middleton's gardens, and dress to be outside.

If all this leaves you feeling peckish, head over to the cozy Middleton Place Restaurant for excellent Lowcountry specialties for lunch and dinner. For a peaceful retreat from the city, you can also stay overnight at the contemporary Inn at Middleton Place, where floor-to-ceiling windows splendidly frame the Ashley River. ⊠ *4300 Ashley River Rd., West Ashley* ☎ *800/782–3608, 843/556–6020* ⊕ *www.mid-dletonplace.org* ⊠ *General admission $28; house tour $15.*

WORTH NOTING

★ FodorsChoice **Charles Towne Landing.** There's plenty to see and
FAMILY do in this park marking the original 1670 settlement of Charles Towne, the first permanent European settlement in South Carolina. Begin with the visitor center's 12-room, interactive museum and exhibit hall that tells the history of the early settlers and the natives here before them. Kids will make a beeline for the *Adventure,* a full-size replica of the colonists' 17th-century tall ship that's docked on the creek running through the park. The grounds are threaded with 6 miles of paths through forest and marsh, including an Animal Forest zoo where you can see black bear, bobcat, puma, and bison. All in all, there are 664 acres of gardens and forest, including an elegant live oak alley. Leashed dogs are allowed (although not in the Animal Forest) and

rental bikes are available for $5/hour. ✉ *1500 Old Towne Rd.* ☎ *843/852–4200* ⊕ *southcarolinaparks.com/charles-towne-landing* ⛁ *$10.*

Deep Water Vineyard & Firefly Distillery. Located in idyllic countryside 40 minutes from downtown Charleston, Deep Water's 48-acre property grows native muscadine grapes on Wadmalaw Island. Formerly Irvin-House Vineyards, the business changed hands and rebranded in 2017. All nine varietals can be tasted for $7, which includes a wine glass to take home. Next door is Firefly Distillery, which achieved notoriety for its sweet tea vodka. Sample this and their other spirits for $6 in a barn that's also outfitted with everything country, from fried peanuts to preserves. ✉ *6775 Bears Bluff Rd., Wadmalaw Island* ☎ *843/559–6867* ⊕ *www.deepwatervineyard.com* ⛁ *Free.*

Drayton Hall. Considered the nation's finest example of Palladian-inspired architecture, Drayton Hall is the only plantation house on the Ashley River to have survived the Civil War intact. A National Trust Historic Site built between 1738 and 1742, it's an invaluable lesson in history as well as in architecture. The home has been left unfurnished to highlight the original plaster moldings, opulent hand-carved woodwork, and other ornamental details. Regular tours, with guides known for their in-depth knowledge, depart on the half hour and paint a vivid picture of the people who once inhabited this fabled house. Visitors can also see the African American cemetery and even take part in the 45-minute "Connections" program that uses maps and historic documents to trace the story of Africans from their journey to America, through slavery, and into the 20th century. ✉ *3380 Ashley River Rd., West Ashley* ☎ *843/769–2600* ⊕ *www.draytonhall.org* ⛁ *$22.*

SIDE TRIPS FROM CHARLESTON

Gardens, parks, and the great outdoors are good reasons to travel a bit farther afield for day trips. As Charleston and the surrounding suburbs—particularly Mount Pleasant—keep on growing, Southern country towns still exist in the vicinity. Sit out on a screen porch after some good home cooking, paddle around a haunting cypress swamp, and take a hike through the towering pines of the Francis Marion National Forest. If the closest you have ever been to an abbey is watching *The Sound of Music,* you can visit Mepkin Abbey and see the simplicity of the monastic life.

Charleston Preserved

When the Civil War ended in 1865, Charleston was left battered and bruised—both physically and economically. Because locals had little money for building new homes and businesses in the coming decades, they made do with those they had, effectively saving from destruction the grand structures seen today. As development in the city began to pick up in the early 1900s, many of these historic buildings could have been lost were it not for the spirit of community activism that sprang into being in the 1920s.

According to Jonathan Poston, author of *Buildings of Charleston*, the preservation movement took off when an Esso gas station was slated to take the place of the Joseph Manigault House. Irate citizens formed the Society for the Preservation of Old Dwellings (the first such group in the nation), whose efforts managed to save what is now a vastly popular house museum. By 1931, Charleston's City Council had created the Board of Architectural Review and placed a designated historic district under its protection as a means of controlling unrestrained development—two more national firsts. The Historic Charleston Foundation was established in 1947, and preservation is now second nature (by law).

As you explore, look for Charleston single houses: one room wide, they were built with the narrow end street-side with multistory Southern porches (called piazzas) to catch prevailing breezes. Wide-open windows allow the cool air that drifts across these shaded porches to enter the homes.

You'll see architectural vestiges of the past on homes situated along Charleston's preserved streets. Many houses have plaques detailing their history; some exhibit Carolopolis Awards, which were received for responsible stewardship of historic architecture. Old fire insurance plaques are rarer; they denote the company that insured the home and that would extinguish the flames if a fire broke out. Notice the "earthquake bolts"—some in the shape of circles or stars and others capped with lion heads—that dot house facades along the Battery. These are attached to iron rods installed in the house to reinforce it after the great earthquake of 1886. Note also the iron spikes along the top of residential gates, doors, walls, and windows. Serving the same purpose as razor wire seen today atop prison fences, most of these *chevaux de frises* ("Frisian horses") were added to deter break-ins—or escapes—after a thwarted 1822 slave rebellion.

Along the way, turn off the air-conditioning, breathe in the fresh air, and enjoy the natural beauty of these less-touristed parts of South Carolina.

Visitor Information **Santee Cooper Visitors Center.** ✉ *9302 Old Number 6 Hwy., Santee* ☎ *803/854–2131* ⊕ *www.santeecooper-country.org.*

MONCKS CORNER

30 miles northwest of Charleston on U.S. 52.

This town is a gateway to a number of attractions in Santee Cooper Country. Named for the two rivers that form a 171,000-acre basin, the Santee Cooper area brims with outdoor pleasures, centered on Lakes Marion and Moultrie.

EXPLORING

Francis Marion National Forest. Pack a picnic and your fishing poles, or hit the hiking, biking, horseback-riding, and motorbike trails in 260,000 acres of swamps, lakes, oaks, and pines. Bring a canoe to explore the peaceful black water of the Wambaw Creek Wilderness Canoe Trail, hike the Swamp Fox Passage of the Palmetto Trail, or pitch a tent at one of five rustic campgrounds within the forest. ✉ *Francis Marion National Forest Ranger Station, 2967 Steed Creek Rd., Huger* ☎ *843/336–2200* ⊕ *www.fs.usda.gov/scnfs* 🖘 *Free.*

Mepkin Abbey. This active Trappist monastery overlooking the Cooper River is on the site of the former plantation home of Henry Laurens. It was later the home of noted publisher Henry Luce and his wife Clare Boothe Luce, who commissioned renowned landscape architect Loutrell Briggs to design a garden in 1937. That garden remains a stunning place for a serene walk or contemplative rest on a waterfront bench. You can take a guided tour of the church or even stay here for a spiritual retreat in the sleek, modern facility with individual rooms and private baths. Hearing the monks sing during their normal daily routine and attending the annual Piccolo Spoleto Festival concerts here are peaceful and spiritual experiences. The gift shop sells oyster mushrooms and garden compost from the abbey's farm as well as candies, preserves, and creamed honey from other Trappist abbeys. ✉ *1098 Mepkin Abbey Rd., off Dr. Evans Rd., Moncks Corner* ☎ *843/761–8509* ⊕ *www.mepkinabbey.org* 🖘 *Free admission; $5 tours* ⊙ *No tours on either the 1st or 2nd Fri. of each month for a day of silence.*

FAMILY **Old Santee Canal Park.** Four miles of boardwalks and unpaved paths take you through Biggin Swamp and along the last portion of the country's first true canal. An interpretive center details the history of the canal, which was used to transport goods from upstate South Carolina to the port of Charleston for the first half of the 19th century. The circa-1840 Stony Landing Plantation House is furnished with period reproductions, offering a glimpse into what a planter's secondary home might have been like in that era. Also on-site (and included in admission) is the Berkeley County Museum and Heritage Center, which tells the story of the county's cultural and natural history. Prefer to explore by boat? Rent a canoe and venture up the canal for $5 per half hour. ⊠ *900 Stony Landing Rd., off Rembert C. Dennis Blvd., Moncks Corner* ☎ *843/899–5200* ⊕ *www. oldsanteecanalpark.org* ⚓ *$3.*

SUMMERVILLE

25 miles northwest of Charleston via I–26 and Rte. 165.

Victorian homes, many of which are listed on the National Register of Historic Places, line the public park. Colorful gardens brimming with camellias, azaleas, and wisteria abound. Many downtown and residential streets have been laid out to curve around tall pines, as a local ordinance prohibits their destruction. Enjoy a stroll in the park, or go antiquing on the downtown shopping square. Summerville D.R.E.A.M.—the Downtown, Restoration, Enhancement, and Management organization—is doing an outstanding job preserving the past while also promoting the present with events such as an old-fashioned Christmas festival.

Summerville was built by wealthy planters and is now attracting young, professional families and well-to-do retirees transplanted from colder climes. It has an artsy bent to it and some trendy eateries have opened.

ESSENTIALS

Visitor Information Greater Summerville/Dorchester County Chamber of Commerce and Visitor Center. ⊠ *402 N. Main St., Summerville* ☎ *843/873–2931* ⊕ *www.greatersummerville.org.*

WHERE TO STAY

$$$ ▣ **Woodlands Mansion.** *All-Inclusive.* With the distinct feel of an English country estate, this 1906 property is one of the most celebrated event destinations of the South. **Pros:** a country retreat excellent for de-stressing; well suited for

weddings; luxurious bedding and electronic blinds (with drapes) make it ideal for sleeping. **Cons:** far (45 minutes) from downtown Charleston; rooms are only available when the mansion is not booked for a wedding or event. [$] *Rooms from: $call for rates and availability* ✉ *125 Parsons Rd., Moncks Corner* ☎ *843/875–2600, 800/774–9999* 🌐 *www.woodlandsinn.com* ⊗ *Sun.–Tues. only open for group business* 🛏 *18 rooms* 🍴 *No meals.*

EDISTO ISLAND

44 miles southwest of Charleston via U.S. 17 and Rte. 174.

On rural Edisto (pronounced *ed*-is-toh) Island, you'll find magnificent stands of age-old oaks festooned with Spanish-moss, and side roads that lead to Gullah hamlets and aging wooden churches; wild turkeys may still be spotted on open grasslands and amid palmetto palms. Twisting tidal creeks, populated with egrets and herons, wind around golden marsh grass. A big day on the island may include shelling and shark-tooth hunting.

The small "downtown" beachfront is a mix of public beach-access spots, restaurants, and old, shabby-chic beach homes that are a far cry from the palatial villas rented out on other area islands. It's also the access point to wild, remote Botany Bay Plantation, while nearby Edisto Beach State Park offers more pristine wilderness and is a camper's delight.

Despite weathering the storm surge of two hurricanes in the last decade, the beach community has rebuilt and retained its remote, forgotten feel. There are a number of privately owned rental accommodations—condos, villas, and homes—and Wyndham Ocean Ridge Resort offers time-share units that can be rented when available. None are on the beach, however.

GETTING HERE AND AROUND

Edisto is connected to the mainland by a bridge over the intracoastal waterway. The only way here is by private car.

ESSENTIALS

Visitor Information Edisto Chamber of Commerce. ✉ *42 Station Ct.* ☎ *843/869–3867* 🌐 *www.edistochamber.com.*

TOURS

★ Fodor'sChoice **Botany Bay Ecotours.** This naturalist-owned outfit
FAMILY offers boat tours of the ACE Basin, including dolphin tours
and sunset cruises. There's also a Gullah/Geechee ecotour,
led by local Gullah icon Sarah Burnell, who "sings" dolphins to the boat. The company also offers private tours
to Morgan Island, home to a colony of rhesus monkeys.
⊠ *3702 Dock Site Rd., Edisto Beach ✦ Dock Slip D 2*
☎ *843/869–2998* ⊕ *www.botanybayecotours.com.*

FAMILY **Edisto Watersports & Tackle.** Hop aboard one of Edisto Water-
sports & Tackle's two-hour sunset river cruises through
the beautiful ACE Basin. With commentary on history
and wildlife offered up along the way, the tour through
this vast wilderness on a 24-foot Carolina Skiff costs $40.
You can also charter a fishing boat, set out on an Otter
Island shelling excursion, or opt for a kayak or paddleboard tour. ⊠ *3731 Docksite Rd.* ☎ *843/869–0663* ⊕ *www.
edistowatersports.net.*

FAMILY **The Pink Van Tour.** Edisto native Marie Elliott leads entertaining tours full of history and facts. There are multiple
stops of interest, from historic churches to a plantation,
and the cost is $25 for 2½ hours. Trips leave from various
locations, and phone reservations are required. ⊠ *Edisto
Island* ☎ *843/603–0967.*

EXPLORING

Botany Bay Plantation Heritage Preserve. This 3,363-acre wildlife management area was deeded to the state by a private
owner in the early 2000s and is now one of the most popular publicly accessible natural beaches in South Carolina.
Hurricane Matthew destroyed much of the boneyard beach
in 2016, so beach access is now only possible at low tide. A
driving tour passes through impoundments and maritime
forest and past saltwater marsh, making it one of the most
diverse and car-accessible nonisland coastal habitats in the
Southeast. For birders, it's the Lowcountry's closest thing
to paradise. If you're visiting in the fall, note that most
weekends and some entire weeks are closed to allow for
deer hunting. ⊠ *Botany Bay Rd.* ⊕ *scgreatoutdoors.com/
park-botanybay.html* ⊘ *Closed Tues.*

FAMILY **Edisto Beach.** Edisto's south edge has 4 miles of public beach.
At its western end, the beach faces St. Helena Sound and
has smaller waves. There is beach access at each intersection
along Palmetto Boulevard and free public parking along
the road. The beach itself has narrowed because of ero-

sion from recent hurricanes, so you'll have more room to spread out if you time your visit for low tide. These clean coastal waters teem with both fish and shellfish, and it's common to see people throwing cast nets for shrimp. It's a great beach for beachcombing. Alcohol is allowed as long as it is not in glass containers. There's little shade and no food stands, so be sure to pack snacks. **Amenities:** none. **Best for:** solitude; sunset; swimming. ⊠ *Palmetto Blvd., from Coral St. to Yacht Club Rd., Edisto Beach* ⊕ *www. townofedistobeach.com.*

★ Fodor'sChoice **Edisto Beach State Park.** This 1,255-acre park
FAMILY includes a 1½-mile-long beachfront with some of the area's best shelling, marshland, and tidal rivers, and a lush maritime forest with a 7-mile trail running through it. The trail is hard-packed shell sand, suitable for bikes and wheelchairs. Overnight options include two campgrounds and seven handsome, fully furnished cabins with marshfront vistas. The park stays extremely busy, so you have to reserve cabins and campsites as far as 11 months in advance. The small ranger station has some fishing poles to lend and firewood for sale. Pets on leashes are allowed. The park's Environmental Learning Center features animal exhibits and a touch tank. It's an excellent jumping-off point for exploring the natural history of Edisto Island and the surrounding ACE Basin. ⊠ *8377 State Cabin Rd.* ☎ *843/869–2756* ⊕ *www.southcarolina- parks.com/edisto-beach* ⬙ *$5.*

FAMILY **Edisto Island Serpentarium.** This fabled attraction, run by a pair of brothers, features an indoor display of snakes from around the world, plus a meandering outdoor garden with sprawling habitats for snakes, turtles, and alligators. Educational programs and alligator feedings enrich the experience, and kids love the gift shop. Call ahead, as hours vary. ⊠ *1374 Hwy. 174* ☎ *843/869–1171* ⊕ *www.edistoser- pentarium.com* ⬙ *$15* ☉ *Closed Dec.–Mar.*

FAMILY **Geechie Boy Market and Mill.** Driving down Highway 174, look out for a giant red roadside chair. It welcomes folks to stop for a photo op and a trip inside a vintage-style grocery selling Geechie Boy's stone-ground cornmeal and grits (which you'll find served in many a fine Charleston restaurant). A 1945 grits separator presides over one side of the store; ask for a demo if you'd like to see it in action. Hit the road with fresh produce from the family farm and homemade cornmeal donuts. Crafts by area artists, cookbooks, and other gifts round out the offerings. ✉ *2995 Hwy. 174* ☎ *843/631–0077* 🌐 *www.geechieboymill.com.*

MYSTERY TREE. **Truly unique, this tree across the highway (Route 174) from the entrance to Botany Bay Plantation is wildly decorated according to the season. A mystery person who prefers to be anonymous changes the tree's decorations during the night.**

2

WHERE TO EAT

★ Fodor's Choice ✕ **Ella & Ollie's.** *Seafood.* The chef and man-
$$$$ agement team behind this seasonal seafood- and produce-driven eatery gained experience at the Old Post Office and in downtown Charleston's fine dining scene before opening this new local hot spot on Edisto. It's the only restaurant in Edisto Beach that emulates the sophisticated, thoughtful menus of Charleston. **Known for:** special Thai menu on Tuesday night; daily blue plates at lunch; grapefruit margaritas with chipotle sea salt. [$] *Average main: $25* ✉ *21 Fairway Dr., Edisto Beach* ☎ *843/869–4968* 🌐 *www.ellaandollies.com* 🕓 *Closed Sun. and Mon.*

$$$ ✕ **Old Post Office Restaurant.** *Southern.* The old metal cages remain at this converted post office, but instead of mail you'll find Southern-inspired fare from Chef Cherry Smalls. Try the cherrywood-smoked Atlantic salmon with a sour-cream-and-mustard-caper sauce for a taste of heaven. **Known for:** relaxed upscale dining out in the country; local seafood cooked near the source; lively local scene on weekends. [$] *Average main: $24* ✉ *1442 Hwy. 174* ☎ *843/869–2339* 🌐 *www.theoldpostofficerestaurant.com* 🕓 *Closed Sun. and Mon. and Jan. No lunch.*

$$$ ✕ **Pressley's at the Marina.** *Seafood.* Enjoy a meal with a view at this relaxed waterfront spot. The dinner menu (also available for a weekend lunch if you want more than tacos, sandwiches, or wraps) offers up fare from land and sea alike. **Known for:** waterfront dining with a horizon view across the marsh; hopping bar scene on Friday and Saturday night; Thursday theme menus during winter. [$] *Average main: $20* ✉ *3702 Docksite Rd.* ☎ *843/869–9226* 🌐 *www.pressleysatthemarina.com* 🕓 *No lunch weekdays.*

$ ✕ **The Seacow Eatery.** *Southern.* This unassuming café is the
FAMILY island's go-to breakfast spot for omelets, biscuits, and piles of pancakes. Lunch shifts to fried seafood platters and an array of sandwich options. **Known for:** John's Omelet, a six-egg beast stuffed to the brim; peel 'n' eat shrimp; pleasant outdoor patio. [$] *Average main: $12* ✉ *145 Jungle Rd.,*

Edisto Beach ☎ *843/869–3222* 🌐 *www.theseacoweatery.com* 🕒 *Dinner only served in summer.*

$$ 🍴 **Whaley's.** *Seafood.* This 1940s-era filling station—the pumps are still outside—has been converted into a fun and eclectic bar and restaurant where you're sure to find some local color. While the interior is a bit rough around the edges, with concrete floors and bathrooms outside, the beer inventory consists of microbrews, and the Monday night karaoke is a lively mix of locals and visitors. **Known for:** a packed house for live bands on Friday and Saturday night; authentic salty-dog vibe; delicious seafood and pub grub. [$] *Average main: $19* ✉ *2801 Myrtle St.* ☎ *843/869–2161* 🌐 *www.whaleyseb.com.*

WHERE TO STAY

$$ 🏨 **Carolina One Kapp Lyons Group.** *Rental.* Kapp Lyons's inventory of privately owned beach homes ranges from a two-bedroom apartment over a gallery to one-bedroom condos and six-bedroom manses smack-dab on the beach. **Pros:** Southern hospitality; sparkling-clean, well-maintained properties; wide diversity of offerings. **Cons:** no resort amenities; if you are a group of singles looking to rent a party house, go elsewhere; units require that you empty your own trash and put away all dishes or be fined. [$] *Rooms from: $170* ✉ *440 Hwy. 174* ☎ *800/945–9667* 🌐 *www.kapplyons.com* 🛏 *160 units* 🍽 *No meals.*

$$$ 🏨 **Wyndham Ocean Ridge Resort.** *Resort.* If you're looking for high-end amenities in a get-away-from-it-all escape, the island's only resort has it all. **Pros:** great choice for golfers; wonderful beach cabana; atmosphere is laid back, unpretentious. **Cons:** no daily housekeeping services; hard to book at peak times; many units are atop two to three flights of stairs. [$] *Rooms from: $219* ✉ *1 King Cotton Rd., Edisto Beach* ☎ *843/869–4500* 🌐 *www.wyndham-oceanridge.com* 🛏 *250 units* 🍽 *No meals* ☞ *Adjacent to The Plantation Course at Edisto.*

SPORTS AND THE OUTDOORS

BIKING

FAMILY **Island Bikes & Outfitters.** Since 1990, Island Bikes & Outfitters has been renting bikes to vacationers. The friendly staff will arm you with a map, orient you to the bike trails, and advise you on how to reach the section of the park that has a boardwalk network for bikers and hikers. Delivery is available. In addition, you can rent golf carts, kayaks, canoes, and paddleboards and buy bait. They sell beachwear, visors, boogie boards, beach chairs, and more. ⊠ *140 Jungle Rd.* ☎ *843/869–4444* ⊕ *islandbikesandoutfitters.com.*

GOLF

The Plantation Course at Edisto. Sculpted from the maritime forest by architect Tom Jackson in 1974, this course mirrors the physical beauty of the island's Lowcountry landscape. Although it's located within the island's only resort, Wyndham Ocean Ridge, it operates as a public course with memberships. The moderate rates are the same for all seasons, with special three-day cards and weekly unlimited-rounds specials. It offers pick-up service within the resort and from the nearby marina. ⊠ *19 Fairway Dr.* ☎ *843/869–1111* ⊕ *www.theplantationcourseatedisto.com* ⌁ *$55–$65* ⚑ *18 holes, 6130 yards, par 70.*

WALTERBORO

44 miles west of Charleston via U.S. 17 and U.S. 64.

This sleepy Southern town makes Charleston look like Manhattan. Its main drag, East Washington Street, still looks much like it did in the 1950s. While continuing to embrace its endearing small-town ways, it is moving in a new, savvy direction. To wit, its marketing slogan is "Walterboro, the Front Porch of the Lowcountry," with a cherry-red rocking chair as its logo. Those rocking chairs can be found outside shops and restaurants, inviting passersby to sit awhile.

Walterboro has become a fun day trip for Charlestonians. The South Carolina Artisans Center has become a major draw, as have the moderately priced antiques and collectible stores. Annual events include the Rice Festival (a street party with live music and performers) and the Downtown Walterboro Criterium International Bike Race in April or May. The town's proximity to Interstate 95 means there's a bevy of inexpensive motels like Days Inn and Hampton Inn nearby. Travelers wanting more local flavor opt for the homey bed-and-breakfasts in restored houses in the historic downtown.

GETTING HERE AND AROUND

The downtown area is walkable and the town is great for bicycling, especially in the Walterboro Wildlife Sanctuary.

ESSENTIALS

Walterboro-Colleton Chamber of Commerce. ⊠ *403 E. Washington St., Suite A* ☎ *843/549–9595* ⊕ *www.walterboro.org.* **Walterboro Welcome Center.** ⊠ *1273 Sniders Hwy.* ☎ *843/538–4353* ⊕ *www. walterborosc.org.*

EXPLORING

FAMILY **Colleton Museum & Farmers Market.** This museum chronicles the history of this small Southern town, displaying everything from butter churns to the country's first anesthesia machine. Particularly charming is the small chapel complete with stained glass, pews, and century-old wedding gowns. Stop in at the outdoor farmers' market held on Tuesday and Saturday. ⊠ *506 E. Washington St.* ☎ *843/549–2303* ⊕ *www. colletonmuseum.org* ⌕ *Free* ☉ *Closed Sun. and Mon.*

★ Fodor'sChoice **Great Swamp Sanctuary.** Boardwalks and hiking, FAMILY biking, and canoe trails weave through this lovely 600-acre park, sometimes referred to as Walterboro Wildlife Sanctuary. One of the paths traces the colonial-era Charleston-to-Savannah Stagecoach Road, where you can still see the cypress remnants of historic bridges. It's a Southern swamp, so douse yourself with insect repellent and be on alert for reptiles. ⊠ *399 Detreville St.* ⊕ *www.walterborosc. org/walterboro-wildlife-sanctuary* ⌕ *Free.*

South Carolina Artisans Center. This lovely center is a showcase for more than 250 South Carolina artists. Look for jewelry, sculptures, glass, woodwork, and more. The loomed shawls and silk scarves make great gifts, and the sweetgrass baskets are treasures. The grounds include sculptures and a rustic cabin with the town's signature red rocking chair, perfect for a photo op. ⊠ *318 Wichman St.* ☎ *843/549–0011* ⊕ *www. scartisanscenter.com* ⌕ *Free* ☉ *Closed Sun.*

WHERE TO EAT AND STAY

$$ ✕**Carmine's Trattoria.** *Italian.* Although some locals call it the "fancy place," Carmine's is a lively pizza joint more than anything. The only high-end furnishing is a baby grand, which is tickled by pianists on Friday and Saturday nights. **Known for:** hearty pizzas and pasta bowls; live piano music; a charming amalgam of Italy and the rural South. Ⓢ *Average main: $18* ⊠ *242 E. Washington St.* ☎ *843/782–3248* ☉ *Closed Sun.*

$$ ✕**Fat Jack's.** *American.* If you're staying near Interstate 95 FAMILY or looking for a friendly bar to watch a game, this independent joint is a step above the array of fast-food and chain restaurants in the vicinity. The menu of sandwiches,

steaks, and seafood is reasonably priced, and the patrons are mostly local. **Known for:** quick, friendly service; generous portions. [$] *Average main: $18* ✉ *2122 Bells Hwy.* ☎ *843/549–5096* 🌐 *www.fatjacksofwalterboro.com.*

2

$ 🍴 **Hiott's Pharmacy.** *American.* Hiott's Pharmacy is one of those delightful throwbacks—a drugstore with a soda fountain where the news of the day is discussed and young people share a Coca-Cola float. You can get a pimento cheese on white bread for $2.30. **Known for:** old-school malts and floats; authentic '50s vibe that isn't contrived; daily gathering of the town's patriarchs at 10 am. [$] *Average main: $3* ✉ *373 E. Washington St.* ☎ *843/549–7222* 💳 *No credit cards* ⏲ *Closed Sun.*

FAMILY

$ 🍴 **Main Street Grille.** *American.* Grab a window seat at this casual spot for a pleasant view of East Washington Street while you dig into shrimp and stone-ground grits, a Philly-style cheese steak, or a juicy burger on a kaiser roll. Desserts like bourbon pecan pie are house made and served in generous portions. **Known for:** hearty takes on American classics; convenient place to recharge before more antiques shopping; local hospitality. [$] *Average main: $12* ✉ *256 E. Washington St.* ☎ *843/782–4774* ⏲ *Closed Sun.*

$ 🏨 **The Hampton House Bed & Breakfast.** *B&B/Inn.* Built in 1912 by the patriarch of the prominent Fishburne family, this B&B has all of the accoutrements of a Lowcountry mansion, from its high ceilings to the charming literary nook, as well as modern-day luxuries like a crescent-shape pool. **Pros:** caring and hospitable owners; small dogs allowed for extra fee; Forde Doll & Doll House Collection on-site. **Cons:** less private than a contemporary hotel; some areas could use a refresh. [$] *Rooms from: $125* ✉ *500 Hampton St.* ☎ *843/542–9498* 🌐 *www.hamptonhousebandb.com* 💳 *No credit cards* 🔑 *3 rooms* 🍽 *Breakfast.*

$ 🏨 **Nine O'Seven Bed & Breakfast.** *B&B/Inn.* With hardwood floors, soaring ceilings, and an elongated front porch, this 1920s Walterboro cottage demonstrates excellent taste in its traditional decor. **Pros:** good value; exquisite interior decor; four-room suite has its own entrance and kitchenette. **Cons:** no credit cards; two rooms share a bathroom; long walk to downtown Washington Street. [$] *Rooms from: $75* ✉ *907 Hampton St.* ☎ *843/542–2943* 🌐 *www.nineoseven.com* 💳 *No credit cards* 🔑 *3 rooms* 🍽 *Breakfast.*

Bachelor Hill Antiques. David Evans displays an eclectic mix of fine furnishings, antiques, art, and '50s finds in inspiring roomlike tableaux. Designers nationwide know about this spot, and the store's eclectic offerings have furnished major motion pictures. The fair prices mean items here move fast. ✉ *255 E. Washington St.* ☎ *843/549–1300* ⊕ *www. bachelorhillantiques.com* ⊗ *Closed Sun.*

Choice Collectibles. On the site of the former Ritz Theater, Choice Collectibles is as retro as the sign for the theater's box office displayed over the cash register. You could get lost in time perusing the fascinating and inexpensive finds from decades past. ✉ *329 E. Washington St.* ☎ *843/549–2617.*

WHERE TO EAT IN CHARLESTON

Updated
by Stratton
Lawrence

CHARLESTON IS BLESSED WITH A bevy of Southern-in-flected selections, from barbecue parlors to fish shacks to casual places serving Lowcountry fare like shrimp and grits. If you'd like to try something new, there are plenty of places serving updated, inspired versions of classic dishes. Before you leave, you'll definitely see why Charleston is considered one of the greatest food cities in the world.

The city's dining scene status continues to rise, boosted by a group of James Beard Foundation repeat award winners. Robert Stehling of Hominy Grill, Mike Lata of FIG and The Ordinary, Jason Stanhope of FIG, and Sean Brock of McCrady's and Husk each earned the designation of Best Chef: Southeast, in successive years. The city boasts other prodigious talents, too: Alex Lira of Bar Normandy, Jeremiah Bacon of the Macintosh, Michelle Weaver of Charleston Grill, Ken Vedrinski of Trattoria Lucca, Jacques Larson of Wild Olive and The Obstinate Daughter, and Josh Walker of Xiao Bao Biscuit. It's the establishment of the New South, circa now.

As for attire, Charleston invites a crisp yet casual atmosphere. Don't forget, it was recognized as the Most Mannerly City in the country by Marjabelle Young Stewart, which means that residents are slow to judge (or, at the least, that they're doing so very quietly). On the whole, the city encourages comfort and unhurried, easy pacing. The result is an idyllic setting in which to enjoy oysters on the half shell and other homegrown delicacies from the land and sea that jointly grant the city its impressive culinary standing.

PRICES

Fine dining in Charleston can be expensive. One fun option to keep costs down is to roam around for a day trying small plates at several restaurants. Another way to save money is to drive over the bridges to Mount Pleasant or James and Johns islands, where inspired food can be found at a lower price tag.

WHAT IT COSTS				
	$	$$	$$$	$$$$
Restaurants	under $15	$15–$19	$20–$24	over $24

Restaurant prices are for a main course at dinner, not including taxes (7.5% on food, 8.5% tax on liquor).

RESTAURANT REVIEWS

The following reviews have been condensed for this book. Please go to Fodor.com for full reviews.

NORTH OF BROAD

$$$$ 🍴**Anson.** *Southern.* Nearly a dozen windows here afford picturesque views of the passing horse-drawn carriages. The softly lighted, gilt-trimmed dining room is ideal for romantic occasions, though some locals prefer the more casual scene downstairs. **Known for:** several steps above most of the tourist-oriented fare on Market Street; addictive fried oysters. [$] *Average main: $28* ✉ *12 Anson St., Market* ☎ *843/577–0551* 🌐 *www.ansonrestaurant.com* 🕒 *No lunch.*

★ Fodor's Choice 🍴**Basic Kitchen.** *Vegetarian.* The stars aligned **$** when two designers, Ben and Kate Towill, decided to open a restaurant built around flavors that don't sacrifice our health to tantalize our taste buds. Their striking addition to the downtown scene serves a vegan- and vegetarian-friendly breakfast, lunch, and dinner every day of the week in a bright and cheery space. **Known for:** the Basic Bowl, a build-your-own produce-and-protein meal; smoothies; bright ambience. [$] *Average main: $14* ✉ *82 Wentworth St., College of Charleston Campus* ☎ *843/789–4568* 🌐 *www.basickitchen.com.*

$ 🍴**Basil.** *Thai.* There's a reason that this corner restaurant in the heart of downtown has been lauded again and again for its Asian fare. Dinner hours generate extended wait times—no reservations allowed—as patrons angle for an outdoor or window table to sample the eclectic dishes. **Known for:** sidewalk dining in the heart of Upper King Street; tons of vegetarian options; long waits for a table on weekends. [$] *Average main: $12* ✉ *460 King St., Upper King* ☎ *843/724–3490* 🌐 *www.eatatbasil.com.*

Where to Eat in
Downtown Charleston

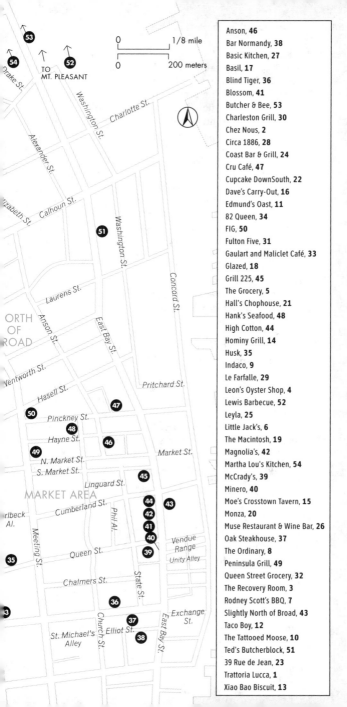

0   1/8 mile

0   200 meters

TO
MT. PLEASANT

Drake St.

Washington St.

Charlotte St.

Alexander St.

Elizabeth St.

Calhoun St.

Washington St.

Concord St.

Laurens St.

East Bay St.

NORTH
OF
BROAD

Anson St.

Wentworth St.

Hasell St.

Pritchard St.

Pinckney St.

Hayne St.

N. Market St.

S. Market St.

Market St.

Linguard St.

MARKET AREA

Horlbeck
Al.

Cumberland St.

Phil Al.

Meeting St.

Queen St.

Vendue
Range

Unity Alley

Chalmers St.

State St.

Church St.

Elliot St.

Exchange
St.

East Bay St.

St. Michael's
Alley

$$$ ✕**Blossom.** *Seafood.* Exposed rafters, wood-paneled walls, and unadorned tables make this place casual and yet upscale. The terrace has a view of St. Philip's majestic spire, and the dining room and bar are heavily populated with young professionals. **Known for:** patio dining; locally sourced seafood; fine dining without pretension. Ⓢ*Average main: $23* ✉ *171 E. Bay St., Market* ☎ *843/722–9200* ⊕ *www.blossomcharleston.com.*

★ Fodor'sChoice ✕**Butcher & Bee.** *Modern American.* Healthy and
$ light but always satisfying, this local favorite has grown into new digs and expanded its lunch and dinner menus. The seasonal menu features creative salads, craft sandwiches, rice bowls, and a scrumptious breakfast menu that leaves patrons wanting to stick around for lunch. **Known for:** locally sourced, seasonal ingredients used in eclectic ways; drool-worthy sandwiches; big patio for outside dining. Ⓢ*Average main: $12* ✉ *1085 Morrison Dr., North Morrison* ☎ *843/619–0202* ⊕ *www.butcherandbee.com.*

★ Fodor'sChoice ✕**Charleston Grill.** *Southern.* Quite simply, this
$$$$ restaurant provides what many regard as the city's highest gastronomic experience. Chef Michelle Weaver creates the groundbreaking New South cuisine, while sommelier Rick Rubel stocks 1,300 wines in his cellar, with many served by the glass. **Known for:** impeccable service; a wine selection that rivals the world's best; nightly tasting menu that spans genres. Ⓢ*Average main: $37* ✉ *Charleston Place Hotel, 224 King St., Market* ☎ *843/577–4522* ⊕ *www.charlestongrill. com* ⊗ *No lunch.*

★ Fodor'sChoice ✕**Chez Nous.** *French.* The menu may be nearly
$$$$ illegible, the space miniscule, and the tucked-away location like finding Waldo, but the food is almost always sublime. Each night only two appetizers, two entrées (like snapper with a vin jaune sauce or gnocchi with chanterelles), and two desserts are offered. **Known for:** romantic hideaway dining; unique French, Spanish, and Italian fare; constantly changing menu. Ⓢ*Average main: $26* ✉ *6 Payne Ct., off Coming St., Upper King* ☎ *843/579–3060* ⊕ *cheznouschs. com* ⊗ *Closed Mon.*

$$$$ ✕**Circa 1886.** *Modern American.* Located on-site at the Wentworth Mansion, this former residential home is full of hand-carved marble fireplaces and stained-glass windows. The award-winning eatery emphasizes seasonal offerings, while also showing off the chef's Texas roots. **Known for:** outdoor dining in the courtyard; city views from the cupola atop the mansion; jerk-brined antelope. Ⓢ*Average main:*

Best Bets for Charleston Dining

CLOSE UP

With hundreds of restaurants to choose from, how will you decide where to eat? Fodor's writers and editors have selected their favorite restaurants by price, cuisine, and experience in the Best Bets lists *below*. The Fodor's Choice properties represent the "best of the best" in every price category. You can also search by neighborhood for excellent eats—just peruse our reviews on the following pages.

Fodor's Choice: Bar Normandy, Basic Kitchen, Bowens Island, Charleston Grill, Chez Nous, Edmund's Oast, Extra Virgin Oven, FIG, The Grocery, Husk, Indaco, Le Farfalle, Lewis Barbecue, Little Jack's, The Macintosh, Martha Lou's Kitchen, McCrady's, Minero, NICO, The Obstinate Daughter, The Ordinary, Rodney Scott's BBQ, Ted's Butcherblock, Tomato Shed Cafe, Trattoria Lucca, The Wreck of the Richard & Charlene, Wild Olive, Xiao Bao Biscuit

Best American: The Grocery, Little Jack's, Ted's Butcherblock

Best Asian: Basil, Xiao Bao Biscuit

Best Brunch: The Glass Onion, High Cotton, Hominy Grill

Best Budget Eats: The Glass Onion, Hominy Grill, Martha Lou's Kitchen, Minero, The Tattooed Moose

Best Business Dining: Slightly North of Broad

Best French: Chez Nous, Gaulart & Maliclet Café, NICO

Best Italian: Le Farfalle, Trattoria Lucca, Wild Olive

Best Lunch: The Glass Onion, Poe's Tavern, Tomato Shed Cafe

Best Southern: Hominy Grill, Husk, Red Drum

Child-Friendly: Jack's Cosmic Dogs, The Wreck of the Richard & Charlene

Great View: Bowen's Island, The Wreck of the Richard & Charlene

Hotel Dining: Charleston Grill

Hot Spots: Hall's Chophouse, Xiao Bao Biscuit

Late-Night Dining: Recovery Room, Voodoo Tiki Bar & Lounge

Most Romantic: Chez Nous, Fulton Five

Outdoor Seating: Poe's Tavern

3

$32 ⊠149 Wentworth St., Lower King ☎*843/853–7828* ⊕*www.circa1886.com* ☉*Closed Sun. No lunch.*

$$$ ✕**Coast Bar & Grill.** *Seafood.* Off a little alley in a restored indigo warehouse, Coast Bar & Grill has a stripped-down look with exposed brick walls and wood columns. Wood-fired seafood and heavy sauces are staples, but lighter dishes like fish tacos and ceviche make it a standout. **Known for:** wood-fired oven; live acoustic music on Sunday; gatherings before shows at the adjacent Charleston Music Hall. [$] *Average main: $24* ✉ *39D John St., Upper King* ☎ *843/722–8838* 🌐 *www.coastbarandgrill.com* ⏲ *No lunch.*

$$$ × **Cru Café.** *Southern.* The sunny wraparound porch in this 18th-century house lures people to this eatery, but it's the inventive menu that keeps them coming back. Fried chicken breasts are topped with poblano peppers and mozzarella, and duck confit is served with caramelized pecans, goat cheese, and fried shoestring onions. **Known for:** local produce and seafood; four-cheese macaroni; cozy dining in a centuries-old Charleston single home. [$] *Average main: $24* ✉ *18 Pinckney St., Market* ☎ *843/534–2434* 🌐 *www.crucafe.com* ⏲ *Closed Sun. and Mon.*

$ × **Cupcake DownSouth.** *Bakery.* This cute shop features more FAMILY than 50 flavors of cupcakes. A daily flavor chart reveals the collection of pocket-sized pleasures on offer. **Known for:** sweet treats to please all ages; catering for parties and weddings; flavors like peanut butter banana fluff, praline, and death by chocolate. [$] *Average main: $4* ✉ *433 King St., Upper King* ☎ *843/853–8181* 🌐 *www.freshcupcakes.com.*

$ × **Dave's Carry-Out.** *Southern.* A vestige of a past era in Cannonborough-Elliottborough, this stalwart soul food joint still boxes up fried shrimp, deviled crab, and juicy pork chops. The menu changes daily, and it's wise to follow the recommendations of the chef just behind the counter in the open kitchen. **Known for:** authentic South Carolina soul food; neighborhood hub for locals; fried shrimp and fish that rival the waterfront spots. [$] *Average main: $10* ✉ *42 Morris St., #C, Cannonborough* ☎ *843/577–7943* ⏲ *Closed Sun. and Mon.*

★ Fodor's Choice × **Edmund's Oast.** *Southern.* It's not just what's $$$$ in the pint glasses at this upscale brewpub that has locals raving. The kitchen dishes up heritage chicken and Carolina Gold rice porridge, roasted grouper with cowpea-and-fennel salad, and braised lamb meatballs. **Known for:** the best of the best for beer nerds; foodie-oriented Sunday brunch; sunshine-filled patio. [$] *Average main: $25* ✉ *1081 Morrison Dr., North Morrison* ☎ *843/727–1145* 🌐 *www.edmundsoast.com* ⏲ *No lunch.*

$$$$ × **82 Queen.** *Southern.* This landmark mainstay continues to thrive, even amid the restaurant boom around it. Wildly popular as a social meeting ground in the 1980s, it has settled down into its primary role as an atmospheric, fine-dining establishment. **Known for:** one of the city's iconic she-crab soups; romantic dining; in the heart of the

LOWCOUNTRY CUISINE

Although you can find Low-country cuisine along most of coastal South Carolina all the way down to Savannah, its foundation feeds off the Holy City of Charleston, where, several centuries ago, European aristocrats would share kitchens with their African slaves. The result was a colonial European fusion with Caribbean and West African, otherwise known as Gullah, influences.

Hoppin' John. This rice-and-bean concoction is not only a favorite Lowcountry dish but a lucky one at that. Families throughout the Lowcountry prepare hoppin' John on New Year's Day for lunch or dinner in hopes that it will provide them with a year's worth of good luck. It's all in the classic Lowcountry ingredients: black-eyed peas symbolize pennies (a side of collard greens adds to the wealth in the new year). Rice, chopped onions, bacon (or ham), and peppers are added to the peas. Add garnishes like a spoonful of salsa or a dollop of sour cream for an interesting Southwest spin.

Perlau. South Carolina takes great pride in its perlau (aka perloo), more lovingly known at the dinner table as chicken bog. This rice-based dish is cooked with chunks of tender chicken and sausage slices, simmered in the chef's choice of classic Southern seasonings. For more than 30 years, in fact, the tiny town of Loris has been hosting its annual Loris Bog-Off Festival, where hundreds of chefs compete to be awarded with the best bowl of bog.

She-Crab Soup. Rich and creamy, with lumps of crabmeat and a splash of dry sherry, she-crab soup is to the Lowcountry as chowder is to New England. The "she" of this signature dish actually comes from the main ingredient: a female crab's orange crab roe. It is delicious as an appetizer, and quite filling as an entrée.

Shrimp and Grits. If you're not convinced that South Carolina is serious about grits, consider this: in 1976, it declared grits the official state food. To be truly decadent, you need to finish this starch off with heavy cream and a slab of butter. Each chef has his or her own guarded recipe, but traditionally, local wild shrimp is sautéed with onions, garlic, and fresh tomatoes. Today, foodies will delight in discovering the dish to be dressed up with everything from sausage, bacon, and Cajun seasoning to cheese, gravy, and tomato-based sauces.

Lower King area. $ *Average main: $29* ✉ *82 Queen St., Lower King* ☎ *843/723–7591* 🌐 *www.82queen.com.*

★ Fodor's Choice 🍴 **FIG.** *Southern.* Spend an evening at this
$$$$ trendsetter for fresh-off-the-farm ingredients cooked with unfussy, flavorful finesse—the kitchen has produced two James Beard Best Chef: Southeast winners. The menu changes frequently, but the family-style vegetables might be as simple as young beets in sherry vinegar served in a plain white bowl. **Known for:** local, seasonal fare; nationally recognized wine program; lively bar scene. $ *Average main: $30* ✉ *232 Meeting St., Market* ☎ *843/805–5900* 🌐 *www.eatatfig.com* ⊗ *Closed Sun. No lunch.*

$$$$ 🍴 **Fulton Five.** *Italian.* Tucked away in the antiques district of Lower King, this romantic northern Italian restaurant is appropriately decorated with chartreuse walls studded with brass accents. In warm weather you can opt for a seat on the second-floor terrace. **Known for:** classic Italian dinner experience; seasonal menu of pastas and entrées; succinct but impressive wine list. $ *Average main: $34* ✉ *5 Fulton St., Lower King* ☎ *843/853–5555* 🌐 *www.fultonfivecharleston.com* ⊗ *Closed Sun. No lunch.*

$ 🍴 **Glazed.** *Bakery.* Three words: maple bacon doughnuts.
FAMILY If that's not enough to get you in the door, any number of other creative options—think raspberry nutella or berries and mascarpone—should do the trick. **Known for:** unconventional doughnut flavors; made from scratch; constantly rotating daily specials. $ *Average main: $3* ✉ *481 King St., Upper King* ☎ *843/577–5557* 🌐 *www.glazedgourmet.com.*

$$$$ 🍴 **Grill 225.** *Steakhouse.* This atmospheric establishment has been stockpiling accolades for years, and it's never been better. The cuisine—combined with a staggering array of excellent wines and professional, caring service—make Grill 225 a popular special-occasion spot. **Known for:** glitz and glamour; one of the best steaks in town; signature Nitrotini cocktail. $ *Average main: $40* ✉ *Market Pavilion Hotel, 225 E. Bay St., Market* ☎ *843/723–0500* 🌐 *www.marketpavilion.com/grill225.cfm.*

★ Fodor's Choice 🍴 **The Grocery.** *Modern American.* Executive
$$$$ chef and owner Kevin Johnson's restaurant sits in impressive quarters near the corner of Cannon and King streets. The menu suggests a humble, considerate approach, as the dishes represent local flavors: the wood-roasted carrots come with feta, raisins, and pistachio crumble, while the wood-roasted whole fish is delivered with salsa verde. **Known for:** down-to-earth dishes designed for sharing; a monstrous wood-fired oven; decadent cassoulet. $ *Average*

main: $28 ✉ *4 Cannon St., Market* ☎ *843/302–8825* 🌐 *www.thegrocerycharleston.com* ⏲ *No lunch.*

$$$$ 🍴 **Hall's Chophouse.** *Steakhouse.* Thanks to its impressive 28-day-aged USDA steaks, Hall's Chophouse is regarded as one of the top steak houses in town. Recommended are the 28-ounce Tomahawk rib eye, the New York strip, and the slow-roasted prime rib. **Known for:** hopping upscale bar scene; first-class service from the Hall family; amazing variety of steaks. [$] *Average main: $45* ✉ *434 King St., Upper King* ☎ *843/727–0090* 🌐 *www.hallschophouse.com* ⏲ *No lunch* ☞ *Sun. brunch features live gospel singers.*

3

$$$$ 🍴 **Hank's Seafood.** *Seafood.* This upscale fish house serves such Southern adaptations as Lowcountry bouillabaisse and seafood platters that come with sweet-potato fries and coleslaw. With a community table flanked by paper-topped private tables, the lively spot hearkens back to an earlier time in Charleston's culinary history. **Known for:** maintaining quality and a local following; seafood platters; oyster happy hour 4:30–6 on weekdays. [$] *Average main: $28* ✉ *10 Hayne St., at Church St., Market* ☎ *843/723–3474* 🌐 *www.hanksseafoodrestaurant.com* ⏲ *No lunch.*

$$$$ 🍴 **High Cotton.** *Southern.* This Charleston classic remains unchanged by time: lazily spinning paddle fans, lush palm trees, and exposed brick walls. The kitchen serves up regional classics like Lowcountry boil and bacon-wrapped stuffed rabbit loin. **Known for:** live jazz and bluegrass music at the bar; one of the city's finest weekend brunches; high-rising peanut butter pie for dessert. [$] *Average main: $34* ✉ *199 E. Bay St., Market* ☎ *843/724–3815* 🌐 *www.highcottoncharleston.com* ⏲ *No lunch weekdays.*

$$ 🍴 **Hominy Grill.** *Southern.* The wooden barber poles from the last century still frame the door of this homespun café and Lowcountry landmark. Chef Robert Stehling is a Carolina boy who lived in New York; that dichotomy shows in his "uptown" comfort food. **Known for:** the standard bearer for shrimp and grits; the Charleston Nasty, a heart-stopping chicken biscuit with gravy; low-key Southern charm and hospitality. [$] *Average main: $18* ✉ *207 Rutledge Ave., Cannonborough* ☎ *843/937–0930* 🌐 *www.hominygrill.com* ⏲ *No dinner.*

★ Fodor's Choice 🍴 **Husk.** *Southern.* With an abundance of accolades, Husk serves an ambitious menu steeped in the South, and the South alone—celebrated chef Sean Brock forbids the inclusion of items from other regions or provinces. A large chalkboard lists the ever-changing artisanal dishes available, as the menu sometimes varies twice daily. **Known**

$$$$

for: the Husk burger, modeled after In-N-Out's famous offering; the throwback stand-alone bar with its great bourbon menu; smoky bacon corn bread for a side. $ *Average main: $29* ⊠ *76 Queen St., Market* ☎ *843/577–2500* ⊕ *www.huskrestaurant.com.*

$$$ ✕**Indaco.** *Italian.* For sophisticated Italian fare in a vibrant (and sometimes boisterous) setting, this hip spot on Upper King is the place. A modern aesthetic of exposed wood and an open kitchen may drive the design, but the food isn't putting on airs. **Known for:** an open kitchen that spills into the dining room, putting on a show; Negroni cocktail on tap. $ *Average main: $24* ⊠ *526 King St., Upper King* ☎ *843/872–6828* ⊕ *www.indacocharleston.com* ⊘ *No lunch.*

★ Fodor'sChoice ✕**Le Farfalle.** *Italian.* When this ambitious Italian
$$$ osteria opened in 2016 in a vast space that had seen failed ventures before it, locals questioned whether it would thrive or crash and burn. Fortunately for everyone, it soared. **Known for:** parmigiano reggiano shavings served as an amuse-bouche; inventive pasta dishes; happy hour snacks like $5 roasted pork sandwiches. $ *Average main: $24* ⊠ *15 Beaufain St., Lower King* ☎ *843/212–0920* ⊕ *www. lefarfallecharleston.com.*

$$ ✕**Leon's Oyster Shop.** *Southern.* Casual, quirky, and a tad Wes Anderson-y, this oysters-and-fried-chicken joint sports a kitschy ambience and blues-heavy sound track. Fried catfish, oyster, and chicken sammies come towering, dressed in fresh slaw or "comeback sauce" and nestled on perfectly prepared rolls. **Known for:** lively stand-up bar scene; extensive champagne list; old-school soft-serve ice cream. $ *Average main: $15* ⊠ *698 King St., Upper King* ☎ *843/531–6500* ⊕ *www.leonsoystershop.com.*

★ Fodor'sChoice ✕**Lewis Barbecue.** *Barbecue.* Austin pitmaster
$ John Lewis transformed Charleston's smoked meat scene when he opened this Texas-style joint that serves prime rib, pulled pork, and "hot guts" by the pound. Opt for the monster "El Sancho Loco" sandwich if you just can't decide. **Known for:** Tex-Mex Tuesdays and smoked prime rib Wednesdays; inducing food comas; margaritas and other refreshing cocktails. $ *Average main: $12* ⊠ *464 N. Nassau St., North Morrison* ☎ *843/805–9500* ⊕ *www.lewisbarbecue.com* ⊘ *Closed Mon.*

$$$ ✕**Leyla.** *Lebanese.* This Lebanese restaurant brings the authentic flavors of the Middle East to Charleston. The fragrance of beef, lamb, and chicken shawarma wafts from the glass front doors. **Known for:** authentic Middle Eastern fare; unconventional options; unique desserts like osmalieh (crispy

CLOSE UP

Fodor's Interview with Eric Doksa

Eric Doksa is the food critic for *Charleston City Paper*, a barbecue nut, and a self-proclaimed beer nerd. Here, he talks with Fodor's about some of his favorite places in the Holy City.

Q: She-crab soup is probably the most iconic Charleston dish. Where do you go for the best version?

A: When I think of she-crab soup, **The Wreck of the Richard & Charlene** (106 Haddrell St., Mount Pleasant ☎ *843/884–0052*) immediately comes to mind. It's quintessentially Shem Creek, low key, but makes a great she-crab.

Q: Where do you go for the best shrimp and grits?

A: It's a tie for me. **Husk** (76 Queen St., Market area ☎ *843/577–2500*) and **Hominy Grill** (207 Rutledge Ave. ☎ *843/937–0930*).

Q: Are there any new places that you're excited about?

A: **Edmund's Oast** (1081 Morrison Dr., North Central ☎ *843/727–1145*). It's such a great concept and it touches all the bases—beer, food, atmosphere.

Q: Do you have a favorite local's joint?

A: **Dave's Carry-Out** (42 Morris St., Upper King ☎ *843/577–7943*). It's a hole-in-wall seafood spot.

3

shredded dough with pistachios). [$] *Average main: $24* ✉ *298 King St., College of Charleston Campus* ☎ *843/501–7500* 🌐 *www.leyla-charleston.com* ⏲ *Closed Mon.*

★ FodorsChoice ✕ **Little Jack's.** *Diner.* You couldn't be blamed for
$$ thinking that this burger joint and chophouse has been here for nearly a century—it's designed to look that way, and the effect works. Leather booths, checkered tablecloths, and plenty of black-and-white imagery create the perfect scene to sip a martini before chowing down on a pastrami on rye. **Known for:** classic cocktails, mixed with high-end flair; the simple but addictive tavern burger; old-school atmosphere that doesn't feel contrived. [$] *Average main: $18* ✉ *710 King St., Hampton Park Terrace* ☎ *843/531–6868* 🌐 *www.littlejackstavern.com.*

★ FodorsChoice ✕ **The Macintosh.** *Modern American.* Here's
$$$$ another name to tuck into your sweetgrass basket filled with great Charleston chefs: Jeremiah Bacon. In his lauded kitchen, he shows off his fondness for the little-regarded deckle—a highly marbled, delicious piece of rib eye—as well as local cobia, clams, and grouper. **Known for:** creative seasonal starters; bone marrow bread pudding for dessert;

sophistication without pretense. $\boxed{S}$ *Average main: $30* $\boxtimes$ *478 King St., Upper King* $\textcircled{\tiny\blacksquare}$ *843/789–4299* $\oplus$ *www.themacintoshcharleston.com* $\odot$ *No lunch except for Sun. brunch.*

$$$$ $\times$ **Magnolias.** *Southern.* The theme at this extremely popular—and worthy—tourist destination is evident in the vivid paintings of creamy white blossoms that adorn the walls. A visit from Oprah Winfrey revived the reputation of "Mags," a pioneer here of innovative Lowcountry cuisine. **Known for:** collard-green-and-tasso-ham egg rolls that spawned a Southern-fusion revolution; classic upscale Southern fare; affordable Sunday brunch. $\boxed{S}$ *Average main: $28* $\boxtimes$ *185 E. Bay St., Market* $\textcircled{\tiny\blacksquare}$ *843/577–7771* $\oplus$ *www. magnoliascharleston.com.*

CHITTERLINGS. Do not be afraid, be informed. Chitterlings, better known as chitlins (and sometimes chit'lins), can be sampled from several soul food establishments in Charleston, including Martha Lou Gadsden's eponymous restaurant. A quick primer: chitterlings are made up of the small intestines of a pig, and usually served fried or steamed after being boiled for several hours. They're not for everyone, but withhold judgment before tasting (possibly with cider vinegar or hot sauce).

$ $\times$ **Martha Lou's Kitchen.** *Southern.* Martha Lou Gadsden has made her pink cinder-block building into a palace of soul food. Although the building is quirky, with a huge mural of the owner visible from a mile down the road, the food—chicken perfectly cooked to golden brown, divine fried pork chops—is taken seriously. **Known for:** authentic Southern soul food; humble dining room; collard greens, giblet rice, and chitterlings. $\boxed{S}$ *Average main: $12* $\boxtimes$ *1068 Morrison Dr.* $\textcircled{\tiny\blacksquare}$ *843/577–9583* $\oplus$ *www.marthalouskitchen. com* $\equiv$ *No credit cards.*

$\star$ Fodor'sChoice $\times$ **McCrady's.** *Eclectic.* The old McCrady's is now
$$$$ McCrady's Tavern (serving the most elevated pub fare in town), and the new McCrady's—tucked into a nook around the corner—is a 22-seat, prix-fixe menu experience that plays out over a dozen ever-changing courses. This is chef Sean Brock's personal playground—over the course of a meal, diners may find themselves sampling uni with persimmons, a quail egg tart, eggplant jerky, and Ossabaw pork with sorghum. **Known for:** communal dinner style at a wraparound bar; menu changes nightly; walk-ins are welcome, but reservations are recommended. $\boxed{S}$ *Average main: $115* $\boxtimes$ *115 E. Bay St., Market* $\textcircled{\tiny\blacksquare}$ *843/577–0025* $\oplus$ *www.mccradysrestaurant. com* $\odot$ *Closed Mon. and Tues. No lunch.*

★ Fodor's Choice 🍴 **Minero.** *Mexican.* Everything that has Sean
$ Brock's name on it turns to gold, and his foray into Mexican food is no exception. Wings are served in a paper bag, doused in Valentina and shaken table-side. **Known for:** the monstrous $10 burrito; charcoal grilled shrimp, steak, and chicken; vast list of single village and wild agave mescals. [$] *Average main: $12* ✉ *153 E. Bay St., Market* ☎ *843/789–2241* 🌐 *www.minerorestaurant.com.*

$ 🍴 **Moe's Crosstown Tavern.** *American.* The decidedly old-school Moe's Tavern earns a perennial place on the area's best-burger list. The big, half-pound, Angus beef chuck patties are cooked to order. **Known for:** local watering hole for watching games; friendly neighborhood vibe; huge BLT sandwiches. [$] *Average main: $10* ✉ *714 Rutledge Ave., Hampton Park* ☎ *843/641–0469* 🌐 *www.moescrosstowntavern.com.*

$$ 🍴 **Monza.** *Pizza.* An homage to the Italian city of the same
FAMILY name, Monza provides genuine Neapolitan-style pizza and an introduction to one of the world's most historic motor-sport racing circuits: the Autodromo Nazionale Monza. The pizza—baked in a wood-fired oven, in traditional style—boasts a thin, crisp crust and toppings like house-made sausage, pepperoni, eggplant, roasted red peppers, and locally farmed eggs. **Known for:** gourmet pizza named after Formula One drivers; a hip bar scene in the heart of Upper King's action; playful Italian race car theme throughout. [$] *Average main: $15* ✉ *451 King St., Upper King* ☎ *843/720–8787* 🌐 *www.monzapizza.com.*

$$$$ 🍴 **Muse Restaurant & Wine Bar.** *Mediterranean.* Set in a pale yellow building on Society Street, Muse lays bare Mediterranean stylings in sophisticated, relaxed quarters. The bar functions as a drawing room, permitting easy introductions and closer inspection of the restaurant's impressive, 100-plus-bottle wine list. **Known for:** 75 wines by the glass; late-night weekend menu; delicious fried sea bass. [$] *Average main: $26* ✉ *82 Society St., Lower King* ☎ *843/577–1102* 🌐 *www.charlestonmuse.com* 🕒 *No lunch.*

$$$$ 🍴 **Oak Steakhouse.** *Steakhouse.* In a 19th-century bank building, this ornate dining room juxtaposes antique crystal chandeliers with contemporary art. Reserve a table on the third floor for the full effect and the best vistas. **Known for:** excellent wet and dry aged steaks; locally sourced seafood and produce; a massive, carefully selected wine list. [$] *Average main: $40* ✉ *17 Broad St., Market* ☎ *843/722–4220* 🌐 *www.oaksteakhouserestaurant.com* 🕒 *No lunch.*

3

★ Fodor'sChoice × **The Ordinary.** *Seafood.* Award-winning chef
$$$$ Mike Lata delivers every possible type of underwater delight here, from local littleneck clams to wahoo carpaccio. The two-story dining room of this former bank building fills up fast, but you can always belly up to the stunning bar while you wait and enjoy a variety of clever cocktails. **Known for:** heady wine pairings; daily plat du jour; excellent oyster bar. Ⓢ *Average main: $28* ⊠ *544 King St., Upper King* ☎ *843/414–7060* ⊕ *www.eattheordinary.com* ⊘ *Closed Mon. No lunch.*

$$$$ × **Peninsula Grill.** *Seafood.* This fine-dining stalwart melds Lowcountry produce and seafood into traditional but inspired dishes, at once eyeing the past and the future. The dining room fixtures (walls covered in olive-green velvet and 18th-century-style portraits and wrought-iron chandeliers on the ceiling) serve as an excellent backdrop for Angus steaks, jumbo sea scallops, and Berkshire pork chops. **Known for:** sought-after coconut cake dessert; special-occasion splurging; knowledgeable and friendly sommelier. Ⓢ *Average main: $35* ⊠ *Planters Inn, 112 N. Market St., Market* ☎ *843/723–0700* ⊕ *www.peninsula-grill.com* ⊘ *No lunch.*

$ × **Queen Street Grocery.** *French Fusion.* For crepes, breakfast sandwiches, and cold-pressed coffee, locals turn to this venerable Charleston institution. Built in 1922, the corner building has served many purposes throughout the years: butcher shop, candy shop, and late-night convenience store, and now stays true to its roots as a neighborhood grocery store with much of the produce and other goods sourced from local growers. **Known for:** mouthwatering sweet and savory crepes; grab-and-go picnic items (including wine); dependable, old-school corner store. Ⓢ *Average main: $10* ⊠ *133 Queen St., Broad Street* ☎ *843/723–4121* ⊕ *www. queenstreetgrocerycafe.com.*

$ × **The Recovery Room.** *American.* The graffiti-splashed walls and tongue-in-cheek name make the Recovery Room a favorite for hipsters. In addition to cans of Pabst Blue Ribbon, this dive bar under the Crosstown Bridge serves up Sunday brunch, dinner, and a late-night menu with staples like the tater tachos (tater tots covered in shredded cheeses, jalapeños, tomatoes, and onions) and wings available in a dozen different sauces. **Known for:** the top seller of PBR cans in the United States; satisfying late night pub grub; lively, affordable Sunday brunch. Ⓢ *Average main: $7* ⊠ *685 King St., Upper King* ☎ *843/727–0999* ⊕ *www. recoveryroomtavern.com.*

★ Fodor'sChoice ✕**Rodney Scott's BBQ.** *Barbecue.* Rodney Scott
$ became a darling of the Southern BBQ scene in the early
2010s, when he branched out from his family's pit-cooked
joint in Hemingway, SC, to cater events like *Garden &
Gun*'s Jubilee. The growing national acclaim led him to
open his own temple to pulled pork in downtown Charleston. **Known for:** mouthwatering pulled-pork BBQ; Rodney's Sauce, an intoxicating blend of vinegary pucker and
sweetness; quick, friendly counter service. ⓢ *Average main:
$14 ✉ 1011 King St., Hampton Park Terrace* ☎ *843/990–
9535* ⊕ *www.rodneyscottsbbq.com.*

$$$$ ✕**Slightly North of Broad.** *Southern.* Affectionately known as
S.N.O.B., this former warehouse with atmospheric brick-and-stucco walls has a chef's table that looks directly into
the open kitchen. Many of the specialties, including wild
game and other less common meats, are served as small
plates that are perfect for sharing. **Known for:** bustling
lunchtime service; forefather of farm-to-table movement
in Charleston; upscale, authentic Southern fare. ⓢ *Average main: $30 ✉ 192 E. Bay St., Market* ☎ *843/723–3424*
⊕ *www.snobcharleston.com.*

$ ✕**Taco Boy.** *Mexican.* Accommodating locals and out-of-
FAMILY towners alike, Taco Boy delivers tasty Mexican American treats to a bustling patio crowd. The ambience is
half the allure of this eclectic outpost featuring rehabbed
or reclaimed materials—right down to the bar counter,
carved from a fallen North Carolina walnut tree, and the
funky Mexican folk art adorning every inch of wall space.
Known for: funky, eclectic decor; creative, gourmet tacos;
mean margaritas and micheladas. ⓢ *Average main: $12
✉ 217 Huger St., North Morrison* ☎ *843/789–3333* ⊕ *www.
tacoboy.net.*

$ ✕**The Tattooed Moose.** *American.* If it looks like a cross
between a veterans' hall and a dive bar, that's because the
Tattooed Moose is going for a decidedly unpretentious
vibe. With 90-plus beers on the menu and a large moose
head behind the counter, the place cuts a distinctive figure. **Known for:** decadent duck club sandwich; weekend
brunch that's a great value; chill and eclectic vibe. ⓢ *Average main: $12 ✉ 1137 Morrison Dr., North Morrison*
☎ *843/277–2990* ⊕ *www.tattooedmoose.com.*

★ Fodor'sChoice ✕**Ted's Butcherblock.** *Café.* Land at Ted's on a
$ lucky afternoon and you'll likely be conferred a memorable greeting: the scent of smoked meat drifting from a
grill perched near the entrance. Ted's operates as a one-stop butcher shop, supplying beef, game, seafood, and

homemade sausages to complement its selection of artisanal cheeses, wine, and other specialty foods. **Known for:** Ultimate Burger Saturday cooked on the Big Green Egg; Friday night dinner-and-wine pairing; daily sandwiches with memorable flavor profiles. [$] *Average main: $10* ✉ *334 E. Bay St., Ansonborough* ☎ *843/577–0094* 🌐 *www.tedsbutcherblock.com* 🕒 *Closed Sun. and Mon.*

$$$$ ✕ **39 Rue de Jean.** *French.* With a backdrop of classic French-bistro style—gleaming wood, cozy booths, and white-papered tables—Charleston's trendy set wines and dines until the wee hours here on such favorites as steamed mussels in a half dozen preparations. Order them with *pomme frites,* as the French do. **Known for:** lively social scene; top-notch sushi; amazing burgers. [$] *Average main: $26* ✉ *39 John St., Upper King* ☎ *843/722–8881* 🌐 *www.39ruedejean.com.*

MUSTARD SAUCE. **So, you've sampled rich, tomato-based sauces in Kansas City or Memphis, spiked your barbecue with vinegar-flavored concoctions in eastern North Carolina, and maybe even tried the white, mayonnaise-based sauce of Alabama. Now, about that mustard sauce. ... It can be traced to the state's German forebears, and is often called Orangeburg mustard in deference to the city of the same name, situated about 80 miles north of Charleston. Colored golden, the sauce is made up of mustard (naturally), brown sugar, and molasses and is certainly worth pouring over pulled pork or smoked chicken.**

★ Fodor's Choice ✕ **Trattoria Lucca.** *Italian.* Chef Ken Vedrinski's
$$$$ downtown wonder, Trattoria Lucca, is a welcoming invitation to the world of Italian food in Charleston. Come in for the warm cauliflower *sformatino* (with farm-fresh eggs, pancetta, and Parmesan cheese), stay for the pasta dishes made with locally milled organic semolina. **Known for:** Monday night family supper; handmade, authentic pastas and entrées; excellent Italian wine list. [$] *Average main: $26* ✉ *41 Bogard St., Cannonborough* ☎ *843/973–3323* 🌐 *www.luccacharleston.com* 🕒 *Closed Sun. No lunch.*

★ Fodor's Choice ✕ **Xiao Bao Biscuit.** *Asian Fusion.* Amid the boom
$$ in Charleston's dining scene in the early 2010s, one thing was distinctly lacking: international, ethnic flavors. Then "Xiao Bao" came along and changed the city's trajectory. **Known for:** okonomiyaki cabbage pancake topped with a farm egg and pork candy; seasonally updated menu full of surprises; housed in a former gas station. [$] *Average*

main: $18 ✉ 224 Rutledge Ave., Cannonborough 🌐 www.xiaobaobiscuit.com ⏲ Closed Sun.

SOUTH OF BROAD

★ Fodor's Choice 🍴 **Bar Normandy.** *Fusion.* Each evening around
$$ 4 pm, the Normandy Farms Bakery on Broad Street transforms into one of the city's hottest restaurants. Chef Alex Lira prepares three or four unique dishes each night, typically heavy on seasonal produce and seafood. **Known for:** unconventional pop-up atmosphere; staggeringly creative and flavorful meals; raw East Coast oysters. *[$] Average main: $18 ✉ 19 Broad St., South of Broad ☎ 843/789–4509 ⏲ Closed Mon.*

$ 🍴 **Blind Tiger.** *American.* One of Charleston's oldest speakeasies, the Blind Tiger can go toe-to-toe with any newcomer. Name the beer, name the backdrop, and the Tiger can deliver in spades, starting with two indoor bars and a historic, handsome outdoor patio. **Known for:** atmospheric courtyard at both lunchtime and late-night gatherings; pub fare that's a few steps above average; hopping weekend scene that draws Charleston's well-to-do. *[$] Average main: $11 ✉ 36–38 Broad St., South of Broad ☎ 843/872–6700 🌐 www.blindtigerchs.com.*

$$ 🍴 **Gaulart and Maliclet Café.** *French.* This local favorite, also known as Fast and French, has been a fixture in the neighborhood for more than 30 years, thanks to the consistent food, the esprit de corps of the staff, and the family-style tables for sharing breakfast, lunch, or dinner. Their popular fondue grew from a once-a-week special to a daily affair, and you can also get your cheese fix with the wonderful Bucheron cheese salad. **Known for:** gourmet bites in an area of town short of restaurants; charming ambience; nightly specials, including fondue night. *[$] Average main: $18 ✉ 98 Broad St., South of Broad ☎ 843/577–9797 🌐 www.fastandfrenchcharleston.com ⏲ Closed Sun. No dinner Mon.*

MOUNT PLEASANT AND VICINITY

Although most of the region's best-known eateries are within the city limits, you won't have trouble finding a great meal when you're traveling to the more far-flung destinations. Mount Pleasant, in particular, is a foodie favorite.

$ 🍴 **Jack's Cosmic Dogs.** *American.* The Galactic, Krypto, Orbit
FAMILY City, and Blue Galactic hot dog varieties at Jack's Cosmic are otherworldly excellent, with blue-cheese slaw, spicy mustard, sauerkraut, zippy onion relish, and Jack's own

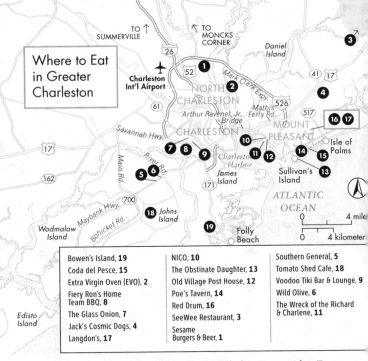

Where to Eat in Greater Charleston

sweet-potato mustard, all swaddled in Pepperidge Farms split-top buns. Akin to a diner, Jack's serves milk shakes and sundaes, real custard soft-serve ice cream, draft root beer, and hand-cut fries. **Known for:** eclectic, one-of-a-kind decor; creative topping combinations; an array of shakes and sundaes. Ⓢ *Average main: $5* ✉ *2805 N. Hwy. 17, Mount Pleasant* ☎ *843/884–7677* ⊕ *www.jackscosmicdogs.com.*

$$$$ ✕ **Langdon's.** *American.* Though it's in a nondescript strip mall across the Cooper River Bridge, this restaurant and wine bar belonging to Mount Pleasant native son Patrick Owens has earned a teetering pile of awards. Owens merges local cuisine with Pan-Asian flavors, exacting a rich menu. **Known for:** fine dining across the Cooper River; excellent wine list; skillet-cooked steaks. Ⓢ *Average main: $30* ✉ *778 S. Shelmore Blvd., Mount Pleasant* ☎ *843/388–9200* ⊕ *www.langdonsrestaurant.com* ⊘ *Closed Sun.*

★ Fodor's Choice ✕ **NICO.** *Seafood.* Chef Nico Romo made his

$$ name at King Street's long-standing upscale seafood restaurant, Fish, before harnessing that name to venture out on his own in Mount Pleasant. Fortunately, his menu still combines his passion for local seafood with his knowledge of

French cuisine, although with perhaps a few more liberties taken. **Known for:** thoughtfully curated raw bar; happy hour oyster deals on weekdays; impressive Scotch collection. [$] *Average main: $18* ✉ *201 Coleman Blvd., Mount Pleasant* ☎ *843/352–7969* 🌐 *www.nicoshemcreek.com.*

$$$$ 🍴 **Old Village Post House.** *Southern.* Many residents of this tree-lined village consider this their neighborhood tavern. Expect contemporary takes on Southern favorites like lump crab cakes, shrimp and grits, and fresh vegetables like a butter beans mélange. **Known for:** charming atmosphere of a 19th-century inn; celebrated Southern cuisine; popular weekend brunch. [$] *Average main: $26* ✉ *101 Pitt St., Mount Pleasant* ☎ *843/388–8935* 🌐 *www.oldvillage-posthouseinn.com.*

$$$$ 🍴 **Red Drum.** *Southwestern.* Locals and visitors alike tend to (mistakenly) overlook this Mount Pleasant staple in favor of the more stylish picks downtown. Chef Ben Berryhill leans on his Texas roots to formulate a South-by-Southwest approach, cooking venison sausage, double-cut pork chops, and rib-eye steaks on a wood-burning grill he calls "The Beast." Also sample savory beef empanadas or large "fork and knife" tacos from the bar, and head out to the outdoor patio for a beer or beverage. **Known for:** bustling evening bar scene; Tex-Mex weekend brunch; local seafood prepared with spice and flair. [$] *Average main: $25* ✉ *803 Coleman Blvd., Mount Pleasant* ☎ *843/849–0313* 🌐 *www.reddrumrestaurant.com* ⏲ *No lunch.*

$ 🍴 **SeeWee Restaurant.** *Southern.* This former general store
FAMILY is about 25 minutes from downtown Charleston, but it's worth the trip for the Southern-style flashback. The veteran waitresses will call you "hon" and recommend their favorites, a lot of which are Southern-fried: pickles, green tomatoes, chicken, oysters, and fresh local shrimp. **Known for:** real Lowcountry cookin'; charm that's not contrived; outdoor seating and live music Saturday nights. [$] *Average main: $12* ✉ *4808 Hwy. 17 N, Awendaw* ☎ *843/928–3609* 🌐 *www.seeweerestaurantinc.com* ⏲ *No dinner Sun.*

★ Fodor's Choice 🍴 **The Wreck of the Richard & Charlene.** *Seafood.* At
$$$$ first glance, the odd name appears to refer to this waterfront
FAMILY restaurant's exterior, topped off with a shabby screened-in porch (in actuality, the *Richard and Charlene* was a trawler that slammed into the building during a hurricane in 1989). Located in the old village of Mount Pleasant, the kitchen serves up Southern tradition on a plate: boiled peanuts, fried shrimp, and stone-crab claws. **Known for:** generous platters of fried seafood; old-school ambience right on the shrimp

docks; boiled peanuts served at every table. $ *Average main:
$25* ⊠ *106 Haddrell St., Mount Pleasant* ☎ *843/884–0052*
⊕ *www.wreckrc.com* ▭ *No credit cards* ⊘ *No lunch.*

GREATER CHARLESTON

★ Fodor'sChoice ✕ **Bowens Island.** *Seafood.* This seafood shack
$$ has survived hurricanes, fires, and the onslaught of trendy
FAMILY restaurants hitting downtown. Littered with oyster shells
and graffiti, the funky spot serves dinner in an enclosed
dock house, on a covered deck, and inside the main build-
ing. **Known for:** one of the last old-school seafood shacks
left; steamed oysters by the bucket; long lines on weekends.
$ *Average main: $16* ⊠ *1871 Bowens Island Rd., James
Island* ☎ *843/795–2757* ⊕ *www.bowensisland.com* ▭ *No
credit cards* ⊘ *Closed Sun. and Mon. No lunch.*

$$$$ ✕ **Coda del Pesce.** *Seafood.* On Isle of Palms, Ken Vedrins-
ki's homage to the sea is not to be missed. Sure, it's a hike
from downtown, but it's worth it because the chef's take
on seafood is—dare we say it—seaworthy. **Known for:**
upscale seafood with Italian fare; oceanfront fine dining;
excellent wine list. $ *Average main: $28* ⊠ *1130 Ocean
Blvd., Isle of Palms* ☎ *843/242–8570* ⊕ *www.codadelpesce.
com* ⊘ *Closed Sun. No lunch.*

★ Fodor'sChoice ✕ **Extra Virgin Oven.** *Pizza.* Known to locals as
$ EVO, this Park Circle pizzeria is considered by many to
be the area's best, doling out Neapolitan-style pies with
super-thin and crunchy crusts. The Food Network chose
EVO's pistachio pesto pie—containing goat, mozzarella,
and Parmesan cheese on a pesto base whipped up with olive
oil, salt, and pistachios—as the state's best slice. **Known
for:** the standard bearer for craft pizza in town; hard-to-
find local beers on tap; on-site bakery for breads to-go.
$ *Average main: $14* ⊠ *1075 E. Montague Ave., North
Charleston* ☎ *843/225–1796* ⊕ *www.evopizza.com.*

$ ✕ **Fiery Ron's Home Team BBQ.** *BarbecueSouthern.* This bar
FAMILY and restaurant has swiftly earned the endorsement of even
the old-school barbecue set (the restaurant's newfangled
pork tacos notwithstanding). And Home Team has done
so with time-honored adherence to the oft-preferred tech-
nique of low-and-slow grilling, producing St. Louis–style
ribs, and traditional smoked pork and chicken. **Known
for:** pulled pork and rich mac 'n' cheese; live blues and
rock music at all three locations; unique table-side sauces.
$ *Average main: $12* ⊠ *1205 Ashley River Rd., West Ashley*
☎ *843/225–7427* ⊕ *www.hometeambbq.com.*

$$$ ✕**The Glass Onion.** *Southern.* The Alabama roots of this eatery's owner/chef shows in the *beaucoup* Southern eats. Take a peek at the ever-changing, seasonal menu: deviled eggs, meat loaf, fried catfish po'boys, and overstuffed pimiento-cheese sandwiches, along with sweets like bread pudding with whiskey sauce. **Known for:** addictive deviled eggs; consistent, seasonal Southern fare; delectable Saturday brunch that often sells out. ⓢ *Average main: $22* ✉ *1219 Savannah Hwy., West Ashley* ☎ *843/225–1717* ⊕ *www. ilovetheglassonion.com* ☾ *Closed Sun.*

★ Fodor'sChoice ✕**The Obstinate Daughter.** *Italian.* Known for
$$ his fine Italian cuisine at Wild Olive on Johns Island, chef Jaques Larson expands his creative touch with the Obstinate Daughter on Sullivan's Island. In the charming blue-and-white space—nautically styled, of course—the music is vintage R&B and the vibe is relaxed. **Known for:** bustling weekend brunch; duck confit pizza, among other creative toppings; buzz-worthy dining at the beach. ⓢ *Average main: $17* ✉ *2063 Middle St., Sullivan's Island* ☎ *843/416–5020* ⊕ *www.theobstinatedaughter.com.*

$ ✕**Poe's Tavern.** *Burger.* The bar and restaurant is beloved
FAMILY among visitors and locals for its fish tacos and gourmet burgers, all named after stories by Edgar Allen Poe, who was stationed on Sullivan's Island with the Army in the late 1820s. His stint inspired "The Gold Bug," a short story about a magical beetle, and then much later, Poe's Tavern. **Known for:** hopping bar and patio scene; signature burgers; vast beer selection. ⓢ *Average main: $12* ✉ *2210 Middle St., Sullivan's Island* ☎ *843/883–0083* ⊕ *www.poestavern.com.*

$ ✕**Sesame Burgers & Beer.** *Burger.* This burger-and-beer joint
FAMILY makes just about everything on the premises—from its house-ground burgers right down to the mustard, ketchup, and mayonnaise. Among the don't-miss burgers are the Charleston, topped with homemade pimiento cheese; the Lonestar, with pulled pork and blue cheese slaw; and the Park Circle, with cheddar cheese, coleslaw, barbecue sauce, and tomatoes. **Known for:** eclectic burger toppings; solid beer selection; char-grilled corn on the cob. ⓢ *Average main: $10* ✉ *4726 Spruill Ave.* ☎ *843/554–4903* ⊕ *www. sesameburgersandbeer.com.*

$ ✕**Southern General.** *Southern.* This no-frills strip mall spot's 18 options include meaty masterpieces like the Super Butt, house-braised pork with smoked sweet onions and potato cream cheese, as well as healthier options like the Southern Shrimp Salad flavored with cucumber, dill, and tomato. The beer list is hearty as well. **Known for:** hearty half-pound burgers; one of the few purveyors of poutine in town; delectable house-made pickles. [$] *Average main: $9* ✉ *3157 Maybank Hwy., Johns Island* ☎ *843/640–3778* 🌐 *www.thesoutherngeneral.com.*

★ FodorsChoice 🍴 **Tomato Shed Cafe.** *Southern.* This Johns Island
$$ roadside joint presents a banquet of locally raised delicacies. Owners and farmers Pete and Babs Ambrose maintain a 135-acre farm on Wadmalaw Island, sourcing grounds for the restaurant. **Known for:** tomato pie when it's in season; take-and-bake meals; true farm-to-table cuisine. [$] *Average main: $16* ✉ *842 Main Rd., Johns Island* ☎ *843/599–9999* 🌐 *www.stonofarmmarket.com* 🕓 *Closed Sun.*

$ 🍴 **Voodoo Tiki Bar & Lounge.** *Eclectic.* Who would you rather share a mai tai with—Bruce Lee, Elvis, or Wile E. Coyote? At Voodoo, all three are set in velvet portraits and framed in the dining room, directly opposite the portholes and gold curtains. **Known for:** half-price tacos during happy hour (4–7) on Monday; great tequila selection; festive tiki drinks. [$] *Average main: $8* ✉ *15 Magnolia Rd., West Ashley* ☎ *843/769–0228* 🌐 *www.voodootikibar.com* 🕓 *No lunch.*

★ FodorsChoice 🍴 **Wild Olive.** *Italian.* What began as a neighbor-
$$$ hood Italian joint on Johns Island was soon discovered by downtowners as a reason to drive off the peninsula. Chef Jacques Larson's amalgam of Italian cuisine and Lowcountry seafood is both authentic and inventive, from handmade Granny Smith apple ravioli to local littleneck clams, served with a spicy lemon-caper zupetta. **Known for:** chocolate pistachio custard; affordable wine list; out-of-the-way location with plenty of parking. [$] *Average main: $24* ✉ *2867 Maybank Hwy., Johns Island* ☎ *843/737–4177* 🌐 *www.wildoliverestaurant.com.*

4

WHERE TO STAY IN CHARLESTON

Updated
by Stratton
Lawrence

CHARLESTON HAS A WELL-EARNED REPUTATION as one of the most historic and beautiful cities in the country. Among travelers, it's also increasingly known for superior accommodations, ranging from lovingly restored mansions converted into atmospheric bed-and-breakfasts to boutique inns to world-class hotels, all found in the residential blocks of the historic downtown peninsula. Most are within walking distance of the shops, restaurants, and museums spread throughout the nearly 800-acre district.

Chain hotels pepper the busy, car-trafficked areas like Meeting Street. In addition, there are chain properties in the nearby areas of West Ashley, Mount Pleasant, and North Charleston, where you'll find plenty of Holiday Inns, Hampton Inns, Marriott Courtyards, and La Quinta Inns. Mount Pleasant is considered the most upscale suburb; North Charleston is the least, but if you need to be close to the airport, are participating in events at the Coliseum complex, or aim to shop the outlet malls there, it is a practical, less expensive alternative.

Overall, a visit to Charleston is a lifetime memory, and to know it is to love it. The city's scorecard for repeat visitors is phenomenal. Charleston is a port of embarkation for cruise ships, and most cruisers wisely plan on a pre- or post-cruise stay. This premier wedding and honeymoon destination also draws many couples back for their anniversaries.

BED-AND-BREAKFAST AGENCIES

Historic Charleston Bed & Breakfast. Rent a carriage house behind a private home in a historic downtown neighborhood through this reservation service. Fully furnished, these properties can be a more economic choice for extended stays than many hotel rooms. Each has a private entrance and one off-street parking space. ☎ 843/722–6606, 800/743–3583 ⊕ www.historiccharlestonbedandbreakfast.com.

VACATION HOME RENTALS

Dunes Properties. For a wide selection of house and condo rentals on Folly Beach, Kiawah and Seabrook islands, and Isle of Palms (including Wild Dunes Resort), call the Isle of Palms branch of locally owned Dunes Properties. ✉ 1400 Palm Blvd., Isle of Palms ☎ 843/886–5600 ⊕ www.dunesproperties.com.

Wyndham Vacation Rentals. For condo and house rentals on Kiawah and Seabrook islands, and Isle of Palms (including Wild Dunes Resort), contact Wyndham Vacation Rentals. ✉ 354 Freshfields Dr., Johns Island ☎ 843/768–5000 ⊕ www.wyndhamvacationrentals.com.

PRICES

Charleston's downtown lodgings have three seasons: high season (March to May and September to November), mid-season (June to August), and low season (late November to February). Prices drop significantly during the short low season, except during holidays and special events like the Southeastern Wildlife Exposition each February. High season is summer at the island resorts; rates drop for weekly stays and during the off-season. Although prices have gone up at the B&Bs, don't forget that a full breakfast for two is generally included, as well as an evening wine reception, which can take the place of happy hour and save on your bar bill. You should factor in, however, the cost of downtown parking; see if your hotel offers free parking. In the areas "over the bridges," parking is generally free. Depending on when you arrive, you can try to find on-street metered parking, as there is no charge after 6 pm and all day Sunday.

■ TIP→ **If you're on a budget, consider lodgings outside the city limits, which tend to be less expensive.** Also remember that longer stays sometimes translate into a better per-night price.

WHAT IT COSTS			
$	$$	$$$	$$$$
Hotels	under $150	$150–$200	$201–$250	over $250

Prices are for two people in a standard double room in high season, excluding tax.

LODGING REVIEWS

Listed alphabetically within neighborhoods. The following reviews have been condensed for this book. Please go to Fodors.com for full reviews of each property.

DOWNTOWN CHARLESTON

NORTH OF BROAD

$$ ☆**Andrew Pinckney Inn.** *B&B/Inn.* Nestled in the heart of Charleston, this West Indies–inspired inn offers a range of accommodations, from charming rooms perfect for couples to two-level suites big enough for the whole family. **Pros:** the town houses are ideal for longer stays; afternoon gourmet tea and coffee service with fresh-baked cookies. **Cons:** elevator access for standard rooms only; bustling neighborhood

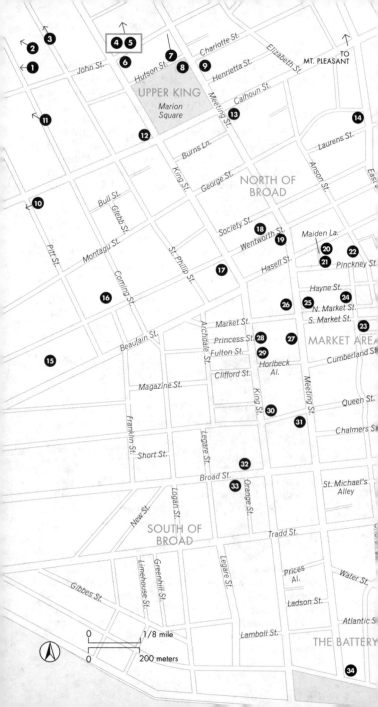

Where to Stay in Downtown Charleston

and nearby horse stables can be noisy. $ *Rooms from: $199* ✉ *40 Pinckney St., Market* ☎ *843/937–8800, 800/505–8983* 🌐 *www.andrewpinckneyinn.com* 🛏 *41 rooms* 🍴 *Breakfast.*

★ Fodor'sChoice 🏨 **Ansonborough Inn.** *B&B/Inn.* At this boutique
$$$ hotel you can relax in your comfortable suite or indulge in evening wine and cheese on the expansive rooftop terrace while enjoying views of the city and Cooper River. **Pros:** lots of period details; 24-hour upscale supermarket across the street; easy walking distance to the Market. **Cons:** gym only has treadmill and weight machine; some rooms open to a central atrium directly over the lobby. $ *Rooms from: $219* ✉ *21 Hasell St., Market* ☎ *800/723–1655* 🌐 *www.ansonboroughinn.com* 🛏 *45 suites* 🍴 *Breakfast.*

★ Fodor'sChoice 🏨 **Belmond Charleston Place.** *Hotel.* Even casual
$$$$ passersby enjoy gazing up at the immense handblown Murano glass chandelier in this hotel's open lobby, clicking across the Italian marble floors, and browsing the gallery of upscale shops that completes the ground-floor offerings of this landmark hotel. **Pros:** every room was recently renovated and updated; at the heart of the city's best shopping district; pet-friendly (with an additional fee). **Cons:** hosts lots of conference groups in shoulder seasons; lacks the charm of more historic properties. $ *Rooms from: $359* ✉ *205 Meeting St., Market* ☎ *843/722–4900, 888/635–2350* 🌐 *www.belmond.com/charleston-place* 🛏 *435 rooms* 🍴 *Some meals.*

$$$ 🏨 **Cannonboro Inn.** *B&B/Inn.* In the MUSC area, this tidy inn features rooms furnished with antiques from the 19th century, when the house was built. **Pros:** free off-street parking; laid-back atmosphere; free use of bicycles for exploring downtown. **Cons:** not so convenient to the tourist area; children under 10 not allowed; breakfast is not as elaborate as at competing B&Bs. $ *Rooms from: $205* ✉ *184 Ashley Ave., Medical University of South Carolina* ☎ *843/723–8572* 🌐 *cannonboro.charleston-sc-inns.com* 🛏 *8 rooms* 🍴 *Breakfast.*

$$ 🏨 **Charleston Marriott.** *Hotel.* The sunset views from the balconies of this river-view hotel get better the higher you go—they're wonderful from the seasonal rooftop Aqua Terrace bar and lounge, where drinks and tapas are served. **Pros:** inexpensive shuttle to downtown; great views of the Ashley River; classy location for conference and business travelers. **Cons:** it's a long walk to King Street and the heart of downtown; fee for Wi-Fi access; no complimentary breakfast. $ *Rooms from: $199* ✉ *170 Lockwood Dr., Medical University of South Carolina* ☎ *843/723–3000* 🌐 *www.marriott.com* 🛏 *340 rooms* 🍴 *No meals.*

$$$ ☰ **Courtyard by Marriott Charleston Historic District.** *Hotel.* Step directly from the heart of the city into the high-tech lobby of this hotel—look for a tucked-away media center with a big-screen TV, a boarding-pass printing station, and a sleek bistro that offers coffee, cocktails, and breakfast and dinner fare. **Pros:** concierge gives great recommendations; families will be right at home in the suites with comfortable seating and kitchenettes. **Cons:** many views are obstructed by other buildings; breakfast not included; overshadowed by upscale newcomers around Marion Square. Ⓢ *Rooms from: $229* ✉ *125 Calhoun St., Upper King* ☎ *843/805–7900* ⊕ *www. marriott.com/hotels/travel/chshd-courtyard-charleston-historic-district* ⤳ *176 rooms* ⦿ *No meals.*

$$$$ ☰ **The Dewberry.** *Hotel.* Built in the renovated Federal Building overlooking Marion Square, the Dewberry exudes style and sophistication from the travertine marble to the mahogany and walnut that adorn the lobby and in-house bar and restaurant. **Pros:** one of the city's best cocktail bars on-site; perfectly central location; world-class spa. **Cons:** sheer indulgence doesn't come free; the planned rooftop bar was shut down by the city. Ⓢ *Rooms from: $499* ✉ *334 Meeting St., Middle King* ☎ *888/550–1450* ⊕ *www.thedewberrycharleston.com* ⤳ *155 rooms* ⦿ *No meals.*

$$$ ☰ **DoubleTree by Hilton Hotel & Suites Charleston–Historic District.**
FAMILY *Hotel.* With a beautifully restored entrance portico from 1874, this former bank building offers spacious suites with nice touches like antique reproductions and canopy beds. **Pros:** it's central to the Market Street tourist district; well-equipped gym; pet-friendly with a $100 deposit. **Cons:** breakfast not included, although there is an on-site café; lacks the historic atmosphere of an independent inn; no self-parking available. Ⓢ *Rooms from: $209* ✉ *181 Church St., Market* ☎ *843/577–2644* ⊕ *www.doubletree.com* ⤳ *212 rooms* ⦿ *No meals.*

★ Fodor'sChoice ☰ **1837 Bed & Breakfast.** *B&B/Inn.* A hospitable
$$ staff helps give you a sense of what it would be like to live in one of Charleston's grand old homes. **Pros:** a very good concierge will help you plan your days; reasonable rates; relaxing porch to rest up after exploring. **Cons:** limited on-site parking; period furniture and decor won't carry as much appeal to younger generations; surrounding college district can be noisy on weekend nights. Ⓢ *Rooms from: $165* ✉ *126 Wentworth St., Market* ☎ *843/723–7166, 877/723–1837* ⊕ *www.1837bb.com* ⤳ *9 rooms* ⦿ *Breakfast.*

PROPERTY TYPES IN CHARLESTON

Charleston's lodgings run the gamut from intimate inns to sophisticated hotels to beachfront resorts where you can pretend you're miles away from civilization.

B&Bs: Although they may be owned by a couple, most B&Bs in Charleston also employ a small staff. Most are within downtown's historic neighborhoods, and many were formerly grand residences, such as the Governor's House Inn or the John Rutledge House Inn.

Inns: In this town, a fine line divides true inns from B&Bs. They are usually larger than B&Bs and often have more professional staff, including a concierge (as at the Planters Inn). The breakfast and evening offerings are often a step above those of B&Bs, and they may even have a restaurant, like the lauded Circa 1886 at the Wentworth Mansion.

Boutique Hotels: Though small by international hotel standards, Charleston's growing array of boutique hotels offer a pampering staff. Those who stay here can experience the good life by day and at night slumber in a sumptuous bed dressed with Egyptian-cotton sheets and cashmere blankets. The Market Pavilion Hotel is perhaps the city's best-known boutique hotel. A newer kid on the boutique hotel block, The Restoration has gained notoriety with visitors and locals alike, thanks to its rooftop bar and restaurant, The Watch.

Full-Service Hotels: Some visitors prefer the amenities and privacy of a large, world-class property (Belmond Charleston Place) or a well-known American chain hotel (such as the Charleston Marriott). In a city where the temperatures are high during the summer months, it may be worth trading historic charm for a hotel pool and vigorous air-conditioning.

Island Resorts: The barrier islands surrounding the city of Charleston are the sites for three major self-contained resorts: Kiawah Island Golf Resort, its neighbor Seabrook Island, and the Wild Dunes Resort on the Isle of Palms. All three have 18-hole golf courses, with Kiawah's being the most famous and most costly (the PGA Championship was played there in 2012), and each has excellent tennis facilities. Seabrook has no hotel accommodations (just villas and condos); Wild Dunes is the most family-friendly.

$$$$ ⊡ **86 Cannon.** *B&B/Inn.* Awash in style and modern luxury yet firmly rooted in historic authenticity, this new arrival caters to the well-to-do with a taste for understated class. **Pros:** posh amenities; thoughtful architectural and design details; wide porches are perfect for an afternoon spent reading. **Cons:** long walk to the heart of town; historic house converted into an inn means fellow guests are always nearby. Ⓢ *Rooms from: $429* ✉ *86 Cannon St., Cannonborough* ☎ *843/779–7700* ⊕ *www.86cannon.com* ⌁ *5 rooms* ⦾ *Breakfast.*

$$$ ⊡ **The Elliott House Inn.** *B&B/Inn.* Listen to the chimes of nearby churches as you sip wine in the greenery-laden courtyard of this inn, then retreat to a cozy room with period furnishings and four-poster beds, or bubble away some social time in the whirlpool tub that can (and often does) hold a dozen people. **Pros:** helpful staff; free bikes and Wi-Fi access; nightly wine-and-cheese reception. **Cons:** street-view rooms can be noisy; no roll-away beds for the kids. Ⓢ *Rooms from: $224* ✉ *78 Queen St., Market* ☎ *843/518–6500* ⊕ *www.elliotthouseinn.com* ⌁ *26 rooms* ⦾ *Breakfast.*

$$$ ⊡ **Embassy Suites Historic Charleston.** *Hotel.* A courtyard where cadets once marched is now a soaring atrium—complete with a glass ceiling, frilly palm trees, and a babbling fountain—in this 1822 building that once served as the Old Citadel. **Pros:** located directly on Marion Square; free made-to-order breakfast; complimentary drinks nightly in the lobby bar. **Cons:** the suites lack charm; some rooms have little or no natural light; it's overshadowed by flashy newcomer neighbors Hotel Bennett and The Dewberry. Ⓢ *Rooms from: $219* ✉ *337 Meeting St., Upper King* ☎ *843/723–6900* ⊕ *www.embassysuites.com* ⌁ *153 suites* ⦾ *Breakfast.*

$$$ ⊡ **Francis Marion Hotel.** *Hotel.* Wrought-iron railings, crown moldings, and decorative plasterwork speak of the elegance of 1924, when the Francis Marion was the largest hotel in the Carolinas. **Pros:** in the midst of the peninsula's best shopping; on-site Spa Adagio; some of the best city views. **Cons:** rooms are small, as is closet space; on a busy intersection; often hosts conferences that fill the hotel. Ⓢ *Rooms from: $219* ✉ *387 King St., Upper King* ☎ *843/722–0600* ⊕ *www.francismarionhotel.com* ⌁ *235 rooms* ⦾ *No meals.*

SOMETHING EXTRA. **Charleston isn't regularly voted among the most romantic cities in the country for nothing. When you book your room, ask about special packages. Extras that are often**

available include romantic carriage rides, dinners, specialty guided tours, and champagne or other goodies delivered to your room. This is the case for most properties downtown.

$$$$ **French Quarter Inn.** *B&B/Inn.* Guests appreciate the lavish seasonal breakfasts with freshly baked pastries (and mimosas and other beverages on weekends), the afternoon wine-and-cheese receptions, and evening cookies and milk at this friendly boutique hotel. **Pros:** a quiet haven in the heart of the Market area; champagne at check-in; free bike rentals. **Cons:** gym access is off-site; neighborhood can be noisy and crowded during peak season; parking is $30/day and valet-only. [$] *Rooms from: $269* ✉ *166 Church St., Market* ☎ *843/722–1900* 🌐 *www.fqicharleston.com* 🛏 *50 rooms* 🍴 *Breakfast* ☞ *Note that the address to enter the hotel is 10 Linguard St.*

$$$ **Fulton Lane Inn.** *B&B/Inn.* This inn is both lovely and quirky: its Victorian-dressed rooms (some with four-poster beds, handsome fireplaces, and jetted tubs) are laid out in a bit of a floor-creaking maze, but it adds to its individuality. **Pros:** location is tops; charming choice of rooms; evening wine, cheese, and sherry. **Cons:** non-suite rooms are a bit cramped; street noise. [$] *Rooms from: $219* ✉ *202 King St., Lower King* ☎ *843/720–2600* 🌐 *www.fultonlaneinn.com* 🛏 *45 rooms* 🍴 *Breakfast.*

$$$$ **Grand Bohemian Charleston.** *Hotel.* One of the entrances to this luxurious Marriott-affiliated hotel steers guests directly into an art gallery, an indication of the modern, creative flair that awaits inside. **Pros:** in-house wine-blending program offered for guests; one of the best rooftop bars in town; central location for walking the Historic District. **Cons:** priced higher than some competitors; the unique emphasis on art won't appeal to everyone. [$] *Rooms from: $425* ✉ *55 Wentworth St., Market* ☎ *843/722–5711* 🌐 *www.grandbohemiancharleston.com* 🛏 *50 rooms* 🍴 *No meals.*

$$ **Hampton Inn Charleston–Historic District.** *Hotel.* Hardwood floors, a central fireplace, and leather furnishings in the lobby of what was once an 1860s railroad warehouse help elevate this chain hotel. **Pros:** hot breakfast; located near numerous restaurant and nightlife options; pleasant outdoor swimming pool area. **Cons:** lacks the charm of independent competitors; rooms are on the small side. [$] *Rooms from: $199* ✉ *345 Meeting St., Upper King* ☎ *843/723–4000* 🌐 *www.hamptoninn.com* 🛏 *170 rooms* 🍴 *Breakfast.*

$$$$ **HarbourView Inn.** *Hotel.* If you ask for a room with a view or even a private balcony here, you can gaze out on Charleston Harbor and onto the fountain at the center of Waterfront

Park. **Pros:** continental breakfast can be delivered to your room or the rooftop; attractive rooftop terrace with soaring views; live music three nights a week, plus weekly beer and wine tastings. **Cons:** chain hotel feel in some parts; not as new and exciting as similarly priced options. [$] *Rooms from: $279* ✉ *2 Vendue Range, Market* ☎ *843/853–8439* 🌐 *www.harbourviewcharleston.com* ⇆ *52 rooms* 🍴 *Breakfast.*

$$ **Hilton Garden Inn Charleston Waterfront.** *Hotel.* A sunny swimming pool and breezy patios overlooking the Ashley River are among the main attractions at this modern hotel that joined the local lodging scene in 2014. **Pros:** complimentary shuttle service to downtown; free parking; near the marinas, MUSC, and The Citadel. **Cons:** too far to walk to King Street; no complimentary breakfast; lacks the character of a historic hotel. [$] *Rooms from: $169* ✉ *45 Lockwood Dr., Medical University of South Carolina* ☎ *843/637–4074* 🌐 *hiltongardeninn3.hilton.com* ⇆ *141 rooms* 🍴 *No meals.*

$$ **Homewood Suites by Hilton Charleston Historic District.** *Hotel.*
FAMILY Centrally located along the Upper King corridor, this new addition balances location, modern amenities, and relative affordability. **Pros:** fitness center features brand new machines; free drinks at the evening happy hour. **Cons:** generic features lack the charm of independent options; the pool area is largely shaded except at midday; parking is valet only. [$] *Rooms from: $179* ✉ *415 Meeting St., Upper King* ☎ *843/724–8800* 🌐 *homewoodsuites3.hilton.com* ⇆ *139 rooms* 🍴 *Breakfast.*

$$$$ **Hotel Bennett.** *Hotel.* This opulent hotel aimed to set the bar even higher for luxury Charleston accommodations with its 2018 opening. **Pros:** the signature spa rivals Charleston Place; state-of-the-art fitness center; rooftop yoga offers the best workout views in town. **Cons:** it may be the most expensive downtown hotel; wedding parties may take over the hotel on weekends; club access is a very pricey upgrade. [$] *Rooms from: $509* ✉ *404 King St., Upper King* ☎ *844/835–2625* 🌐 *www.hotelbennett.com* ⇆ *179 rooms* 🍴 *No meals.*

$$$ **Hyatt House Charleston/Historic District.** *Hotel.* Despite its
FAMILY size, this pair of new hotels (there's a Hyatt Place in the same complex) manages to feel tucked away amidst the buzz of Upper King Street. **Pros:** central location in the booming Upper King district; plenty of space to spread out, especially in the larger suites; a full breakfast is included. **Cons:** sterile atmosphere compared to nearby boutique hotels; Upper King is rapidly becoming a hotel district rather than a local's neighborhood, and this hotel led that

charge. [$] *Rooms from: $220* ✉ *560 King St., Upper King* ☎ *843/207–2299* 🌐 *charlestonhistoricdistrict.house.hyatt.com* 🛏 *113 suites* 🍴 *Breakfast.*

$$ 🏨 **Indigo Inn.** *B&B/Inn.* Repeat guests are the norm thanks to the convenient setting of this family-owned former warehouse with a peaceful vibe, despite its central location near Market Street. **Pros:** excellent location; pets allowed in some rooms; due to its age, it's priced more competitively than other boutique hotels. **Cons:** rooms are not large and some are dark; furniture and decor can feel a little tired. [$] *Rooms from: $199* ✉ *1 Maiden La., Market* ☎ *843/577–5900* 🌐 *www.indigoinn.com* 🛏 *40 rooms* 🍴 *Breakfast.*

$$$ 🏨 **Jasmine House Inn.** *B&B/Inn.* Walking down the quiet, tree-lined street and coming upon this glorious 1843 Greek revival mansion—yellow with white columns—you simply want to make your way inside. **Pros:** complimentary beverages; evening wine-and-cheese spreads on the sideboard; several rooms have working fireplaces. **Cons:** children are not allowed; decor is dated. [$] *Rooms from: $219* ✉ *64 Hassell St., Market* ☎ *843/577–0041* 🌐 *www.jasminehouseinnbnb.com* 🛏 *10 rooms, 1 apartment* 🍴 *Breakfast.*

$$$ 🏨 **Kings Courtyard Inn.** *B&B/Inn.* The three delightful courtyards at this centrally located circa-1853 inn are great places to enjoy your continental breakfast, afternoon sherry, or evening wine and cheese in the open air courtyard. **Pros:** ideal location for walking to shops and restaurants; pets are allowed in four rooms; double-paned windows muffle street noise. **Cons:** walls are thin; guests from Fulton Lane Inn share in the evening receptions in the outdoor courtyard, making it crowded at times. [$] *Rooms from: $219* ✉ *198 King St., Lower King* ☎ *843/723–7000* 🌐 *www.kingscourtyardinn.com* 🛏 *41 rooms* 🍴 *Breakfast.*

$$$$ 🏨 **Market Pavilion Hotel.** *Hotel.* The hustle and bustle of one of the city's busiest corners vanishes as soon as the uniformed bellman opens the lobby door of the Market Pavilion Hotel to reveal wood-paneled walls, antique furnishings, and chandeliers hung from high ceilings; it resembles a European grand hotel from the 19th century, and you'll feel like you're visiting royalty. **Pros:** opulent furnishings; architecturally impressive, especially the tray ceilings; convenient location. **Cons:** gym is small; some may find the interior over-the-top. [$] *Rooms from: $279* ✉ *225 E. Bay St., Market* ☎ *843/723–0500* 🌐 *www.marketpavilion.com* 🛏 *70 rooms* 🍴 *Breakfast.*

$$ 🏨 **The Meeting Street Inn.** *B&B/Inn.* Guest rooms in this 1874 stucco mansion, with porches on the second, third, and fourth floors, overlook a lovely courtyard with fountains

and a hot tub. **Pros:** some rooms have desks and other extras; bathrooms sport nice marble fixtures; fun wine-and-cheese nights. **Cons:** lacy canopy beds and exquisite wallpaper aren't for everyone; some rooms overlook a parking lot; parking is not included and is at the adjacent off-site parking lot. [$] *Rooms from: $159* ✉ *173 Meeting St., Market* ☎ *843/723–1882* 🌐 *www.meetingstreetinn.com* 🛏 *56 rooms* 🍴 *Breakfast.*

$$$ 🏨 **The Mills House.** *Hotel.* A favorite local landmark that serves as a departure point for several historic tours, the Wyndham-managed Mills House is the modern iteration of the original 1853 hotel by the same name. **Pros:** convenient to South of Broad and to Market and King Street shopping; popular Sunday brunch spot; a concierge desk so well regarded that locals call for neighborly assistance and advice. **Cons:** rooms are rather small, which is typical of hotels of this time period; on a busy street; parking is valet-only and expensive. [$] *Rooms from: $209* ✉ *115 Meeting St., Market* ☎ *843/577–2400* 🌐 *www.millshouse.com* 🛏 *215 rooms* 🍴 *No meals.*

$ 🏨 **NotSo Hostel.** *B&B/Inn.* A small enclave of 1840s-era buildings make up this homey, idyllic hostel. **Pros:** great price and sense of camaraderie; historic rooms have character; insider tips from fellow guests and staff. **Cons:** not for travelers who wish to keep to themselves; communal bathrooms. [$] *Rooms from: $68* ✉ *156 Spring St., Cannonborough* ☎ *843/722–8383* 🌐 *www.notsohostel.com* 🛏 *24 dorm beds, 1 room with private bath, 7 rooms with communal baths* 🍴 *No meals.*

$$$$ 🏨 **Planters Inn.** *B&B/Inn.* Part of the Relais & Châteaux group, this boutique property with well-appointed, expansive, and beautifully maintained rooms is a stately sanctuary amid the bustle of Charleston's City Market. **Pros:** double-pane windows render the rooms soundproof; front desk staff knows your name upon arrival; complimentary evening cocktails and bedtime macarons. **Cons:** no pool; gym access is off-site; parking is pricey and by valet only. [$] *Rooms from: $279* ✉ *112 N. Market St., Market* ☎ *843/722–2345* 🌐 *www.plantersinn.com* 🛏 *64 rooms* 🍴 *No meals.*

$$$ 🏨 **Renaissance Charleston Historic District Hotel.** *Hotel.* Marriott aimed for the feel of a boutique hotel with their renovation of this upscale stalwart in the heart of town. **Pros:** located in the King Street shopping district; sizable gym; lively on-site restaurant. **Cons:** parking is either off-site or a pricey valet; charge for in-room Wi-Fi; families may find the pool small. [$] *Rooms*

from: $229 ✉ *68 Wentworth St., Lower King* ☎ *843/534–0300* ⊕ *www.renaissance-charlestonhotel.com* ↪ *166 rooms* ⦿ *No meals.*

★ Fodor's Choice ⊡ **The Restoration.**
$$$$ *B&B/Inn.* Charleston architect Neil Stevenson designed this boutique hotel to be swank and suave to the hilt, even featuring a rooftop terrace with sleek sofas and prime views. **Pros:** complimentary passes to nearby workout facilities; room service comes via neighboring restaurants; free bike rentals. **Cons:** no gym on the premises, but there are some within easy walking distance; prices are steep. ⓢ *Rooms from: $299* ✉ *75 Wentworth St., Market* ☎ *877/221–7202* ⊕ *www.therestorationhotel.com* ↪ *54 suites* ⦿ *Breakfast.*

★ Fodor's Choice ⊡ **The Vendue.** *B&B/Inn.* Thanks to its gorgeous
$$ art-filled space, the Vendue feels as much like a contemporary art museum as it does a boutique hotel. **Pros:** free bike rentals; soundproofing masks street noise; terrific on-site restaurant. **Cons:** no complimentary breakfast; some halls and spaces are small as in centuries past. ⓢ *Rooms from: $179* ✉ *19 Vendue Range, Market* ☎ *843/577–7970* ⊕ *www.thevendue.com* ↪ *84 rooms* ⦿ *No meals.*

$$$$ ⊡ **Wentworth Mansion.** *B&B/Inn.* The grandest inn in town features Second Empire antiques and reproductions, elaborate woodwork, and original stained-glass windows, as well as sweeping views from the rooftop cupola. **Pros:** fantastic on-site restaurant and spa; opulent guest rooms; free parking. **Cons:** style can strike some people as forbidding; outside the tourist areas. ⓢ *Rooms from: $349* ✉ *149 Wentworth St., College of Charleston Campus* ☎ *843/853–1886* ⊕ *www.wentworthmansion.com* ↪ *21 rooms* ⦿ *Breakfast.*

★ Fodor's Choice ⊡ **Zero George.** *Hotel.* Five restored 19th-cen-
$$$$ tury residences have been joined together to create this hideaway in the heart of Charleston's leafy Ansonborough neighborhood that's surrounded by well-heeled homes, and just a short walk from East Bay restaurants, City Market, and Marion Square. **Pros:** convenient and quiet location; local charm; free Wi-Fi and breakfast. **Cons:** it's a bit of a walk to the Market and to King Street; style and luxury

---

DOGGY DAY CARE

Zen Dog. If you brought your dog along but don't want to leave him in your room all day, call Zen Dog, run by Pet Vet Animal Hospital in Mount Pleasant. Their cageless day care includes a backyard for play time. ✉ *307 Mill St., Mount Pleasant* ☎ *843/884–7387* ⊕ *www.petvetmtp.com/zen-dog-daycare.html.*

don't come cheap. $ *Rooms from: $339* ✉ *0 George St., Ansonborough* ☎ *843/817–7900* 🌐 *www.zerogeorge.com* 🛏 *18 rooms* 🍴 *Breakfast.*

SOUTH OF BROAD

$$$$ 🏨 **The Governor's House Inn.** *B&B/Inn.* The stately architecture of this quintessential Charleston lodging radiates the grandeur, romance, and civility of the city's bountiful colonial era. **Pros:** a true taste of the Charleston high life; chairs and beach towels provided for day trips; free off-street parking in an elegant courtyard. **Cons:** kids not allowed in the main-building rooms; the period decor isn't as trendy as newer options; no elevator, so don't book an upstairs room if you need one. $ *Rooms from: $265* ✉ *117 Broad St., South of Broad* ☎ *843/720–2070, 800/720–9812* 🌐 *www.governorshouse.com* 🛏 *11 rooms* 🍴 *Breakfast.*

$$$$ 🏨 **John Rutledge House Inn.** *B&B/Inn.* The New Orleans–esque exterior of this National Historic Landmark (the former residence of politician John Rutledge) has wrought-iron architectural details, and inside, parquet floors sit beneath 14-foot ceilings adorned with plaster moldings. **Pros:** afternoon tea is served in the former ballroom; quiet back courtyard; friendly staff. **Cons:** you can hear some street and kitchen noise in the first-floor rooms; the two carriage houses are not as grand as the main house. $ *Rooms from: $289* ✉ *116 Broad St., South of Broad* ☎ *843/723–7999* 🌐 *www.johnrutledgehouseinn.com* 🛏 *19 rooms* 🍴 *Breakfast.*

$$$ 🏨 **Two Meeting Street Inn.** *B&B/Inn.* As pretty as a wedding cake, this 1892 Queen Anne–style mansion wears overhanging bays, colonnades, balustrades, and a turret; two original Tiffany stained-glass windows (worth as much as the house itself), carved-oak paneling, and a crystal chandelier dress up the public spaces. **Pros:** free on-street parking; community refrigerator on each floor; ringside seat for a Battery view and horse-drawn carriages clipping by. **Cons:** no credit cards accepted; not equipped for handicapped guests; decor can feel dated. $ *Rooms from: $225* ✉ *2 Meeting St., South of Broad* ☎ *843/723–7322* 🌐 *www.twomeetingstreet.com* 💳 *No credit cards* 🛏 *9 rooms* 🍴 *Breakfast.*

MOUNT PLEASANT

★ Fodor's Choice 🏨 **The Beach Club at Charleston Harbor Resort & Marina.** *Resort.* Mount Pleasant's finest hotel sits on
$$$
FAMILY
Charleston Harbor, so you can gaze at the city's skyline with your feet on this resort's sandy beach or from the

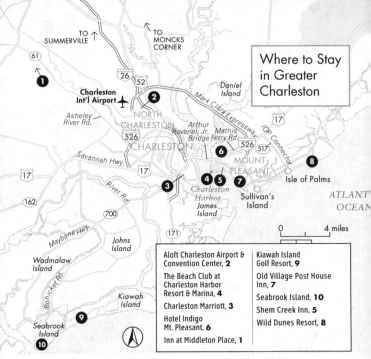

TO
SUMMERVILLE

TO
MONCKS
CORNER

Charleston
Int'l Airport

Asheley
River Rd.

NORTH
CHARLESTON

Daniel
Island

Mark Clark Expressway

Arthur
Ravenel, Jr.
Bridge

Mathis
Ferry Rd.

CHARLESTON

Savannah Hwy.

River Rd.

Charleston
Harbor

James
Island

MOUNT
PLEASANT

Sullivan's
Island

Isle of Palms

ATLANT
OCEAN

Johns
Island

Wadmalaw
Island

Maybank Hwy.

Kiawah
Island

Seabrook
Island

Where to Stay in Greater Charleston

0   4 miles

Aloft Charleston Airport &
Convention Center, **2**

The Beach Club at
Charleston Harbor
Resort & Marina, **4**

Charleston Marriott, **3**

Hotel Indigo
Mt. Pleasant, **6**

Inn at Middleton Place, **1**

Kiawah Island
Golf Resort, **9**

Old Village Post House
Inn, **7**

Seabrook Island, **10**

Shem Creek Inn, **5**

Wild Dunes Resort, **8**

waterfront pool. **Pros:** easy access to downtown but offers an away-from-it-all vibe; large pool and extensive grounds are perfect for enjoying a sunset glass of wine; on-site gym. **Cons:** a bit removed from the action; not pet-friendly; no complimentary breakfast. $ *Rooms from: $225* ⊠ *20 Patriots Point Rd., Mount Pleasant* ☎ *843/856–0028* ⊕ *www. charlestonharborresort.com* ⬩ *92 rooms* ⦶ *No meals.*

$$ ⊡ **Hotel Indigo Mt. Pleasant.** *Hotel.* Just a five-minute drive over the scenic Arthur Ravenel Jr. Bridge from downtown Charleston, this former Holiday Inn underwent a major overhaul in 2017, including full renovations of every room and amenities upgrades designed for business travelers. **Pros:** recently updated pool and fitness center; state-of-the-art business center; pets are allowed with a fee. **Cons:** not downtown; lacks historic atmosphere; a condo complex blocks the bridge view. $ *Rooms from: $159* ⊠ *250 Johnnie Dodds Blvd., Mount Pleasant* ☎ *843/884–6000* ⊕ *mountpleasantlyindigo.com* ⬩ *158 rooms* ⦶ *No meals.*

$$ ⊡ **Old Village Post House Inn.** *B&B/Inn.* This white wooden building anchoring Mount Pleasant's historic Old Village neighborhood is three-in-one—an excellent restaurant, a neighborly tavern, and a cozy inn set at the top of a high

staircase. **Pros:** prices are as affordable as some chain motels on the highway; in the most picturesque and walkable neighborhood in Mount Pleasant; close to Sullivan's Island and Isle of Palms. **Cons:** shares some public spaces with the downstairs restaurant; some minor old building woes including creaky wood floors; not a traditional hotel, so service can be quirky. $ *Rooms from: $200* ✉ *101 Pitt St., Mount Pleasant* ☎ *843/388–8935* 🌐 *www.oldvillagepost-houseinn.com* 🛏 *6 rooms* 🍴 *Breakfast.*

$$ FAMILY **Shem Creek Inn.** *Hotel.* Shem Creek is the heart of Mount Pleasant, and this long-standing inn's recent renovation now makes the charming waterway an attractive place to call home for the night. **Pros:** daily continental breakfast; free on-site parking; easy access to Shem Creek's restaurants and kayak tours. **Cons:** the bars across the creek host live music and can get noisy on weekends; it's a drive or a cab ride to get downtown; the inn's location and affordability guarantee that some guests come here to party. $ *Rooms from: $169* ✉ *1401 Shrimp Boat La., Mount Pleasant* ☎ *843/881–1000* 🌐 *www.shemcreekinn.com* 🛏 *51 rooms* 🍴 *Breakfast.*

4

ELSEWHERE IN AND AROUND CHARLESTON

$ **Aloft Charleston Airport & Convention Center.** *Hotel.* Designed with the young, hip, and high-tech traveler in mind, this chain hotel has everything from touch-screen check-in kiosks to a stylish bar with a pool table. **Pros:** indoor pool; convenient for airport, convention center, and outlet shopping; pet-friendly vibe. **Cons:** noise from planes taking off; somewhat cramped rooms; no complimentary breakfast. $ *Rooms from: $141* ✉ *4875 Tanger Outlet Blvd., North Charleston* ☎ *843/566–7300* 🌐 *www.aloftcharlestonairport.com* 🛏 *136 rooms* 🍴 *No meals.*

★ Fodor's Choice $$ **Inn at Middleton Place.** *B&B/Inn.* On the banks of the Ashley River, this country inn offers a peaceful respite from the city—there are even shady hammocks outside for afternoon naps and a pool fronting the river. **Pros:** beautiful setting for morning and evening walks; bicycle and kayak rentals available; pet-friendly up to 50 pounds. **Cons:** half-hour drive from downtown Charleston. $ *Rooms from: $159* ✉ *4290 Ashley River Rd., West Ashley* ☎ *843/556–0500, 800/543–4774* 🌐 *www.theinnatmiddletonplace.com* 🛏 *55 rooms* 🍴 *Breakfast.*

$$$$ FAMILY **Kiawah Island Golf Resort.** *Resort.* Choose from one- to four-bedroom villas, three- to eight-bedroom private homes, or the Sanctuary at Kiawah Island, a glistening

255-room luxury waterfront hotel and spa that is one of the most prestigious resorts in the country and yet is still kid-friendly. **Pros:** smaller villas are more affordable; restaurant is an ideal venue for an anniversary or a proposal; the golf courses and tennis programs are ranked among the country's best. **Cons:** not all rooms have ocean views; pricey and a long drive from town. [$] *Rooms from: $285* ✉ *1 Sanctuary Beach Dr., Kiawah Island* ☎ *843/768–2121, 800/654–2924* 🌐 *www.kiawahresort.com* ↩ *750 rooms and villas* 🍴 *No meals.*

$$ FAMILY 🏨 **Seabrook Island.** *Resort.* About 350 fully equipped one- to six-bedroom villas, cottages, townhomes, and homes are available on Seabrook, one of the most private of the area's island resorts, on a physically beautiful, relatively unspoiled island. **Pros:** safe haven for kids to play; the only place in the area where you can ride horses on the beach; nearby upscale shopping and restaurants. **Cons:** a 45-minute drive from Charleston; security can be stringent—don't drive over the posted 25 mph speed limit. [$] *Rooms from: $200* ✉ *3772 Seabrook Island Rd., Seabrook Island* ☎ *855/441–4404* 🌐 *www.wyndhamvacationrentals.com* ↩ *350 units* 🍴 *No meals.*

$$ FAMILY 🏨 **Wild Dunes Resort.** *Resort.* Guests at this 1,600-acre island beachfront resort can choose from a long list of recreational options, including Tom Fazio–designed golf courses and a nationally ranked tennis program. **Pros:** golf courses are first-class; family-friendly bike paths parallel every thoroughfare; beach is rarely crowded. **Cons:** in summer, kids dominate the pool areas and the boardwalk; 30-minute drive to downtown Charleston, and summer beach traffic can make day trips a headache. [$] *Rooms from: $189* ✉ *1 Sundial Circle, Isle of Palms* ☎ *866/359–5593* 🌐 *www.destinationhotels.com/wild-dunes* ↩ *493 rooms* 🍴 *No meals.*

5

NIGHTLIFE AND PERFORMING ARTS

Updated
by Stratton
Lawrence

FOR A MIDSIZE CITY, CHARLESTON has a surprisingly varied and sophisticated arts scene, though the city really shines during its major annual arts festival, Spoleto Festival USA. Still, throughout the year, there are ample opportunities to explore higher culture, from productions by the Footlight Players and PURE Theatre, to concerts at the historic Charleston Music Hall.

The nightlife scene is similarly comprehensive, with nocturnal venues for all ages and tastes. If your image of Charleston is a buttoned-down town with men in seersucker suits and bow ties, think again.

Today, Charleston nightlife can be rowdy and more youth-oriented, though there is still a fair share of jazz clubs and other venues that cater to more mellow evenings. Here the nightlife begins at happy hour, which can start as early as 4 pm. Several bars and restaurants have incredible happy hour deals, and a night of barhopping generally includes grazing on small plates. Long lines outside an establishment can indicate a younger crowd, and/or mean that a good band is playing, like at the Music Farm.

PERFORMING ARTS

ANNUAL FESTIVALS AND EVENTS

Spoleto USA is only the beginning—there are dozens of festivals held throughout the city each year. Some focus on food and wine, whereas others are concerned with gardens and architecture. Charleston is one of the few American cities that can claim a distinctive regional cuisine.

Charleston Fashion Week. Toasting emerging designers and models with runway shows, competitions, and exhibitions, the main events at this five-night festival in March are held beneath tents in Marion Square. Smaller shows are hosted by downtown boutiques. The festival has helped several designers launch their fashion careers. But perhaps even more impressive than the festival are the tony after-parties. ⊠ *Marion Square, King and Calhoun Sts., Upper King* ⊕ *www.charlestonfashionweek.com.*

★ Fodor's Choice **Charleston Wine + Food.** Since 2005, this annual fete has served as the city's marquee event for foodies. Spread over five days, it brings together the nation's leading chefs (including local James Beard award winners), food writers, and, of course, regular diners who love to eat and drink. Held the first full weekend of March, it emphasizes the Lowcountry's culinary heritage. Marion Square serves as the hub with its Culinary Village, but savvy attendees grab up tickets quickly for the numerous dinners and special events held around the city. ⊠ *Charleston* ☎ *843/727–9998* ⊕ *www.charlestonwineandfood.com.*

FAMILY **Cooper River Bridge Run.** Each year in early April, more than 40,000 runners race from Mount Pleasant to the pinnacle of Charleston's highest structure—the Arthur Ravenel Jr. Bridge—and into downtown Charleston. Along the 10K route, live bands keep the runners pumped until they reach the massive finish party at Marion Square. Even if you don't run, the finish line is a celebration worth joining. ■TIP→ **If you're in town during the first weekend of April but not participating, note that traffic between Mount Pleasant and downtown is rerouted through North Charleston during the race, and heavy traffic persists throughout the city until the afternoon.** ☎ *843/856–1949* ⊕ *www.bridgerun.com.*

Fall Tour of Homes. Sponsored every October by the Preservation Society of Charleston, the Fall Tour of Homes provides an inside look at Charleston's private buildings and gardens, from stately mansions on the Battery to intact Revolutionary-era houses. ⊠ *147 King St., Market* ☎ *843/722–4630* ⊕ *www.preservationsociety.org/falltours.*

Festival of Houses & Gardens. More than 100 private homes, gardens, and historic churches are open to the public for tours during the Festival of Houses & Gardens, held annually during March and April. There are also symphony galas in stately drawing rooms, plantation oyster roasts, and candlelight tours. ⊠ *108 Meeting St., Market* ☎ *843/722–3405* ⊕ *www.historiccharleston.org.*

FAMILY **High Water Fest.** Curated by the Charleston-bred musical duo Shovels & Rope, this waterfront music festival features the buzziest national indie and alt-country acts like The Shins, The Avett Brothers, and Band of Horses. There's a fitting emphasis on food, with top local restaurants and food trucks dishing out inspired options that stand above most festival fare. ⊠ *1001 Everglades Ave, North Charleston* ⊕ *www.highwaterfest.com* 🎫 *$159.*

FAMILY **MOJA Arts Festival.** Held each year in late September and early October, this festival celebrates the region's African heritage and Caribbean influences on local culture. It includes theater, dance, and music performances, lectures, art shows, and films. The free Sunday afternoon finale, featuring concerts, dancing, and plenty of food, is a marquee city event each year. ✉ *Charleston* ☎ *843/724–7305* ⊕ *www.mojafestival.com.*

FAMILY **Piccolo Spoleto Festival.** The spirited companion festival of Spoleto Festival USA showcases the best in local and regional talent from every artistic discipline. There are as many as 700 events—from jazz performances to puppet shows, chamber music concerts, and expansive art shows in Marion Square—from mid-May through early June. Many of the performances are free or inexpensive, and hundreds of these cultural experiences are kid-friendly. ✉ *Charleston* ☎ *843/724–7305* ⊕ *www.piccolospoleto.com.*

FAMILY **Southeastern Wildlife Exposition.** One of Charleston's biggest annual events, this celebration of the region's flora and fauna takes place in mid-February, offering fine art by renowned wildlife artists, bird of prey demonstrations, dog competitions, an oyster roast, and a gala. Spread across three days, the expo generally attracts more than 500 artists and 40,000 participants to various venues around the city. ✉ *Charleston* ☎ *843/723–1748* ⊕ *www.sewe.com.*

★ Fodor'sChoice **Spoleto Festival USA.** For 17 glorious days in late
FAMILY May and early June, Charleston gets a dose of culture from the Spoleto Festival USA. This internationally acclaimed performing-arts festival features a mix of distinguished artists and emerging talent from around the world. Performances take place in magical settings, such as the College of Charleston's Cistern beneath a canopy of ancient oaks or inside a centuries-old cathedral.

A mix of formal concerts and casual performances is what Pulitzer Prize–winning composer Gian Carlo Menotti had in mind when, in 1977, he initiated the festival as a complement to his opera-heavy Italian festival. He chose Charleston because of its European look and because its residents love the arts—not to mention any cause for celebration. He wanted the festival to be a "fertile ground for the young" as well as a "dignified home for the masters."

Some 45 events—with most tickets averaging between $25 and $50—include everything from improv to Shakespeare, from rap to chamber music, from ballet to salsa. Because events sell out quickly, buy tickets several weeks in advance (book hotel rooms and make restaurant reservations early, too). Tickets to midweek performances are a bit easier to secure. ✉ *Charleston* ☎ *843/579–3100* ⊕ *www.spoletousa.org.*

CLASSICAL MUSIC

Charleston Symphony Orchestra. With a season that runs from late September through April, the Charleston Symphony Orchestra hosts full-scale symphonic performances, chamber ensembles, a pops series, family-oriented events, and holiday concerts at the newly renovated Gaillard Performance Hall. This symphony is nationally renowned and serves as the Spoleto Festival Orchestra. ✉ *Charleston* ☎ *843/723–7528* ⊕ *www.charlestonsymphony.com.*

FILM

FAMILY **Regal Palmetto Grande Stadium 16.** This grand art-deco-style multiplex is Charleston's most modern cinema, with comfortable stadium-style seats and the usual popcorn and treats. ✉ *1319 Theater Dr., Mount Pleasant* ☎ *844/462–7342* ⊕ *www.regmovies.com.*

FAMILY **Terrace Theater.** About 10 minutes from downtown, this local favorite hosts its own film festival every March. Its carpeted halls and theaters have the feel of an old-school cinema, screening a mix of new releases and indie films. Concessions include beer and wine. ✉ *1956 Maybank Hwy., James Island* ☎ *843/762–4247* ⊕ *www.terracetheater.com.*

THEATER

FAMILY **Charleston Stage at the Dock Street Theatre.** The original Dock Street Theatre opened in 1736, as the first dedicated theater in America. A major renovation in 2010 reopened the historic building to the public. Charleston Stage produces musicals and plays throughout the year, including many geared toward families and children. ✉ *135 Church St., Downtown Historic District* ☎ *843/720–3968* ⊕ *www. charlestonstage.com.*

Footlight Players. In a charming theater built in a former cotton warehouse tucked into the French Quarter, this troupe—in continuous operation since 1931—produces original plays, musicals, and other events throughout the year. ✉ *20 Queen St., Market* ☎ *843/722–4487* ⊕ *www. footlightplayers.net.*

PURE Theatre. In a cozy space facing Upper King Street, this local troupe produces timely comedies and thoughtful classics throughout the year, as well as special holiday performances. ✉ *477 King St., Upper King* ☎ *843/723–4444* ⊕ *www.puretheatre.org.*

VENUES

Charleston Gaillard Center. This city-owned grand performance hall reopened in 2015 after a $142 million complete renovation. It now hosts symphony, theater, and ballet companies, as well as concerts by renowned musicians and numerous events during Spoleto Festival USA. ⊠ *77 Calhoun St., Upper King* ☎ *843/242–3099* ⊕ *gaillardcenter.org.*

★ Fodor'sChoice **Charleston Music Hall.** Regularly hosting big-name bluegrass, blues, and country acts, the beautiful 900-seat Charleston Music Hall shines. Home to the Charleston Jazz Orchestra, it's in the heart of Upper King and within easy walking distance of numerous popular bars and restaurants for pre- and postshow refreshments. ⊠ *37 John St., Upper King* ☎ *843/853–2252* ⊕ *www.charlestonmusichall.com.*

North Charleston Performing Art Center. Touring Broadway productions and big-name bands frequent the 2,300-seat North Charleston Performing Art Center. In recent years, performers such as Bon Iver, Tony Bennett, and Willie Nelson have taken the stage. ■ TIP→ **It's worth paying extra for seats in the front half of the venue.** ⊠ *5001 Coliseum Dr., North Charleston* ☎ *843/529–5000* ⊕ *www.northcharlestoncoliseumpac.com.*

Simons Center for the Arts. Performances by the College of Charleston's theater department and chamber and classical musical recitals are presented here during the school year. ⊠ *54 St. Phillips St., College of Charleston Campus* ☎ *843/953–6315* ⊕ *music.cofc.edu/concerts.*

NIGHTLIFE

Charleston loves a good party, and the city boasts an ever-growing array of choices for a night on the town. The more mature crowd goes to the sophisticated spots, and there are many wine bars, clubs featuring jazz groups, and trendy lounges with craft cocktail menus. Rooftop bars are a particular Charleston tradition, and the city has several good ones. Many restaurants offer live entertainment on at least one weekend night, catering to crowds of all ages. The Upper King area has grown exponentially in recent years, overtaking the Market area in terms of popularity and variety of bars and lounges. ■ TIP→ **A city ordinance mandates that bars must close by 2 am, so last call is usually 1:30.**

NORTH OF BROAD

LOWER KING

BARS AND PUBS

Bin 152. Husband-and-wife Patrick and Fanny Panella ply their guests with selections from more than 130 bottles of wine and 40 varieties of cheeses and charcuterie, freshly baked breads, contemporary art, and tasteful antique furniture. All of it is imminently available, too, from the Sauvignon Blanc and Shiraz to the tables and chairs. Cast in low lighting, the wine bar serves as a comfortable backdrop for a pre- or post-dinner drink, or an entire evening. ⊠ *152 King St., Lower King* ☎ *843/577–7359* ⊕ *www.bin152.com.*

MARKET AREA

BARS AND PUBS

Cane Rhum Bar. Just off of Market Street, this classy but colorful cocktail lounge serves creative island-inspired concoctions and Caribbean street food to a mixed crowd of visitors, weekend revelers and after-work professionals. Funky, laid-back decor lightens the mood, making it a welcome escape from the bustle of the Market. ⊠ *251 E. Bay St., Market* ☎ *843/277–2764.*

★ Fodor'sChoice **The Gin Joint.** The cocktails here—frothy fizzes, slings, smashes, and juleps—are retro, some dating back to before Prohibition. The bartenders don bow ties and suspenders, but the atmosphere is utterly contemporary, with slick gray walls, butcher block table tops, and subtle lighting. The kitchen serves up small plates like oysters, arugula salad, and Coca-Cola braised ham. ⊠ *182 E. Bay St., Market* ☎ *843/577–6111* ⊕ *www.theginjoint.com.*

The Griffon. Dollar bills cover just about every square inch of the Griffon, helping the bar achieve nearly legendary status around the city. Its wood interior is dark, dusty, and well worn, yet charming. A rotating selection of draft beers comes from local breweries like Westbrook, Coast, and Holy City. It's a popular lunchtime and happy hour watering hole, and hosts live music on weekend nights. ⊠ *18 Vendue Range, Market* ☎ *843/723–1700* ⊕ *www.griffoncharleston.com.*

Henry's. The longest continuously operating restaurant and bar in South Carolina, Henry's House has evolved since it opened in 1930. On the first floor is a large horseshoe bar and dining room with floor-to-ceiling windows looking out to the Market. The second floor is a classic jazz bar with exposed brick and rafters, and dim chandelier lighting. A few steps up is a rooftop deck and an enclosed dance lounge that attracts a younger crowd on weekends. ⊠ *54 N. Market, Market* ☎ *843/723–4363* ⊕ *www.henryshousecharleston.com.*

UP ON THE ROOF. Locals head to the city's rooftop bars on summer evenings where cool breezes offer relief from the heat. Establishments like the Pavilion Bar, the Rooftop at Vendue, and Henry's have made rooftop terraces into bars and lounges. At sunset, you can watch the horizon change colors and view the boats in the harbor.

★ Fodor's Choice **Pavilion Bar.** Atop the Market Pavilion Hotel, the swanky outdoor Pavilion Bar offers panoramic views of the city and harbor, set around the hotel's posh swimming pool. Enjoy appetizers like lobster ceviche and duck nachos with a specialty mojito or martini. The dress code dictates no flip-flops, baseball caps, visors, or tank tops. ⊠ *Market Pavilion Hotel, 225 E. Bay St., Market* ☎ *843/723–0500* ⊕ *www.marketpavilion.com.*

Pearlz Oyster Bar. People come here from far and wide for the raw or steamed oysters—fat, juicy, and plucked from the Louisiana Gulf, Nova Scotia, and various points in between. Try the oyster shooters: one oyster in a shot glass, topped with Absolut Peppar vodka and a few squirts of spicy cocktail sauce. Consider it an opening sortie before popping in at the other East Bay Street–area hot spots in downtown Charleston. ⊠ *153 E. Bay St., Market* ☎ *843/577–5755* ⊕ *www.pearlzoysterbar.com.*

The Rooftop Bar at Vendue. Have a cocktail and appetizer as you watch the colorful sunset behind the church steeples. There are actually two bars at this venue atop the recently renovated Vendue Inn; the lower Deck Bar has tables and chairs shaded by umbrellas, but the view of the water is partially obscured by condo towers. Keep going to the upper-level bar, which offers a 360-degree panorama and an open-air atmosphere. You'll find live music by local and regional bands on weekends. Get here early—they close at 10 pm on weekdays and at midnight on weekends. ⊠ *Vendue Inn, 19 Vendue Range, Market* ☎ *843/577–7970* ⊕ *www.thevendue.com.*

JAZZ CLUBS

★ FodorsChoice **Charleston Grill.** The elegant Charleston Grill hosts live jazz seven nights a week, drawing from the city's most renowned musicians. Performers range from the internationally acclaimed Brazilian guitarist Duda Lucena to the Bob Williams Duo, a father and son who play classical guitar and violin. The place draws an urbane crowd that spans generations. Down the hall, the neighboring Thoroughbred Club offers nightly live music and an impressive selection of bourbons. ⊠ *Charleston Place Hotel, 224 King St., Market* ☎ *843/577–4522* ⊕ *www.charlestongrill.com.*

LIVE MUSIC

Halls Chophouse. This pricey bar and restaurant, which caters to a crowd of professionals young and old, has a contemporary, minimalist interior design. A piano-and-sax duo serenades the first-floor dinner patrons and the bar crowd several nights a week. During Sunday brunch, the Plantation Singers gospel group belts out the spiritual blues. A "must-have" is Halls's signature martini—lavender-infused vodka with rosemary and a trio of berries. ⊠ *434 King St., Market* ☎ *843/727–0090* ⊕ *www.hallschophouse.com.*

Salty Mike's. This bar offers fine service to sailors, college kids, and out-of-towners alike, with cheap domestic beer and old-fashioned cocktails. Situated beneath the Marina Variety Store restaurant—itself a Charleston landmark dating back to 1963—Salty Mike's provides a crusty, no-frills ambience and a dreamy seaside view of the Ashley River and Charleston City Marina. ⊠ *17 Lockwood Dr., North of Broad* ☎ *843/937–0208* ⊕ *www.varietystorerestaurant.com.*

The Thoroughbred Club. The Thoroughbred Club is fun and has more than a touch of class, with a horse-racing theme and excellent appetizer menu. You can order three appetizers for $25—a great deal when you consider dishes like seared diver scallops with wild mushrooms and pancetta. Go for the impressive afternoon tea offered Thursday through Sunday, or sip a cocktail and enjoy the soothing piano being played Monday through Friday, and Sunday from 4 to 11 and Saturday from 1 to 11. Each of the pianists has a different repertoire, so depending on the song requests, they can infect the patrons with a wonderful spirit and camaraderie. ⊠ *Charleston Place Hotel, 130 Market St., Market* ☎ *843/722–4900* ⊕ *www.charlestonplace.com.*

Tommy Condon's. Enjoy Irish music by local group, the Bograts, on most weekends at this rollicking, traditional Irish pub. If you're hungry, dig into the Irish nachos—cubed potatoes, cheddar cheese, jalapeños, tomatoes, and ranch dressing—with a Guinness or Harp. ⊠ *160 Church St., Market* ☎ *843/577–3818* ⊕ *www.tommycondons.com.*

UPPER KING

BARS AND PUBS

★ Fodor'sChoice **The Belmont.** This place doesn't seek attention—heck, it won't even list its phone number. But with a soaring tin ceiling, exposed-brick walls, and a penchant for projecting black-and-white films onto the wall, the charisma comes naturally. An inventive cocktail menu served up by sharply dressed mixologists helps, too. Try their take on the spicy-sweet Brown Derby, a bourbon drink made with jalapeño-infused honey, or the Bells of Jalisco, featuring *reposado* tequila, more jalapeño honey, and lime juice. There's also a light menu of panini, charcuterie, and homemade pop tarts. ⊠ *511 King St., Upper King* ⊕ *www.thebelmontcharleston.com.*

Burns Alley. You'll do well just to find this place. Tucked into an alley behind the Walgreen's at King and Calhoun streets, Burns Alley offers cozy quarters for sports fans in need of cheap beers and a giant projection screen. A small upstairs area overlooks the action, offering a premium vantage point during crowded evenings. ⊠ *354B King St., Upper King* ☎ *843/723–6735* ⊕ *www.burnsalley.com.*

Charleston Beer Works. This friendly watering hole with 40 draft beers on tap offers a late-night menu of wings and pub grub. Live music on weekends and ample screens for sports events make this a popular hangout for the college crowd. ⊠ *480 King St., Upper King* ☎ *843/727–2151* ⊕ *www.charlestonbeerworks.com.*

Closed for Business. This "draught emporium" offers more than 40 taps pouring pints and liters of local and seasonal brews. With pale wood paneling, leather club chairs, and light bulbs flickering in a fireplace, the place has plenty of charm. CFB also features a tasty menu of upscale pub fare, including Chicago-style hot dogs and a fried pork cutlet sandwich called the Pork Slap. ⊠ *453 King St., Upper King* ☎ *843/853–8466* ⊕ *www.closed4business.com.*

The Cocktail Club. This establishment characterizes the craft cocktail movement with its "farm-to-shaker" seasonal selection of creative concoctions. The bar showcases exposed-brick walls and wooden beams inside its lounge areas, though warm evenings are best spent outside on the rooftop patio. Inside, some of Charleston's best bartenders muddle and shake clever mixtures like the Allan Greenspoon, made with green chili vodka, aloe vera liqueur, and lime juice, and the Double Standard, a serrano-pepper-infused gin-and-cucumber vodka blend. ✉ *479 King St., #200, Upper King* ☎ *843/724–9411* ⊕ *www.thecocktailclubcharleston.com.*

Dudley's on Ann. A local landmark, the city's oldest gay bar hosts lively karaoke parties, DJs and dancing on weekends, and lively drag shows. ✉ *42 Ann St., Upper King* ☎ *843/577–6779* ⊕ *www.dudleysonann.com.*

O-Ku. Done up in black and white, this edgy Japanese establishment serves exquisite small plates like ceviche with mango, pear, and mint- *yuzu* vinaigrette that pair perfectly with a sake flight. You can lounge on the couches during happy hour—which runs from 5 to 7 Monday, Wednesday, and Friday—and enjoy half-priced sake and signature sushi rolls. On Saturday night, a high-energy DJ cranks out tunes while the place becomes a velvet rope club. ✉ *463 King St., Upper King* ☎ *843/737–0112* ⊕ *www.o-kusushichs.com.*

Pour Taproom. This bar atop the Historic District Hyatt serves beer by the ounce from their 70 taps, allowing patrons to sample ad infinitum. It's biggest draw, however, is the view. From its ninth-floor vantage, it's the highest rooftop bar in the city. ✉ *560 King St., Upper King* ☎ *843/779–0810* ⊕ *charleston.pourtaproom.com.*

Prohibition. This throwback speakeasy mixes signature craft cocktails and offers a respectable beer-and-wine selection to accompany Southern-inspired burgers, pork chops, and duck dishes. A ragtime jazz band plays in the early evening on weekends, then the tables are removed and a DJ transforms the dining room into a full-on dance club. ✉ *547 King St., Upper King* ☎ *843/793–2964* ⊕ *prohibitioncharleston.com.*

Proof. These cozy quarters on King Street, complete with communal tables surrounded by bar stools, bustle at happy hour and on weekend evenings. The upscale bar offers seasonal signature cocktails, as well as a respectful selection of wines and craft beers. ✉ *437 King St., Upper King* ☎ *843/793–1422* ⊕ *www.charlestonproof.com.*

★ Fodor'sChoice **South Seas Tiki Lounge.** The city's most authentic tiki bar transports patrons to a nighttime Polynesian paradise with carefully crafted zombies and mai tais. In addition to the bar, there's a comfy lounge and peaceful patio tucked away just off King Street. ⊠ *23 Ann St., Upper King* ☎ *843/306–0101* ⊕ *www.southseastiki.com.*

Vintage Lounge. There's a Gilded Age vibe at this swanky but relaxed wine bar set in a long, dimly lit room framed with splashes of gold and a massive marble bar. The carefully selected menu of wines by the glass is accompanied by small plates and fondue. ⊠ *545 King St., Upper King* ☎ *843/818–4282* ⊕ *www.vintagechs.com.*

DANCE CLUBS
Trio. Funky sounds from the '70s and '80s mix with the latest club anthems at this perennially popular dance club. Listen to the cover bands at the downstairs bar, mingle on the outdoor patio, or head upstairs for the DJ-led dance party. It's only open Friday and Saturday nights. ⊠ *139 Calhoun St., Upper King* ⊕ *www.triocharleston.com.*

LIVE MUSIC
Music Farm. Once a train depot, this towering space is filled to the max when popular bands like Galactic, Neko Case, and Big Gigantic play. Tickets typically range from $15 to $25. The bar is only open on nights when a concert is scheduled. ⊠ *32 Ann St., Upper King* ☎ *843/577–6989* ⊕ *www.musicfarm.com.*

MOUNT PLEASANT

Spirit of Carolina. Dine and dance the night away aboard the wide-beamed, motor yacht *Spirit of Carolina.* Dinner is three or more courses and includes a choice of five entrées, from shrimp and grits to New York strip. Live musicians perform blues and beach music during the cruise. This three-hour excursion appeals to an older crowd, but everyone enjoys seeing the twinkling lights of the harbor. The ship departs from Patriots Point in Mount Pleasant. Reservations are essential for evening cruises. ⊠ *40 Patriots Point Rd., Mount Pleasant* ☎ *843/722–2628* ⊕ *www.spiritlinecruises.com.*

GREATER CHARLESTON

ISLE OF PALMS

LIVE MUSIC

The Windjammer. An oceanfront bar with well-known rock bands performing on the raised stage, the Windjammer attracts a mix of young people just out of college, salty locals, and visiting tourists. Expect to pay $10–$25 admission when there's a live band, but if you sit on the back deck there's generally no cover charge. The volleyball court and deck play host to bikini contests throughout the summer. ✉ *1008 Ocean Blvd., Isle of Palms* ☎ *843/886–8948* ⊕ *www.the-windjammer.com.*

JAMES ISLAND

LIVE MUSIC

FAMILY **The Pour House.** The heart of Charleston's live music community lies off the peninsula at this colorful club decorated with murals. Touring acts like the Chris Robinson Brotherhood and Keller Williams play the main stage on most nights, while the sprawling outdoor deck hosts family-friendly free concerts by local musicians every evening. There's a Cuban food truck on-site, and the adjacent farm-to-table eatery, The Lot. ✉ *1977 Maybank Hwy., James Island* ☎ *843/571–4343* ⊕ *www.charlestonpourhouse.com.*

SULLIVAN'S ISLAND

BARS AND PUBS

Dunleavy's Pub. Just a block from the beach, this friendly pub is a local favorite, often featuring Irish, folk, and blues music throughout the week. It's also home to the annual Polar Bear Plunge on New Year's Day. ✉ *2213 Middle St., Sullivan's Island* ☎ *843/883–9646* ⊕ *www.dunleavyson-sullivans.com.*

6

SPORTS AND THE OUTDOORS

Updated by Stratton Lawrence

CALLED THE LOWCOUNTRY BECAUSE IT'S at sea level—and sometimes even below—Charleston is surrounded by an array of tidal creeks, estuaries, and rivers that flow out to the deep blue Atlantic Ocean. The region's beaches are taupe sand, and the Carolina sun warms them nine months out of the year. Many are uncrowded, especially in the spring and fall, when it's not hard to find the perfect spot.

Several barrier islands within easy driving distance of the city are studded with lacy palm trees and live oaks hung with Spanish moss. The car-accessible islands are fairly extensively developed, but still shelter plenty of wildlife. Charlestonians will tell you (without bragging) that this is one of the most beautiful regions on this planet. Here you can commune with nature, perhaps like you haven't in years.

Sailing is an increasingly popular activity in this port city. If you already know how to sail, you can rent a small sailboat. If you don't, you can take sailing lessons or head out on a charter boat. Among the annual sailing events are the Sperry Charleston Race Week in April and the much-televised Charleston-to-Bermuda Race in late May.

Many of the region's best outdoor activities can be expensive, and this may give pause to families on a budget. But regularly scheduled dolphin-watching and kayak tours make for relatively inexpensive outings, and crabbing at low tide is free. You'll also find an amazing number of low-cost options, from biking to nature walks. In the warm weather, the beach is the place to be. Those looking for more of an adrenaline rush can rent surfboards and ride the waves.

The area's golf courses are reasonably priced compared with, say, Hilton Head. The championship courses on the nearby islands are the most beautiful, though they can be costly. There are plenty of public courses where you can enjoy the region's scenery without emptying your wallet.

SPORTS AND ACTIVITIES

BASEBALL

Fans who like to hear the crack of the bat and the cheers of the crowd should plan on attending a game at "The Joe" (Joseph P. Riley Jr. Stadium).

TOP OUTDOOR EXPERIENCES

Beaches: Charleston's palm-studded coastline and the beaches of its barrier islands rival those of the Caribbean—and are often cleaner, safer, and less congested. The shoulder seasons of spring and fall are good for beachcombing, and summer is the time for swimming and water sports.

Biking: Charleston's historic downtown is particularly bike-friendly, and setting off on two wheels is a wonderful way to avoid traffic and parking hassles. You can ride through the various in-town parks, like Marion Square, Waterfront Park, and Hampton Park, or take the bike path on the colossal Arthur Ravenel Jr. Bridge. On the island resorts, a bike is the ideal way to get around, especially for families with older kids.

Boating: Charleston's waters offer something for both the blue-water sailor and those who just want to take a waterborne tour. Fishing is a popular pastime, and a charter is an excellent way to spend the day in search of a trophy-size catch.

Golf: The weather is ideal for golf in the spring and fall, or even during the region's relatively mild winter. Summer's strong rays make morning and late afternoon the most popular tee times. Though some inland courses are not quite up to par with the courses of Hilton Head, golf on the nearby island resorts, especially at Kiawah Island Golf Resort, is exceptional.

Kayaking: This relatively inexpensive activity is one of the best ways to explore the Lowcountry's many waterways. Try paddling to keep up with the schools of dolphins you'll encounter while gliding silently along the intracoastal waterway. You can rent kayaks at Middleton Place, offering you the opportunity to push your paddle through former rice fields with views of the famous Butterfly Gardens. In Mount Pleasant, you can kayak in Shem Creek, the center of its shrimping industry, and if you are fit, you can paddle all the way to Sullivan's Island.

6

★ FodorsChoice **Charleston RiverDogs.** The local minor league
FAMILY baseball team—co-owned by actor Bill Murray, who is often in attendance—plays at "The Joe," on the banks of the Ashley River near the Citadel. Kids love the mascot, Charlie T. RiverDog, and adults love the beer deals and the creative, surprisingly tasty food concessions. After Friday night games, fireworks illuminate the summer sky in honor of this all-American pastime. The season runs from April

through September. ⊠ *Joseph P. Riley Jr. Stadium, 360 Fishburne St., Hampton Park Terrace* ☎ *843/577–3647* ⊕ *www.riverdogs.com* ⊑ *$8–$15.*

BEACHES

There are glorious beaches just outside the Charleston city limits. You and your kids can build sand castles, gather seashells after high tide, or bring a kite and let it loose on a long lead. The Charleston area's mild climate means you can swim from late March through October. For amenities, look for sections of public beach operated by Charleston County Parks, which generally have lifeguards in season, snack bars, restrooms and dressing areas, outdoor showers, umbrella and chair rentals, and large parking lots.

FAMILY **Edisto Beach.** Edisto's south edge has 4 miles of public beach. At its western end, the beach faces St. Helena Sound and has smaller waves. There is beach access at each intersection along Palmetto Boulevard and free public parking along the road. The beach itself has narrowed because of erosion from recent hurricanes, so you'll have more room to spread out if you time your visit for low tide. These clean coastal waters teem with both fish and shellfish, and it's common to see people throwing cast nets for shrimp. It's a great beach for beachcombing. Alcohol is allowed as long as it is not in glass containers. There's little shade and no food stands, so be sure to pack snacks. **Amenities:** none. **Best for:** solitude; sunset; swimming. ⊠ *Palmetto Blvd., from Coral St. to Yacht Club Rd., Edisto Beach* ⊕ *www. townofedistobeach.com.*

★ Fodor'sChoice **Folly Beach.** Anchored by the Folly Beach Pier,
FAMILY this is the Lowcountry's most iconic summer playground. Head out early to avoid traffic if you're visiting over a weekend. Street parking is free, but to avoid a ticket, all four wheels have to be off the pavement. If you're a surfer, keep driving until you reach Folly's Washout. Continue to the northeast end of the island to see the iconic Morris Island Lighthouse rise from the water, or head to the southwest end for lifeguards and amenities at the County Park. Stock up on snacks and sandwiches at Bert's Market on E. Ashley Avenue or grab a taco with the locals at Chico Feo across the street. **Amenities:** food and drink; lifeguards; parking (fee); toilets and showers (at Washout, the pier, and the County Park). **Best for:** surfing; swimming. ⊠ *Folly Beach* ⊕ *www.cityoffollybeach.com.*

FAMILY **Folly Beach County Park.** The Folly River, the Stono River, and the Atlantic Ocean form the peninsula that comprises this palmetto-fringed park, 12 miles southwest of Charleston. There are lifeguards in designated swimming areas and the water is generally calm, making this the best bet for families. Depending on the tides, there are often little pools that toddlers can safely enjoy. The sand is the hard-packed taupe variety ideal for making sand castles. Seasonal amenities include a snack bar, beach chairs, and umbrella rentals. This is one of the parks that stay open year-round. During winter, it's possible to watch the sunset over the water without another person in sight. **Amenities:** food and drink; lifeguards; parking; toilets. **Best for:** sunset; swimming. ⊠ *1100 W. Ashley Ave., off Center St., Folly Beach* ☎ *843/762–9960* ⊕ *www.ccprc.com* ⌖ *$10 per car Apr.–Labor Day; $15 on weekends; $5–$10 Sept.–Mar.*

Front Beach at Isle of Palms. If you want a singles scene and beach bars with live music and bikini contests, then this stretch of Isle of Palms is for you. Its string of businesses is the only beachfront commercial district in the area. Bicyclists are welcome, as are pets on leashes. Parking regulations are strictly enforced. **Amenities:** food and drink; parking (fee). **Best for:** partiers; swimming; windsurfing. ⊠ *Ocean Blvd., 10th Ave. to 14th Ave., Isle of Palms.*

NO SWIMMING SIGNS. **The No Swimming signs by the Isle of Palms Bridge from Sullivan's Island over Breach Inlet are there because the current is treacherous. Sadly, numerous drownings have occurred here.**

FAMILY **Isle of Palms County Park.** Play beach volleyball or soak up the sun in a lounge chair on this wide stretch of sand. This beach is as good as the island's idyllic name. The sands are golden, the waves are gentle, and there's a playground, so it's great for families with small children. People seeking to avoid the crowds and those seeking peace and quiet can venture a few blocks north down the beach. The county park is the only lifeguard-protected area on the Isle of Palms. **Amenities:** food and drink; lifeguards; parking (fee); showers; toilets. **Best for:** sunrise; swimming; walking. ⊠ *Ocean Blvd., 1st to 14th Ave., Isle of Palms* ☎ *843/762–9957* ⊕ *www.ccprc.com* ⌖ *May–Labor Day $10 per car weekdays, $15 on weekends; Sept.–Apr. $5–$10.*

BEACH SAFETY. It may seem inviting to walk out to a sandbar at low tide, but the tide sweeps in fast and the sandbars disappear, leaving people stranded far from shore.

★ Fodor'sChoice **Kiawah Beachwalker Park.** This county park about
FAMILY 28 miles southwest of Charleston has a wide beach at low tide, often ranked among the country's best. Stunningly beautiful Kiawah is one of the Southeast's largest barrier islands, with 10 miles of wide, immaculate ocean beaches. You can walk safely for miles, shelling and beachcombing to your heart's content. The beach is complemented by the Kiawah River, with lagoons filled with birds and wildlife, and golden marshes that make the sunsets even more glorious. **Amenities:** food and drink; lifeguards; parking (fee); showers; toilets. **Best for:** solitude; sunset; swimming; walking. ☒ *1 Beachwalker Dr., Kiawah Island* ☎ *843/762–9964* ⊕ *www.ccprc.com* ☒ *May–Labor Day $10 per car weekdays, $15 on weekends; Sept.–Apr. $5–$10.*

★ Fodor'sChoice **Sullivan's Island Beach.** This is one of the most
FAMILY pristine beaches in the Charleston area. The beachfront is owned by the town, including 200 acres of walkable maritime forest overseen by the Lowcountry Open Land Trust. The downside is that there are no amenities like public toilets and showers. There are, however, a number of good small restaurants on nearby Middle Street, the island's main drag. There are approximately 30 public-access paths (four are wheelchair accessible) that lead to the beach. "Sully's" is a delightful island with plenty to see, including Fort Moultrie National Monument. When parking or getting directions, note that the blocks are referred to as "Stations" on Sullivan's. **Amenities:** none. **Best for:** sunrise; sunset; walking; windsurfing. ☒ *Atlantic Ave., Sullivan's Island* ⊕ *www.sullivansisland-sc.com.*

BIKING

As long as you stay off the busier roads, the historic district is ideal for bicycling. Many of the city's green spaces, including Colonial Lake and Palmetto Islands County Park, have bike trails. If you want to rent a bike, expect to pay about $25 a day.

Cycling at your own pace is one of the best ways to see Charleston. Those staying at the nearby island resorts, particularly families with children, almost always rent bikes, especially if they are there for a week.

Affordabike. The name says it all: bike rentals at this shop start at $25 for 24 hours (or $55 a week), and that includes a helmet, lock, and basket. Conveniently located in the Upper King area, it's open on Sunday—the best day for riding around downtown Charleston or across the Ravenel Bridge. ✉ *563 King St., Upper King* ☎ *843/789–3281* ⊕ *www.affordabike.com.*

The Bicycle Shoppe. Open seven days a week, this shop rents simple beach cruisers for $7 per hour, $28 per day, or $50 per week, and that includes a helmet, basket, and lock. For those wanting to tackle the Ravenel Bridge, the store offers city commuter bikes at the same rates. There's a second branch at 1539 Johnnie Dodds Boulevard in Mount Pleasant, and they offer free delivery to local beaches. ✉ *281 Meeting St., Market* ☎ *843/722–8168* ⊕ *www.the-bicycleshoppecharleston.com.*

Charleston Bicycle Tours. You'll see the quiet streets and hidden secrets of Charleston when you take a multiday tour with Charleston Bicycle Tours. You'll ride past plantations as well as over the Ravenel Bridge, exploring the nearby islands and quaint surrounding towns. Tours include bikes, accommodations, and dining in the area's best restaurants. There's a van shuttle, licensed guide, and even a mechanic. Prices range from $1,295 for a three-day trip visiting the area's plantations to $2,790 for a six-day tour to Savannah. ✉ *164 Market St., Suite 104, College of Charleston Campus* ☎ *843/881–9898* ⊕ *charlestonbicycletours.com.*

Island Bike & Surf Shop. Rent beach bikes for a very moderate weekly rate (starting at $35 per week), or check out hybrids, mountain bikes, bicycles built for two, and a wide range of equipment for everyone in the family. The shop will even deliver to Kiawah and Seabrook islands. They also rent surf and paddleboards. ✉ *3665 Bohicket Rd., Johns Island* ☎ *843/768–1158* ⊕ *www.islandbikeandsurf.com.*

BOATING

Kayak through isolated marshes and estuaries to outlying islands, or explore Cape Romain National Wildlife Refuge. Rates vary depending on your departure point and whether you go it alone or join a guided tour. Rentals are about $20 per hour, and a two-hour guided tour will run you about $50. The nearby resort islands, especially Kiawah and Wild Dunes, tend to have higher rates.

The boating options are incredibly varied, from a small john-boat with an outboard motor to a chartered sailboat. If you're a newcomer to sailing, arranging lessons is no problem.

AquaSafaris. If you want a sailboat or yacht charter, a cruise to a private beach barbecue, or just a day of offshore fishing, AquaSafaris offers it all. Captain John Borden takes veteran and would-be sailors out daily on *Serena,* a 50-foot sloop, leaving from Shem Creek and Isle of Palms. A sunset cruise on the *Palmetto Breeze* catamaran offers panoramic views of Charleston Harbor set to a sound track of Jimmy Buffett tunes. Enjoy beer and cocktails as you cruise in one of the smoothest sails in the Lowcountry. ⊠ *A-Dock, 24 Patriots Point Rd., Mount Pleasant* ☎ *843/886–8133* ⊕ *www.aqua-safaris.com.*

FAMILY **Charleston Kayak Company.** Guided kayak tours with Charleston Kayak Company depart from the grounds of the Inn at Middleton Place. You'll glide down the Ashley River and through brackish creeks in a designated State Scenic River Corridor. Naturalists tell you about the wetlands and the river's cultural history. It's not uncommon to spot an alligator, but thankfully they take no interest in kayakers. Tours last two hours (reservations essential) and start at $49 per adult. There are private tours available, as well as trips through an adjacent swamp and to the marshes behind Folly Beach. For self-guided trips, both single and tandem kayak rentals are available starting at $20, including all safety gear. ⊠ *Middleton Place Plantation, 4290 Ashley River Rd., West Ashley* ☎ *843/628–2879* ⊕ *www.charlestonkayakcompany.com.*

★ Fodor's Choice **Coastal Expeditions.** Outings for individuals, families, and large groups are arranged by Coastal Expeditions.
FAMILY A kayak or SUP tour with a naturalist guide starts at $52 per adult, and kayak rentals start at $45 for a half day. The company provides exclusive access to Cape Romain National Wilderness Area on Bulls Island via the Bulls Island Ferry. The ferry departs from Garris Landing in Awendaw and runs Tuesday, and Thursday to Saturday, from April through November. It costs $40 round-trip. Bulls Island has rare natural beauty, a "boneyard beach," shells galore, and nearly 300 species of migrating and native birds. Coastal Expeditions has additional outlets at Crosby's Seafood on Folly Beach and at Isle of Palms Marina. ⊠ *Shem Creek Maritime Center, 514B Mill St., Mount Pleasant* ☎ *843/884–7684* ⊕ *www.coastalexpeditions.com.*

★ Fodor'sChoice **Flipper Finders.** The Folly River and its adjoin-
FAMILY ing marsh and creek system are one of the best spots in
Charleston to view bottlenose dolphins, and this aptly
named tour company knows where to find them. Captain
Dickey Brendel offers rentals; $50 naturalist-guided day-
time, sunset, and full-moon kayak tours; and boat trips to
Morris Island, allowing guests to pack a picnic lunch and
explore on bikes for the day. Flipper Finder's sister company, Charleston SUP Safaris, offers paddleboard tours,
rentals, and SUP yoga out of the same office, just across
the bridge onto Folly Beach. ✉ *83 Center St., James Island*
☎ *843/588–0019* ⊕ *www.flipperfinders.com.*

Ocean Sailing Academy. Learn how to command your own
26-foot sailboat on Charleston's beautiful harbor with the
guidance of an instructor. This academy can teach you and
your family how to sail comfortably on any size sailboat,
and can take you from coastal navigation to ocean profi-
ciency. Instructors are fun and experienced, and are U.S.
Sailing–certified professionals. Skippered charters and laid-
back sunset cruises are also available. ✉ *24 Patriots Point
Rd., Mount Pleasant* ☎ *843/971–0700* ⊕ *www.osasail.com.*

Pegasus Charters. Pegasus Charters has a four-boat fleet that
includes a 40-foot pleasure yacht and an 80-passenger pontoon catamaran. A couple can charter their classic sailboat
for a romantic sunset sail; groups can book the 36-passen-
ger *Inlet Scout* pontoon boat for a celebratory reunion. This
is a good alternative for large groups, or those who don't
want to be corralled in by a set tour schedule. ✉ *Mount
Pleasant* ☎ *843/276–4203* ⊕ *www.pegasuscharters.com.*

St. John's Kayaks. Located on Johns Island near the entrance
to Kiawah and Seabrook islands, St. John's Kayaks offers
guided ecotours by kayak, fishing expeditions, and pow-
erboat excursions. Safe and stable, easy-boarding kayaks
are ideal for everyone from kids to seniors. Local owners
share their love and passion for the barrier sea islands. They
welcome groups and offer discounted rates. ✉ *4460 Betsy
Kerrison Pkwy., Johns Island* ☎ *843/330–9777* ⊕ *www.
stjohnskayaks.com.*

FISHING

Fishing can be a real adventure in and around Charleston.
If you travel offshore with an experienced guide, you'll
probably come back with enough fish stories to last until
your next trip. This is a pricey adventure best shared with

as many of your fishing buddies as possible. Expect to pay about $120 an hour, including bait and tackle. For inshore fly-fishing, guides generally charge $350 for two people for a half day. Deep-sea fishing charters cost about $1,400 for 12 hours for a boatload of anglers. There are dozens of excellent captains and charters in Charleston, so the best approach is to choose the marina you'd like to leave from and the type of fishing you want to do, and then hone in on the right fit. It's a good idea to chat with a captain on the phone before your trip to set expectations. The free local fishing magazine *Tideline,* available at any local tackle shop, is also an excellent resource.

Bohicket Marina. If you want to catch the big one, Bohicket Marina has half- and full-day charters on 24- to 48-foot boats. Small boat rentals are also available, as well as sunset dolphin-watching cruises. This marina is the closest to Kiawah and Seabrook islands, and has a long-standing reputation. For a half day of inshore fishing, expect to pay $450 for up to four people, including bait, tackle, and licenses. Waterdog Paddle Company is also based here, offering guided SUP tours of Bohicket Creek. ⊠ *1880 Andell Bluff Blvd., Johns Island* ☎ *843/768–1280* ⊕ *www. bohicket.com.*

FAMILY **Folly Beach Pier.** Anglers can rent rods for $10 and cast a line at this 1,000-foot fishing pier. Baby sharks are commonly on the end of your line, but if luck is with you, you can reel in bluefish, black drum, tarpon, pompano, or sea trout. You'll pay $5 for a fishing pass. If you're a nonfisherman and just want to walk the pier, it's free. ⊠ *101 E. Arctic Ave., Folly Beach* ☎ *843/762–9516* ⊕ *www.ccprc.com.*

GOLF

With fewer golfers than Hilton Head, the courses in the Charleston area have more prime tee times available. Even if you're not a guest, you can arrange to play at private island resorts, such as Kiawah Island, Seabrook Island, and Wild Dunes on Isle of Palms. There you will find breathtaking ocean views within a pristine setting. Don't be surprised to find a white-tailed deer grazing on a green or an alligator floating in a water hole. For top courses like Kiawah's Ocean Course, expect to pay in the $200 to $300 range during peak season in spring and early fall.

Municipal golf courses are a bargain, often costing around $25 for 18 holes. Somewhere in between are well-regarded courses at Shadowmoss Plantation Golf Club in West Ashley and the Links at Stono Ferry in Hollywood.

Charleston Golf Guide. For everything from green fees to course statistics and vacation packages in the area, contact the Charleston Golf Guide. ☎ *800/774–4444 ⊕ www. charlestongolfguide.com.*

Charleston Municipal Golf Course. Affectionately called "The Muni," this walker-friendly public course isn't as gorgeous as the resort courses—a highway bisects it—but it does have a lot of shade trees, and the price is right. About 6 miles from downtown and 20 miles from the resort islands of Kiawah and Seabrook, the course has a simple snack bar serving breakfast and lunch, as well as beer and wine. ✉ *2110 Maybank Hwy., James Island ☎ 843/795–6517 ⊕ www.charleston-sc.gov/golf ⚑ $17–$32; carts are an additional $16* ⚐ *18 holes, 6432 yards, par 72.*

Charleston National Golf Club. The best nonresort golf course in Charleston tends to be quiet on weekdays, which translates into lower prices. The setting is captivating, carved along the intracoastal waterway and traversing wetlands, lagoons, and pine and oak forests. Finishing holes are set along golden marshland. Diminutive wooden bridges and a handsome clubhouse that looks like an antebellum mirage add to the natural beauty of this well-maintained course. ✉ *1360 National Dr., Mount Pleasant ☎ 843/203–9994 ⊕ www.charlestonnationalgolf.com ⚑ $66–$95* ⚐ *18 holes, 7064 yards, par 72.*

Dunes West Golf Club. Designed by Arthur Hill, this championship course has great marsh and river views and lots of modulation on the Bermuda-covered greens shaded by centuries-old oaks. The generous fairways have greens that may be considered small by today's standards, making approach shots very important. Located about 15 miles from downtown Charleston, it's in a gated residential community with an attractive antebellum-style clubhouse. ✉ *3535 Wando Plantation Way, Mount Pleasant ☎ 843/856–9000 ⊕ www.duneswestgolfclub.com ⚑ $52–$92* ⚐ *18 holes, 6859 yards, par 72.*

Links at Stono Ferry. Built atop a Revolutionary War battlefield, the reasonably priced Links at Stono Ferry is 30 minutes from downtown Charleston or from Kiawah, off of Highway 17 south toward Savannah. In 2011, it was selected as the S.C. Golf Course of the Year by the state's

6

Golf Course Owners Association, and it's home to the College of Charleston's men's and women's golf teams. Set in a rural area with three holes along the intracoastal waterway, the course is in an upscale residential community with a focus on golf and horses. Its clubhouse has Southern style, including the menu at the on-site Stono Ferry Grill. There's also a top-notch instructional facility, including private lessons and club fittings. ⊠ *4812 Stono Links Dr., Hollywood* ☎ *843/763–1817* ⊕ *www.stonoferrygolf.com* ⊠ *$65–$95* ⅂ *18 holes, 6814 yards, par 72.*

Patriots Point Links. A partly covered driving range and spectacular harbor views of downtown Charleston and Fort Sumter make this golf course feel special. In addition to driving here across the Ravenel Bridge, you can also take the water taxi from downtown and arrange for a staffer to pick you up. Four pros offer one-on-one instruction, as well as lessons and clinics. There's a junior camp during the summer. ⊠ *1 Patriots Point Rd., Mount Pleasant* ☎ *843/881–0042* ⊕ *www.patriotspointlinks.com* ⊠ *$50–$89* ⅂ *18 holes, 6900 yards, par 72.*

Seabrook Island Golf Resort. On this island with acres of untamed maritime forests you'll find two championship courses: Crooked Oaks, designed by Robert Trent Jones Sr., and Ocean Winds, by Willard Byrd. Crooked Oaks, which follows an inland path, is the more player friendly of the two. Ocean Winds is aptly named for three holes that run along the Atlantic; when the wind is up, those ocean breezes make it challenging. Both courses are run out of the same pro shop and have the same green fee, and each is a certified member of the Audubon Cooperative Sanctuary Program for golf courses—expect to see birds and wildlife. A first-class practice facility includes five target greens, two putting greens, and a short game fairway. This is a private island, but visitors not staying on Seabrook can play if their hometown golf pro calls to make a reservation for them. ⊠ *3772 Seabrook Island Rd., Seabrook Island* ☎ *843/768–2529* ⊕ *www.discoverseabrook.com* ⊠ *$125–$180* ⅂ *36 holes, 6800 yards, par 72.*

Shadowmoss Plantation Golf Club. This forgiving course has one of the best finishing holes in the area. It's just off Highway 61, about 17 miles from downtown and 20 miles from the resort islands of Kiawah and Seabrook. A seasoned, well-conditioned course, it meanders through the residential enclave that grew up around it. It's a good value for the money. ⊠ *20 Dunvegan Dr.* ☎ *843/556–8251* ⊕ *www.shad-owmossgolf.com* ⌁ *$36–$55* ⛳ *18 holes, 6701 yards, par 72.*

ISLE OF PALMS

Wild Dunes Resort is a 1,600-acre oceanfront resort on the tip of the Isle of Palms some 30 minutes from downtown Charleston. It has two nationally renowned, Tom Fazio–designed courses, the **Links** and the **Harbor** courses.

Wild Dunes Resort Harbor Course. Tom Fazio designed this course, shaping millions of dollars' worth of dirt into an unforgettable landscape that blends into the surrounding marsh. The dunes are adorned with greens, and hazards can be found around every bend. Nine holes are situated along the intracoastal waterway, several of which require shots across water. ⊠ *Wild Dunes Resort, 5757 Palm Blvd., Isle of Palms* ☎ *855/998–5351* ⊕ *www.wilddunes.com* ⌁ *$55–$115* ⛳ *18 holes, 6446 yards, par 70.*

★ Fodor'sChoice **Wild Dunes Resort Links Course.** With prevailing ocean breezes, undulating dunes, and natural water hazards, this course has been called a seaside masterpiece. It's architect Tom Fazio's first Lowcountry layout, and is still considered one of his best. The Links Course is consistently ranked among the top 100 courses in the country, and is challenging enough for the most avid golfer. Players are permitted to walk the length of the course, regardless of time of day. The clubhouse features an excellent restaurant, Huey's Southern Eats, which has a welcoming patio for after-golf drinks. There's a driving range and putting green just across the street from the clubhouse. ⊠ *Wild Dunes Resort, 10001 Back Bay Dr., Isle of Palms* ☎ *855/998–5351* ⊕ *www.wild-dunes.com* ⌁ *$75–$165* ⛳ *18 holes, 6396 yards, par 70.*

KIAWAH ISLAND

Kiawah Island Golf Resort is home to five championship courses: the world-famous **Ocean Course,** designed by Pete Dye; the Jack Nicklaus–designed **Turtle Point; Osprey Point,** designed by Tom Fazio; **Cougar Point,** designed by Gary Player; and **Oak Point,** redesigned by Clyde Johnston. Kiawah is also home to the Tommy Cuthbert Golf Learning Center, featuring computerized swing analysis, private instruction in covered hitting bays (a good option on rainy days), and Titleist and Callaway personalized club fitting.

Cougar Point Golf Course. Gary Player designed this challenging but popular course, which follows the outline of tidal marshes and offers panoramic views of golden spans of spartina grass and the shimmering Kiawah River. The driving range and putting green are conveniently located directly beside the first tee box. Reservations are essential. ✉ *Kiawah Island Golf Resort, 12 Kiawah Beach Dr., Kiawah Island* ☎ *843/266–4020* ⊕ *www.kiawahresort.com* 🍽 *Resort guest $130–$203; nonresort guest $152–$238* ⛳ *18 holes, 6814 yards, par 72.*

Oak Point Golf Course. Outside the gate of the Kiawah Island, this Clyde Johnston–designed, Scottish-American-style course sits in the center of Hope Plantation, a residential enclave and former indigo plantation. Centered on a classy clubhouse, it makes full use of the area's rolling sand dunes. Reservations are essential. ✉ *Kiawah Island Golf Resort, 4394 Hope Plantation Dr., Kiawah Island* ☎ *843/266–4100* ⊕ *www.kiawahresort.com* 🍽 *Resort guest $130–$203; nonresort guest $152–$238* ⛳ *18 holes, 6701 yards, par 72.*

★ Fodor'sChoice **The Ocean Course.** Considered one of Pete Dye's most superb designs, this seaside course is famous for hosting the Ryder Cup in 1991 and both the 2012 and upcoming 2021 PGA Championships. The course, which offers spectacular views along 2½ miles of beachfront, starred in Robert Redford's film *The Legend of Bagger Vance*. The superbly manicured fairways and greens challenge amateurs and professionals alike. Carts are included in the green fee, as are caddies (but not their gratuities, which are recommended at $100/bag for caddies and $50/bag for forecaddies). Forecaddies are mandatory for anyone utilizing a cart. Before noon (10 am from June through August), this is a walking-only course. At the clubhouse, the Atlantic Room seafood restaurant and lauded Ryder Cup bar at the clubhouse are exceptional. Reservations are essential. ✉ *Kiawah Island Golf Resort, 1000 Ocean Course Dr., Kiawah Island* ☎ *843/266–4670* ⊕ *www.kiawahresort.com* 🍽 *Resort guest $254–$349; nonresort guest $280–$383* ⛳ *18 holes, 7356 yards, par 72.*

★ Fodor'sChoice **Osprey Point Golf Course.** This Tom Fazio–designed course offers some of the best views the Lowcountry has to offer: maritime forests, pristine lagoons, natural lakes, and saltwater marshes. Every hole has picturesque vistas. It's a favorite of residents and resort guests alike. The impressive clubhouse has 14,000-square-foot pro shop selling high-quality apparel; fully staffed locker rooms; and a semiprivate dining room at the popular on-site restaurant, Cherrywood BBQ & Ale House. ✉ *Kiawah Island Golf*

Resort, 700 Governors Dr., Kiawah Island ☎ *843/266–4640* ⊕ *www.kiawahresort.com* ✆ *Resort guest $130–$203; nonresort guest $152–$238* ⚑ *18 holes, 6902 yards, par 72.*

Turtle Point Golf Course. With three spectacular oceanfront holes, this famed Jack Nicklaus–designed course has hosted many amateur and professional tournaments over the years. The undulating course flows seamlessly through interior forests of hardwoods and palmettos and along backwater lagoons. The $7.5 million clubhouse is built in a classic Lowcountry style and features Tomasso at Turtle Point, an upscale Italian restaurant, and a bar with patio seating overlooking the 18th green. Reservations are essential. ✉ *Kiawah Island Golf Resort, 1 Turtle Point Dr., Kiawah Island* ☎ *843/266–4050* ⊕ *www.kiawahresort.com* ✆ *Resort guest $130–$203; nonresort guest $152–$238* ⚑ *18 holes, 7061 yards, par 72.*

HORSEBACK RIDING

Put your foot in the stirrup and get a leg up! Half an hour from Charleston, you can tour Seabrook Island's beaches, maritime forests, and marshlands all on horseback.

★ Fodor'sChoice **Seabrook Island Equestrian Center.** This classy FAMILY equestrian center 24 miles south of Charleston has walking trails for beginning and advanced riders. Beach rides are $150 per rider and include beginner options and advanced tours for riders who can handle a horse competently at a walk, trot, and canter. Trail rides through the woods of Seabrook Island are $75. Parent-led pony rides are $45 for a half hour, while private lessons are $65 for a half hour. Boarding is available. ✉ *3772 Seabrook Island Rd., Seabrook Island* ☎ *843/768–7541* ⊕ *www. discoverseabrook.com.*

SCUBA DIVING

Charleston's offshore waters have a host of man-made reefs teeming with aquatic life. Experienced divers can also independently explore the Cooper River Underwater Heritage Diving Trail, upriver from Charleston. The 2½-mile-long trail has six submerged sites, including ships that date to the Revolutionary War.

Charleston Scuba. Whether you're just learning or an old pro, this dive outfitter offers everything from introductory classes to open-water dives to equipment rentals. The company frequents 16 open-water dive sites in between Charleston Harbor and the Gulf Stream, and prices range from $145 to $175 for two-tank dives. ⊠ *335 Savannah Hwy., West Ashley* ☎ *843/763–3483* ⊕ *www.charlestonscuba.com.*

SOCCER

Charleston Battery. Charleston's soccer team plays on Daniel Island at MUSC Health Stadium, which features a 3,000-square-foot jumbotron and a classy English pub, The Three Lions Club. Games are played from March through September and feature fun-filled giveaways and promotions. The stadium seats 5,100, and tickets range from $20 to $38. ⊠ *MUSC Health Stadium, 1990 Daniel Island Dr., Daniel Island* ☎ *843/971–4625* ⊕ *www.charlestonbattery.com.*

TENNIS

The Charleston area offers tennis options for every skill level. Spring and fall are ideal for play at the area's inexpensive municipal courses. The resort islands have excellent facilities but can be costly.

Charleston is the home of the world-class Volvo Car Open (formerly the Family Circle Cup), a professional women's tournament. Held over nine days every April at the Family Circle Tennis Center, it attracts some 90,000 fans from around the globe and boasts a roster of former champions, including Chris Evert, Martina Navratilova, Jennifer Capriati, and Venus and Serena Williams.

Charleston Tennis Center. With 15 outdoor hard courts lighted for nighttime matches, this tennis center is among the city's most popular and affordable, at $10/hour for nonresidents. There are restrooms on the premises and lessons are available. ⊠ *19 Farmfield Ave., West Ashley* ☎ *843/769–8258* ⊕ *www.charleston-sc.gov.*

★ FodorsChoice **Family Circle Tennis Center.** This world-class facil-
FAMILY ity is one of the top places to play tennis in the Southeast. Open to the public, the 17 courts (13 clay, 4 hard) are lighted for night play. Hourly rates are $10 for the hard courts, $15 for clay. Four miniature courts for kids ages four to eight make this a destination for the whole family. With one of the best-qualified teaching staffs in the country, the MW Tennis Academy offers private lessons and clinics for players of all ages. The Volvo Car Open, a signature

event for women's tennis, is hosted here each April. Not coincidentally, this is also the city's top venue for concerts under the stars. ⊠ *161 Seven Farms Dr., Daniel Island* ☎ *843/849–5300* ⊕ *www.familycircletenniscenter.com.*

Maybank Tennis Center. This James Island complex's eight lighted hard courts and five clay courts are $10 an hour for nonresidents. There are restrooms on the premises. Reservations are recommended. ⊠ *1880 Houghton Dr., James Island* ☎ *843/406–8814* ⊕ *www.charleston-sc.gov.*

ISLE OF PALMS

Wild Dunes Tennis Center. This tennis complex sits in the center of Wild Dunes Resort, where 17 Har-Tru courts include 5 that are lighted for night play—one has stadium-style seating if you expect to draw a crowd. The pros gear their lessons to players of all levels, from novice to expert. There's even a "tiny tot" program for the kids. The full-service pro shop sells, rents, and repairs racquets. Wild Dunes guests get a free hour of access per bedroom, while nonguests must pay $25/hour. ⊠ *Wild Dunes Resort, 5757 Palm Blvd., Isle of Palms* ☎ *866/359–5593* ⊕ *www. wilddunes.com.*

KIAWAH ISLAND

Roy Barth Tennis Center. In Kiawah Island Golf Resort's East Beach Village, the Roy Barth Tennis Center is a short walk from the resort's luxurious oceanfront hotel and spa. Open year-round, it has 19 Har-Tru courts (1 lighted) that were resurfaced in early 2018, 3 hard courts (1 lighted), and a unique practice court with a ball machine and an automated ball retrieval system. Court time is $36 an hour for guests and $46 for everyone else. Lessons range $80–$105/hour (at the higher end, you can take a lesson from Mr. Barth himself), while group lessons are as low as $33/hour. The classy locker room includes showers so you can head straight from the courts to dinner. ⊠ *Kiawah Island Golf Resort, East Beach Village, 1 Sanctuary Dr., Kiawah Island* ☎ *843/768–2838* ⊕ *www.kiawahresort.com/tennis.*

WATER SPORTS

When it comes to water sports, Charleston is a great place to get your feet wet. Surfboards can be rented for as little as $9 an hour. An hour of surf lessons will run you about $40, and includes use of a board.

★ Fodor'sChoice **McKevlin's Surf Shop.** The pros at McKevlin's Surf Shop can teach you what you need to know about riding the waves at Folly Beach. Surfboards start at $9 per hour, and an hour of instruction is $40 and includes the rental. ⊠ *8 Center St., Folly Beach* ☎ *843/588–2247* ⊕ *www.mckevlins.com.*

FAMILY **Tidal Wave Water Sports.** This Jet Ski rental and parasailing outfit operates at the Isle of Palms Marina, offering easy access to the undeveloped waterways behind Capers and Bulls islands. Explore the wet wilderness on a Waverunner Safari Tour, or see it from the air on a parasailing trip. The company also offers tubing, banana boat rides, and wakeboarding, as well as boat and paddleboard rentals. ⊠ *69 41st Ave., Isle of Palms* ☎ *843/886–8456* ⊕ *www. tidalwavewatersports.com.*

SHOPPING

Updated
by Stratton
Lawrence

ONE-OF-A-KIND BOUTIQUES MAKE UP AN important part of the contemporary Charleston shopping experience. Long-established Christian Michi anchors the corner of Market and King; its window displays are like works of art, and its innovative and European designs are treasured by well-heeled, sophisticated clients. Some department stores cater to younger shoppers, and high-end shops sell either their own designer fashions, or carry names that are found in Paris, New York, and South Beach, like Kate Spade in the Shops at Belmond Charleston Place.

The number and quality of shoe stores on King Street is surprising for the city's size. Family-owned shops like Berlin's are city institutions. Newer shops like Sugar Snap Pea are popular with families.

The Upper King District is interspersed with clothing boutiques and restaurants. The revival of this neighborhood has sparked a new wave of home-fashion stores; long-term antiques hunters, accustomed to buying on Lower King, have been lured uptown as well. Charleston has more than 25 fine-art galleries, making it one of the top art towns in America. Local Lowcountry art, which includes both traditional landscapes of the region as well as more contemporary takes, is among the most prevalent styles here. Such innovative artists as Betty Anglin Smith and Fred Jamar, a Belgian known for his whimsical nighttime cityscapes, can give you a piece of Charleston to keep close until your next visit. Collectors will find nationally and internationally renowned work in such exquisite galleries as Ann Long Fine Art and the more contemporary Martin Gallery.

SHOPPING DISTRICTS

FAMILY **Charleston City Market.** This cluster of shops, covered stands, and restaurants fills Market Street between Meeting and East Bay streets. Sweetgrass basket weavers work here amid trinket and souvenir booths, T-shirt shops, and upscale clothing boutiques. In the covered market, vendors have stalls selling everything from jewelry to purses to paintings of Rainbow Row. The middle section of the market is enclosed and air-conditioned. From April through December, there's a night market on Friday and Saturday from 6:30 until 10:30 pm, featuring local craftspeople and street musicians. ✉ *E. Bay and Market Sts., Market* ⊕ *www. thecharlestoncitymarket.com.*

Sweetgrass Baskets

For centuries, Gullah artisans have been weaving and selling handwoven Charleston sweetgrass baskets in the City Market, where they sit busily in their chairs and place their wares on the sidewalk around them. Other places where they are known to set up are beside the downtown post office on Meeting and Broad streets, and on the right side of Highway 17 North, past Mount Pleasant (where you'll find the best prices). Prices range from about $60 for a small basket up into the hundreds for the larger sizes. Be respectful of the renowned presence of the "basket ladies" in this city. Before taking their photograph, ask permission, and offer a tip to show your appreciation.

King Street. The city's main shopping strip is divided into informal districts: Lower King (from Broad Street to Market Street) is the Antiques District, lined with high-end dealers; Middle King (from Market Street to Calhoun Street) is the Fashion District, with a mix of national chains like Anthropologie and Pottery Barn and locally owned boutiques; and Upper King (from Calhoun Street to Spring Street) has been dubbed the Design District, known for both its restaurant scene and clothing and interior-design stores. Check out Second Sundays on King, when the street closes to cars all afternoon from Calhoun Street to Queen Street. Make sure to visit the Saturday farmers' market in Marion Square throughout the spring and summer months. ⊠ *Charleston.*

SHOPPING

SOUTH OF BROAD

ART

Ann Long Fine Art. Serious art collectors head to Ann Long Fine Art for neoclassical and modern works. This world-class gallery features outstanding, albeit pricey, works by gifted American and European artists. Many are painted with Old Master techniques. In addition, the gallery manages the estate of German Expressionist Otto Neumann. ⊠ *54 Broad St., South of Broad* ☎ *843/577–0447* ⊕ *www. annlongfineart.com.*

Charleston Renaissance Gallery. This gallery carries museum-quality art—in fact, more than half of the beautifully framed works are sold to museums. We recommend a visit nonetheless—these are paintings of rare beauty. ✉ *103 Church St., South of Broad* ☎ *843/723–0025* ⊕ *www.fineartsouth.com* ☉ *Closed weekends.*

Corrigan Gallery. Owner Lese Corrigan displays her own Impressionist-influenced paintings of Charleston and the works of some 20 other painters and photographers. Most pieces fit the genre of contemporary Southern art. ✉ *7 Broad St., South of Broad* ☎ *843/722–9868* ⊕ *www.corrigangallery.com* ☉ *Closed Sun.*

Ellis-Nicholson Gallery. With works by painters and sculptors, from those just starting their careers to veterans with international reputations, this gallery has a top-of-the-line selection of contemporary art. They also have an impressive selection of handcrafted jewelry. ✉ *1½ Broad St., South of Broad* ☎ *843/722–5353* ⊕ *www.ellis-nicholsongallery.com* ☉ *Closed Sun.*

★ **Fodor's Choice** **Martin Gallery.** In a former bank building, this light-filled, grand space is the city's most impressive gallery. It sells works by nationally and internationally acclaimed artists, sculptors, and photographers, and is especially well known for its bronzes and large wooden sculptures, as well as glass pieces and custom-designed jewelry. ✉ *18 Broad St., South of Broad* ☎ *843/723–7378* ⊕ *www.martingallerycharleston.com.*

SHOES, HANDBAGS, AND LEATHER GOODS

Farushga. Farushga sells high-quality, cutting-edge handbags and Italian shoes for both men and women, from chic daytime looks to pulling-out-all-the-stops evening glamour. But the real beauty of Farushga is that you will not find the same fine brands sold at every other upscale Italian shoe store. This boutique carries only one pair per size for every style, so if you see something you like, you may want to buy it on the spot. ✉ *25 Broad St., South of Broad* ☎ *843/714–1701* ⊕ *www.farushga.com* ☉ *Closed Sun.*

NORTH OF BROAD

LOWER KING

ANTIQUES AND COLLECTIBLES

George C. Birlant & Co. You'll find mostly 18th- and 19th-century English antiques here, but keep your eye out for a Charleston Battery bench (seen at White Point Garden), for which they are famous. Founded in 1922, Birlant's is fourth-generation family-owned, and is home to the oldest working freight elevator in the country. ⊠ *191 King St., Lower King* ☎ *843/722–3842* ⊕ *www.birlant.com* ⊗ *Closed Sun.*

Jacques' Antiques. As the name suggests, most of the antiques here are imported from France, and the rest are either European or English from the 17th to the 20th century. Decorative arts include ceramics, porcelains, and crystal. From the candlesticks to the armoires, all are in exquisite taste. ⊠ *160 King St., Lower King* ☎ *843/577–0104* ⊕ *www. jacantiques.com* ⊗ *Closed Sun.*

CLOTHING

Ben Silver. Charleston's own Ben Silver, premier purveyor of blazer buttons, has more than 800 designs, including college and British regimental motifs. The shop also sells British neckties, embroidered polo shirts, and blazers. This Charleston institution was founded in the 1960s. ⊠ *149 King St., Lower King* ☎ *843/577–4556* ⊕ *www.bensilver. com* ⊗ *Closed Sun.*

Berlin's. Family-owned since 1883, this Charleston institution has a reputation as a destination for special-occasion clothing. The store, which for generations sold preppy styles, has also added European designers. There's a women's store next door to the men's shop. There is a complimentary parking lot across the street. ⊠ *114–116 King St., Lower King* ☎ *843/722–1665* ⊕ *www.berlinsclothing. com* ⊗ *Closed Sun.*

Billy Reid. The darling of Southern tailors offers fashion-forward shoppers the best in aristocratic men's and women's clothing. Be sure to check out the basement sale racks—in one of the few true basements in Charleston—where prices are slashed as much as 50%. ⊠ *150 King St., Lower King* ☎ *843/577–3004* ⊕ *www.billyreid.com.*

Christian Michi. This shop carries tony women's clothing and accessories. Designers from Italy, such as Piazza Sempione, are represented, as is European line Intropia. Known for its evening wear, the shop has pricey but gorgeous gowns and a fine selection of cocktail dresses. High-end fragrances add to the luxurious air. ⊠ *220 King St., Lower King* ☎ *843/723–0575* ⊗ *Closed Sun.*

Copper Penny. This longtime local clothier sells trendy dresses and women's apparel from designers like Trina Turk, MILLY, Tibi, and Diane von Furstenberg. There's also an accompanying shoe store next door, and two satellite locations in Mount Pleasant. ✉ *311 King St., Lower King* ☏ *843/723–2999* ⊕ *www.shopcopperpenny.com.*

Finicky Filly. This mother/daughter-owned boutique carries exceptional women's apparel, jewelry, and handbags by such designers as Lela Rose, Tory Burch, All Dressed Up, and Etro. ✉ *303 King St., Lower King* ☏ *843/534–0203* ⊕ *www.thefinickyfilly.com.*

★ Fodor'sChoice **Hampden Clothing.** One of the city's trendiest boutiques attracts the young and well-heeled, who come here for an edgier, New York–influenced style. Hot designers like Yigal Azrouël, Vena Cava, Alexander Wang, and Jenni Kayne help make it a premier destination for the latest in fashion. ✉ *314 King St., Lower King* ☏ *843/724–6373* ⊕ *www.hampdenclothing.com.*

House of Sage. Fashionable, affordable women's fashions have made this locally owned boutique a mainstay on the College of Charleston campus for nearly a decade. The wide selection of shirts, dresses, and shoes are almost all priced under $100. ✉ *51 George St., Unit B, College of Charleston Campus* ☏ *843/573–7256* ⊕ *www.houseofsage.com.*

Ibu. Artisans from 34 countries contribute the elaborate and intricate textiles used to make the mostly women's clothing for sale here. The brightly colored shop is nestled in an upstairs nook on Lower King. Purchases support the communities where the clothing and supplies originate. ✉ *183B King St., Lower King* ☏ *843/327–8304* ⊕ *www. ibumovement.com* ⊘ *Closed Sun.*

Jordan Lash. Fashionable men are drawn to the casual threads and sharp styles at this upstart boutique offering everything from suits to swimwear. Trendy Southern brands like Collared Greens bow ties and Cotton Brothers shirts can be found. ✉ *305 King St., Lower King* ☏ *843/804–6710* ⊕ *www.jordanlash.com* ⊘ *Closed Sun.*

FAMILY **Kids on King.** This shop's world-traveling owners offer the finest in children's apparel, accessories, and toys from just about everywhere. You'll be transported to other lands with the handcrafted designs. ✉ *310 King St., Lower King* ☏ *843/720–8647* ⊕ *www.kidsonking.com.*

FAMILY **Sugar Snap Pea.** This sweet shop stocks the ultimate in kids' wear, from Petit Bateau to Jellycat and Tea Collection. Owner Zhenya Kuhne keeps the clothing options fresh and new. There's also a Mount Pleasant branch at 320 Coleman Boulevard, and an outpost on Kiawah at Freshfields Village. ⊠ *233 King St., Lower King* ☎ *843/793–2621* ⊕ *www. sugarsnappea.com* ⊗ *Closed Sun.*

FOOD AND WINE

Caviar & Bananas. This upscale specialty market and café features out-of-the-ordinary items like a duck confit sandwich and pad thai sushi rolls. It's an ideal spot to prep for a picnic. Note the locally produced items such as Callie's Pimiento Cheese and Jack Rudy Cocktail Co. Small Batch Tonic Syrup. There are also locations on Market Street and in the airport. ⊠ *51 George St., College of Charleston Campus* ☎ *843/577–7757* ⊕ *www.caviarandbananas.com.*

GIFTS AND SOUVENIRS

Candlefish. Created by the people who started the wine bottle candle craze Rewined, this eclectic shop is the motherland for all things candle. Choose from dozens of fragrances and styles, or opt for a make-your-own candle kit souvenir. ⊠ *71 Wentworth St., Lower King* ☎ *843/371–1434* ⊕ *www. candlefish.com.*

Vieuxtemps. This is where Charlestonians go to pick out wedding china and build a bridal registry. Possibly the only Charleston store to offer Herend, Royal Crown Derby, Haviland, and Spode, the store is a discerning bride's dream. Linens and cookware are also great reasons to pop by. ⊠ *180 King St., Lower King* ☎ *843/577–6811* ⊕ *www.vieuxtemps.net* ⊗ *Closed Sun.*

★ Fodor'sChoice **Worthwhile.** Designer women's clothing, shoes, and jewelry make it fun to shop at this boutique in a 19th-century historic home. You can also find artsy and hip baby gear. ⊠ *268 King St., Lower King* ☎ *843/723–4418* ⊕ *www.shopworthwhile.com.*

JEWELRY AND ACCESSORIES

★ Fodor'sChoice **Croghan's Jewel Box.** Ring the doorbell for fine new jewelry as well as antiques at this shop, a Charleston institution that's been facilitating proposals, weddings, and anniversaries for more than 100 years. You'll also find wonderful wedding gift items. Should the need arise, Croghan's does excellent repair work. ⊠ *308 King St., Lower King* ☎ *843/723–3594* ⊕ *www.croghansjewelbox. com* ⊗ *Closed Sun.*

MARKET AREA

ART

Anglin Smith Fine Art. This gallery exhibits contemporary paintings by Betty Anglin Smith and her talented triplets, Jennifer, Shannon, and Tripp. Her son, Tripp, is a nature photographer specializing in black-and-white images. The bronze wildlife sculptures are by nationally recognized Darrell Davis; the acclaimed oil paintings by Kim English are attention-getters. ⊠ *9 Queen St., Market* ☎ *843/853–0708* ⊕ *www.anglinsmith.com.*

CHARLESTON'S FRENCH QUARTER. The downtown neighborhood known as the French Quarter, named after the founding French Huguenots, has become a destination for art lovers. The Charleston Gallery Association consists of roughly 40 art galleries, most of which are within the original walled city. Galleries here host a delightful art walk, with wine and refreshments, from 5 to 8 pm on the first Friday in March, May, October, and December. Member galleries and upcoming art events are listed at ⊕ www. charlestongalleryassociation.com.

Gallery Chuma. This gallery showcases Gullah art, ranging from inexpensive prints to original works by artists like Jonathan Green. The vibrantly colored paintings of this highly successful South Carolina artist have helped popularize Gullah culture. ⊠ *188 Meeting St., #N1, Market* ☎ *843/722–1702* ⊕ *www.gallerychuma.com.*

Horton Hayes Fine Art. This gallery carries sought-after Lowcountry paintings by 14 artists, including paintings of coastal life and architecture by Mark Kelvin Horton and the whimsical work of Shannon Runquist, known for her paintings of blue crabs. ⊠ *30 State St., Market* ☎ *843/958–0014* ⊕ *www.hortonhayes.com.*

★ Fodor'sChoice **Robert Lange Studios.** The most *avant* of the contemporary galleries, this striking, minimalist space is a working studio for Robert Lange and other exceptionally talented young artists. Most of the work has a hyperrealistic style with surreal overtones. This is also home base for the work of lauded, whimsical painter Nathan Durfee and local-scene veteran Karen Ann Myers. ⊠ *2 Queen St., Market* ☎ *843/805–8052* ⊕ *www.robertlangestudios.com.*

CLOTHING

ellington. Chic and classy, this shop is known for its washable, packable women's clothing made of feel-good fabrics like silk, linen, and cashmere. Its fashions have classic lines, but always feel up-to-date. ⊠ *24 State St., Market* ☎ *843/722–7999* ⊗ *Closed Sun.*

The Trunk Show. This upscale consignment shop sells designer dresses, handbags, and shoes. The back room has been converted into a men's department, with mostly new clothes but some vintage items as well. The shop is also known for its estate jewelry and custom-made jewelry from semiprecious stones. There's an excellent selection of gowns and evening wear. ⊠ *281 Meeting St., Market* ☎ *843/722–0442* ⊗ *Closed Sun.*

FOOD AND WINE

FAMILY **Market Street Sweets.** Stop here for melt-in-your-mouth pralines, bear claws, fudge, and the famous glazed pecans—cinnamon and sugar is the favorite. It's a sister location of Savannah's River Street Sweets. ⊠ *100 N. Market St., Market* ☎ *843/722–1397* ⊕ *www.riverstreetsweets.com.*

O'Hara & Flynn. One of Charleston's best-known wineshops also has a wine bar, open Monday through Saturday. If you buy a bottle of wine at retail price, you can drink it at the tables or right at the wine bar for a $10 corkage fee. Meats (including imported sausage and salami), cheeses, and fresh olive oil are sold here, and you can order some as small appetizer plates. There's often live jazz and acoustic music on Thursday through Saturday evenings. ⊠ *225 Meeting St., Market* ☎ *843/534–1916* ⊗ *Closed Sun.*

FAMILY **Savannah's Candy Kitchen of Charleston.** This sweets shop sells freshly made fudge, pralines, and pecan pies. It's an outpost of an original store in Savannah. ⊠ *32 N. Market St., Market* ☎ *843/723–4626* ⊕ *www.savannahcandy.com.*

GIFTS AND SOUVENIRS

Indigo Home. Indigo stocks funky home and garden accessories. In addition, there are both locally made and handmade products that come from unique vendors, from quirky clothes to artisan jewelry. ⊠ *4 Vendue Range, Market* ☎ *843/723–2983* ⊕ *www.indigohome.com.*

HOME DECOR

★ Fodor's Choice **Historic Charleston Foundation Shop.** Bring home superb replicas of Charleston books, furniture, china, and decorative accessories. These Charleston mementos, including bags of Carolina Rice, make treasured gifts. ✉ *108 Meeting St., Market* ☎ *843/724–8484* ⊕ *www.historiccharleston.org.*

Le Creuset Boutique. Charleston is the U.S. base of this iconic French cookware company. Their Market Street boutique shows off a rainbow of colorful cast iron cookware ready to inspire any home chef. ✉ *112 N. Market St., Market* ☎ *843/720–5911* ⊕ *www.lecreuset.com.*

SHOES AND ACCESSORIES

Gucci of Charleston. In the Shops at Charleston Place, this branch of the fashion powerhouse carries a full line of handbags, luggage, jewelry, and even a dress or two. ✉ *Shops at Charleston Place, 132 Market St., Market* ☎ *843/722–3788* ⊕ *www.gucci.com.*

SPAS

★ **Fodor's Choice Earthling Day Spa.** With a Southeast Asian design, this soothing spa has an extensive menu of treatments that includes an Indian herbal rub, a Thai detox ritual that wraps you in banana leaves, and a Javanese beauty regimen that includes time in a steam capsule. A Turkish-style steam bath uses exotic spices like cardamom and olive stones to invigorate the circulation and lymphatic systems. Facials are the specialty here, and the algae mineral mask will leave you glowing. There is also a Pilates studio, and a boutique offers spa products galore. ✉ *245 E. Bay St., Market* ☎ *843/722–4737* ⊕ *www.earthlingdayspa.com.*

The Spa at Belmond Charleston Place. This truly deluxe day spa has nine treatment rooms, and a wet room where you can indulge in exotic body wraps like the Seaweed Detox wrap. For a piece of heaven, try the scalp, neck, and shoulder massage with Moroccan oil. Locker rooms for men and women have showers and saunas; men also have a steam room. There's even a selection of kids' offerings, including the Cinderella facial and Lollipop Pedicure. Adjacent is a fitness room, an indoor/outdoor pool with retractable roof and a spacious hot tub, plus a gift shop and the Elysium Salon. ✉ *Belmond Charleston Place, 130 Market St., Market* ☎ *843/722–4900* ⊕ *www.charlestonplacespa.com.*

UPPER KING

BOOKS

★ **Fodor's Choice Blue Bicycle Books.** Look for out-of-print and rare books, including hardcover classics and a large selection of

CLOSE UP

Charleston's Sweet Tooth

Pralines, glazed pecans, bear claws, and benne wafers—Charleston has plenty of unique and local offerings for visitors with a sweet tooth. You can't walk around the Market area without breathing in the irresistible aroma of pralines.

Employees of candy shops like **Market Street Sweets** (*100 N. Market St.*) stand outside offering samples of their wares, including pralines and cinnamon-and-sugar-glazed pecans.

Benne wafers, which are sweet cookies rather than sesame crackers as the name might suggest, are a Charleston original. Benne is the African word for sesame seeds, which were brought over on slave ships. Once in Charleston, all it took was a little brown sugar, and a confection was born. A traditional recipe for benne wafers can be found in the classic cookbook *Charleston Receipts.* These diminutive cookies, the size of a quarter, can be sampled at Charleston's Farmers' Market, downtown in Marion

Square on Saturday mornings. They are also found at **Harris Teeter** (*290 E. Bay St.*), packaged appropriately for gift-giving by local company Food For the Southern Soul.

If you develop an addiction to them, they can be ordered online at ⊕ *www.foodforthe-southernsoul.com,* along with benne candy, praline pecans, and more.

For more locally made sweets, **Cupcake DownSouth** (*433 King St.*) sells the latest flavors popularized in Manhattan, like dark chocolate with caramel frosting sprinkled with sea salt. The adorably quaint **Sugar Bakeshop** (*59½ Cannon St.*) specializes in cupcakes such as grapefruit and chocolate raspberry, homemade ice cream, and cookies. For macaron lovers, the French-influenced confection can be bought at the **Macaroon Boutique** (*45 John St.*). Raspberry is the flavor of choice, matching one of Charleston's favorite colors—pink.

7

Lowcountry fiction and nonfiction, at this locally adored bookstore offering everything from military history to cookbooks. They host frequent signings by local authors like Dorothea Benton Frank and the Lee Brothers. ⊠ *420 King St., Upper King* ☎ *843/722–2666* ⊕ *www.bluebicy-clebooks.com.*

CLOTHING

Las Olas. This locally owned surf-themed shop is the go-to shop for College of Charleston students when bikini season arrives in the spring. There's also an array of men's T-shirts, board shorts, and hats. Satellite locations are at Freshfields Village on Kiawah and at Towne Centre in Mount Pleasant. ✉ *441 King St., Upper King* ☎ *843/737–0488* ⊕ *www. lasolascharleston.com.*

CANNONBOROUGH

CLOTHING

Indigo & Cotton. This men's store is the go-to boutique for the latest in gentlemen's tailoring featuring brands such as Gitman Vintage, Filson Red Label bags, and Raleigh Denim. The Cannonborough shop is also brimming with bow ties, handkerchiefs, and other accessories. ✉ *79 Cannon St., Cannonborough* ☎ *843/718–2980* ⊕ *www.indigoandcotton. com* ⊙ *Closed Sun.*

GIFTS AND SOUVENIRS

Mac & Murphy. This hole-in-the-wall is for anyone who favors old-fashioned methods of communication, with the trendiest in notepads, pens, wrapping paper, and stationery, including Cheree Berry, Crane & Co., and Dude and Chick. ✉ *74½ Cannon St., Cannonborough* ☎ *843/576–4394* ⊕ *www.macandmurphy.com* ⊙ *Closed Sun.*

NORTH MORRISON DRIVE

FOOD AND WINE

★ FodorsChoice **Edmund's Oast Exchange.** This impressive bottle shop in a soaring wood-built space next to the restaurant that shares its name, boasts the city's best selection of beer and wine. An in-house sommelier and cicerone are on hand to help with selections and pairings. ✉ *1081 Morrison Dr., North Morrison* ☎ *843/990–9449* ⊕ *www.edmundsoast. com* ⊙ *Closed Mon.*

MOUNT PLEASANT AND VICINITY

ANTIQUES AND COLLECTIBLES

Page's Thieves Market. Specializing in furniture—especially tables, desks, and chests—this antiques market frequently hosts auctions on weekends. There's also plenty of whimsical local artwork and historical knickknacks. Drop by on your way to the beach at Sullivan's Island or Isle of Palms. ✉ *1460 Ben Sawyer Blvd., Mount Pleasant* ☎ *843/884–9672* ⊕ *www.pagesthievesmarket.com* ⊙ *Closed Sun.*

CLOTHING

Bits of Lace. When this exclusive lingerie shop opened in 1976, no one thought it would make it in such a conservative town, but they were wrong. It's still here, with locations off King Street, and in Mount Pleasant—and stocks beautiful sleepwear and swimsuits. It's known for its bra-fitting service, especially for bigger cup sizes. ⊠ *453 Coleman Blvd., Mount Pleasant* ☎ *843/531–6625* ⊕ *www.bitsoflace.com* ⊗ *Closed Sun.*

HOME DECOR

Carolina Lanterns. Stop in for custom-made copper gas and electric lanterns based on designs from downtown's Historic District, as well as a host of other lights and accessories. ⊠ *1362 Chuck Dawley Blvd., Mount Pleasant* ☎ *843/881–4170* ⊕ *www.carolinalanterns.com* ⊗ *Closed Sun.*

MALLS AND SHOPPING CENTERS

Mount Pleasant Towne Centre. Across the Ravenel Bridge, this mall has 60 stores, including Old Navy, Barnes & Noble, and the locally owned Copper Penny. It's also home to the area's best movie theater, the wide-screen Palmetto Grande Stadium 16. ⊠ *1218 Belk Dr., Mount Pleasant* ☎ *843/216–9900* ⊕ *www.mtpleasanttownecentre.com.*

GREATER CHARLESTON

JOHNS ISLAND

ART

Wells Gallery. Showcasing the talents of many fine artists dating back centuries (including 18th-century naturalist Mark Catesby), this gallery at The Sanctuary on Kiawah Island shows still-life paintings, black-and-white photographs, bronze sculptures, and handblown glass. Everything here is done in excellent taste, from the contemporary decor to the meet-the-artist receptions. ⊠ *1 Sanctuary Beach Dr., Kiawah Island* ☎ *843/576–1290* ⊕ *www.wellsgallery.com.*

MALLS AND SHOPPING CENTERS

Freshfields Village. At the crossroads of Kiawah and Seabrook islands, this shopping area includes a variety of homegrown stores. There are French and Italian restaurants, an ice cream shop, a sports outfitter, and stores selling upscale apparel. More than just a shopping destination, Freshfields has become a major social center, offering everything from wine and beer tastings to movies and concerts on the green. ⊠ *165 Village Green La., Kiawah Island* ☎ *843/768–6491* ⊕ *www.freshfieldsvillage.com.*

NORTH CHARLESTON

MALLS AND SHOPPING CENTERS

Tanger Outlet. If you are a dedicated outlet shopper, head to Tanger Outlet in North Charleston. This spiffy, contemporary mall houses 80 name-brand outlets like LOFT, J.Crew, Under Armour, and Saks OFF 5TH. ⊠ *4840 Tanger Outlet Blvd., North Charleston* ☎ *843/529–3095* ⊕ *www.tangeroutlet.com.*

WEST ASHLEY

SPAS

Stella Nova. This spa got its start on King Street before expanding to two spacious locations in West Ashley and Mount Pleasant. They offer treatments from body wraps to salt scrubs and waxing to pedicures. Couples can enjoy romantic aromatherapy massages. There's a top-of-the-line salon with specially trained stylists and makeup artists as well. The spa is a go-to for bridal parties and girlfriend getaways. ⊠ *2048 Sam Rittenberg Blvd., West Ashley* ☎ *843/766–6233* ⊕ *www.stella-nova.com* ⊗ *Closed Sun.*

HILTON HEAD AND THE LOWCOUNTRY

Updated
by Sally
Mahan

HILTON HEAD ISLAND IS A unique and incredibly beautiful resort town that anchors the southern tip of South Carolina's coastline. What makes this semitropical island so unique? At the top of the list is the fact that visitors won't see large, splashy billboards or neon signs. What they will see is an island where the environment takes center stage, a place where development is strictly regulated.

There are 12 miles of sparkling white-sand beaches, amazing world-class restaurants, top-rated golf courses—Harbour Town Golf Links annually hosts the Heritage Golf Tournament, a PGA Tour event—and a thriving tennis community. Wildlife abounds, including loggerhead sea turtles, alligators, snowy egrets, wood storks, great blue heron, and, in the waters, dolphins, manatees, and various species of fish. There are lots of activities offered on the island, including parasailing, charter fishing, kayaking, and many other water sports.

The island is home to several private gated communities, including Sea Pines, Hilton Head Plantation, Shipyard, Wexford, Long Cove, Port Royal, Indigo Run, Palmetto Hall, and Palmetto Dunes. Within these you'll find upscale housing (some of it doubling as vacation rentals), golf courses, shopping, and restaurants. Sea Pines is one of the most famous of these communities, as it is known for the iconic candy-cane-striped Hilton Head Lighthouse. There are also many areas on the island that are not behind security gates.

ORIENTATION AND PLANNING

GETTING ORIENTED

Hilton Head is just north of South Carolina's border with Georgia. The 42-square-mile island is shaped like a foot, hence the reason locals often describe places as being at the "toe" or "heel" of Hilton Head. This part of South Carolina is best explored by car, as its points of interest are spread across a flat coastal plain that is a mix of wooded areas, marshes, and sea islands. The more remote areas are accessible only by boat or ferry.

Hilton Head's neighbor, Bluffton, is an artsy town rich with history. In the last several years the tiny community has grown to cover about 50 square miles. South of Hilton Head is the city of Savannah, which is about a 45-minute

TOP REASONS TO GO

Beachcombing: Hilton Head Island has 12 miles of beaches. You can swim, soak up the sun, or walk along the sand.

Beaufort: This small antebellum town offers large doses of heritage and culture; nearly everything you might want to see is within its downtown historic district.

Challenging Golf: Hilton Head's nickname is "Golf Island," and its many challenging courses have an international reputation.

Serving Up Tennis: Home to hundreds of tennis courts, Hilton Head is one of the nation's top tennis destinations.

Staying Put: This semitropical island has been a resort destination for decades, and it has all the desired amenities for visitors: a vast array of lodgings, an endless supply of restaurants, and excellent shopping.

drive from the island. North of Hilton Head is Beaufort, a cultural treasure and a graceful antebellum town. Beaufort is also about 45 minutes from Hilton Head.

Hilton Head Island. One of the Southeast coast's most popular tourist destinations, Hilton Head is known for its golf courses and tennis courts. It's a magnet for time-share owners and retirees. Bluffton is Hilton Head's quirky neighbor to the west. The old-town area is laden with history and charm.

Beaufort. This charming town just inland from Hilton Head is a destination in its own right, with a lively dining scene and cute bed-and-breakfasts.

Daufuskie Island. A scenic ferry ride from Hilton Head, Daufuskie is now much more developed than it was during the days when Pat Conroy wrote *The Water Is Wide,* but it's still a beautiful island to explore, even on a day trip. You can stay for a few days at a variety of fine rental properties, tool down shady dirt roads in a golf cart, and delight in the glorious, nearly deserted beaches.

PLANNING

WHEN TO GO

The high season follows typical beach-town cycles, with June through August and holidays year-round being the busiest and most costly. Mid-April, during the annual RBC Heritage Golf Tournament, is when rates tend to be highest.

Thanks to the Lowcountry's mostly moderate year-round temperatures, tourists are ever-present. Spring is the best time to visit, when the weather is ideal for tennis and golf. Autumn is almost as active for the same reason.

To get a good deal, it's imperative that you plan ahead. The choicest locations can be booked six months to a year in advance, but booking agencies can help you make room reservations and get good deals during the winter season, when the crowds fall off. Villa-rental companies often offer snowbird rates for monthly stays during the winter season. Parking is always free at the major hotels, but valet parking can cost from $17 to $25; the smaller properties have free parking, too, but no valet service.

WILL IT RAIN? Don't be discouraged when you see a weather forecast during the summer months saying there's a 30% chance of rain for Hilton Head. It can be an absolutely gorgeous day and suddenly a storm will pop up late in the afternoon. That's because on hot sunny days, the hot air rises up into the atmosphere and mixes with the cool air, causing the atmosphere to become unstable, thereby creating thunderstorms. Not to worry, though: these storms move in and out fairly quickly.

PLANNING YOUR TIME

No matter where you stay, spend your first day relaxing on the beach or hitting the links. After that, you'll have time to visit some of the area's attractions, including the Coastal Discovery Museum or the Sea Pines Resort. You can also visit the Tanger outlet malls on U.S. 278 in Bluffton. Old-town Bluffton is a quaint area with many locally owned shops and art galleries. If you have a few more days, visit Beaufort on a day trip or even spend the night there. This historic antebellum town is rich with history. Savannah is also a short drive away.

GETTING HERE AND AROUND

AIR TRAVEL

Most travelers use the Savannah/Hilton Head International Airport, less than an hour from Hilton Head, which is served by Air Canada, American Airlines, Allegiant, Delta, Frontier, JetBlue, Sun Country Airlines, and United. Hilton Head Island Airport is served by American Airlnes with direct flights available from Charlotte.

Air Contacts Hilton Head Island Airport. ✉ *120 Beach City Rd.,*

North End ☎ *843/255–2950* ⊕ *www.hiltonheadairport.com.* **Savannah/Hilton Head International Airport.** ⊠ *400 Airways Ave., Northwest* ☎ *912/964–0514* ⊕ *www.savannahairport.com.*

BOAT AND FERRY TRAVEL

Hilton Head is accessible via boat, with docking available at Harbour Town Yacht Basin, Skull Creek Marina, and Shelter Cove Harbor.

Boat Docking Information **Harbour Town Yacht Basin.** ⊠ *Sea Pines, 149 Lighthouse Rd., South End* ☎ *843/363–8335* ⊕ *www. seapines.com.* **Shelter Cove Marina.** ⊠ *Shelter Cove, 1 Shelter Cove La., Mid-Island* ☎ *800/466–7894* ⊕ *www.palmettodunes.com/ shelter-cove/marina-hilton-head.* **Skull Creek Marina.** ⊠ *1 Waterway La., North End* ☎ *843/681–8436* ⊕ *www.theskullcreekmarina.com.*

BUS TRAVEL

The Lowcountry Regional Transportation Authority, known as the Palmetto Breeze, has buses that leave Bluffton in the morning for Hilton Head, Beaufort, and some of the islands. The fare is $2, and exact change is required.

Bus Contacts **Lowcountry Regional Transportation Authority.** ☎ *843/757–5782* ⊕ *www.palmettobreezetransit.com.*

CAR TRAVEL

Driving is the best way to get onto Hilton Head Island. Off Interstate 95, take Exit 8 onto U.S. 278 East, which leads you through Bluffton (where it's known as Fording Island Road) and then to Hilton Head. Once on Hilton Head, U.S. 278 forks: on the right is William Hilton Parkway, and on the left is the Cross Island Parkway (a toll road that costs $1.25 each way). If you take the Cross Island (as the locals call it) to the south side where Sea Pines and many other resorts are located, the trip will take about 10 to 15 minutes. If you take William Hilton Parkway the trip will take about 30 minutes. Be aware that at check-in and checkout times on Friday, Saturday, and Sunday, traffic on U.S. 278 can slow to a crawl. ■TIP➔ **Be careful of putting the pedal to the metal, particularly on the Cross Island Parkway. It's patrolled regularly.**

Once on Hilton Head Island, signs are small and blend in with the trees and landscaping, and nighttime lighting is kept to a minimum. The lack of streetlights makes it difficult to find your way at night, so be sure to get good directions.

8

TAXI TRAVEL

There are several taxi services available on Hilton Head, including Hilton Head Taxi and Limousine, and Diamond Transportation, which has SUVs and passenger vans available for pickup at Savannah/Hilton Head International Airport and Hilton Head Airport. Prices range from $20 to $120, depending on where you're headed.

Taxi Contacts **Diamond Transportation.** ☎ 843/247–2156 ⊕ hiltonheadrides.com. **Hilton Head Taxi and Limousine.** ☎ 843/785–8294 ⊕ yellowcabhhi.net.

TRAIN TRAVEL

Amtrak gets you as close as Savannah or Yemassee.

Train Contacts **Savannah Amtrak Station.** ✉ 2611 Seaboard Coastline Dr., Savannah ☎ 800/872–7245 ⊕ www.amtrak.com.

RESTAURANTS

The number of fine-dining restaurants on Hilton Head is extraordinary, given the size of the island. Because of the proximity to the ocean and the small farms on the mainland, most locally owned restaurants are still heavily influenced by the catch of the day and seasonal harvests. Most upscale restaurants open at 11 and don't close until 9 or 10, but some take a break between 2 and 4. Many advertise early-bird menus, and sometimes getting a table before 6 can be a challenge. During the height of the summer season, reservations are a good idea, though in the off-season you may need them only on weekends. There are several locally owned breakfast joints and plenty of great delis where you can pick up lunch or the fixings for a picnic. Smoking is prohibited in restaurants and bars in Bluffton, Beaufort, and on Hilton Head. Beaufort's restaurant scene has certainly evolved, with more trendy restaurants serving contemporary cuisine moving into the downtown area.

HOTELS

Hilton Head is known as one of the best vacation spots on the East Coast, and its hotels are a testimony to its reputation. The island is awash in regular hotels and resorts, not to mention beachfront or golf-course-view villas, cottages, and luxury private homes. You can expect the most modern conveniences and world-class service at the priciest places. Clean, updated rooms and friendly staff are everywhere, even at lower-cost hotels—this is the South, after all. Staying in cooler months, for extended periods of time, or commuting from nearby Bluffton can save money.

WHAT IT COSTS			
$	**$$**	**$$$**	**$$$$**
Restaurants under $15	$15–$19	$20–$24	over $24
Hotels under $150	$150–$200	$201–$250	over $250

Restaurant prices are for a main course at dinner, excluding sales tax. Hotel prices are for two people in a standard double room in high season, excluding service charges and tax.

TOURS

Hilton Head's Adventure Cruises hosts dolphin-watching cruises, sport crabbing, and more. Several companies, including H20 Sports, Live Oac, Outside Hilton Head, and Low Country Nature Tours run dolphin-watching, shark-fishing, kayak, sunset, and delightful environmental trips. Low Country Nature Tours offers a family-friendly fireworks tour during the summer, as well as educational and fun bird-watching tours that children are sure to enjoy.

Gullah Heritage Trail Tours gives a wealth of history about slavery and the Union takeover of the island during the Civil War; tours leave from the Coastal Discovery Museum at Honey Horn Plantation. Tickets are $32.

There's a wide variety of tours available at Harbour Town Yacht Basin, including sunset cruises, fireworks, and dolphin tours. Pau Hana & Flying Circus Sailing Charters offers tours on a catamaran sailboat, and fireworks and sunset cruises. The captains provide an interactive, educational adventure, and the catamaran makes for smooth sailing.

Tour Contacts Adventure Cruises. ⊠ *Shelter Cove Marina, 9 Harbourside La., Mid-Island* ☎ *843/785–4558* ⊕ *www.cruisehiltonhead. com.* **Gullah Heritage Trail Tours.** ⊠ *Coastal Discovery Museum, 70 Honey Horn Dr., North End* ☎ *843/681–7066* ⊕ *www.gullaheritage. com.* **H2O Sports.** ⊠ *Harbour Town Marina, 149 Lighthouse Rd., South End* ☎ *843/671–4386, 877/290–4386* ⊕ *www.h2osports.com.* **Harbour Town Yacht Basin.** ⊠ *Sea Pines, 149 Lighthouse Rd., South End* ☎ *843/363–2628* ⊕ *harbourtownyachtbasin.com.* **Live Oac.** ⊠ *Hilton Head Harbor, 43A Jenkins Rd., North End* ☎ *843/384–4141* ⊕ *www. liveoac.com.* **Low Country Nature Tours.** ⊠ *Shelter Cove Marina, 1 Shelter Cove La., Mid-Island* ☎ *843/683–0187* ⊕ *www.lowcountry-naturetours.com.* **Outside Hilton Head.** ⊠ *Shelter Cove Marina, 1 Shelter Cove La., Mid-Island* ☎ *843/686–6996* ⊕ *www.outsidehilton-head.com.* **Pau Hana & Flying Circus Sailing Charters.** ⊠ *Palmetto Bay Marina, 86 Helmsman Way, South End* ☎ *843/686–2582* ⊕ *www. hiltonheadislandsailing.com.*

VISITOR INFORMATION

As you're driving into town, you can pick up brochures and maps at the Hilton Head Island-Bluffton Chamber of Commerce and Visitor and Convention Bureau.

Visitor Information Hilton Head Island-Bluffton Chamber of Commerce and Visitor and Convention Bureau. ✉ *1 Chamber of Commerce Dr., Mid-Island* ☎ *843/785–3673* ⊕ *www.hiltonhead-island.org.*

HILTON HEAD ISLAND

Hilton Head Island is known far and wide as a vacation destination that prides itself on its top-notch golf courses and tennis programs, world-class resorts, and beautiful beaches. But the island is also part of the storied American South, steeped in a rich, colorful history. It has seen Native Americans and explorers, battles from the Revolutionary War to the Civil War, plantations and slaves, and development and environmentally focused growth.

More than 10,000 years ago, the island was inhabited by Paleo-Indians. From 8000 to 2000 BC, Woodland Indians lived on the island. A shell ring made from their discarded oyster shells and animal bones from that period can be found in the Sea Pines Nature Preserve.

The recorded history of the island goes back to the early 1500s, when Spanish explorers sailing coastal waters came upon the island and found Native American settlements. Over the next 200 years, the island was claimed at various times by the Spanish, the French, and the British. In 1663, Captain William Hilton claimed the island for the British crown (and named it for himself), and the island became home to indigo, rice, and cotton plantations.

During the Revolutionary War, the British harassed islanders and burned plantations. During the War of 1812, British troops again burned plantations, but the island recovered from both wars. During the Civil War, Union troops took Hilton Head in 1861 and freed the more than 1,000 slaves on the island. Mitchelville, one of the first settlements for freed blacks, was created. There was no bridge to the island, so its freed slaves, called "Gullah," subsisted on agriculture and the seafood-laden waters.

Over the years, much of the plantation land was sold at auction. Then, in 1949, General Joseph Fraser purchased

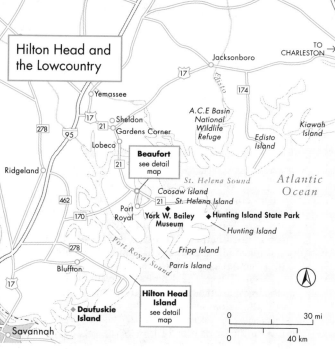

Beaufort
see detail
map

Hilton Head
Island
see detail
map

17,000 acres, much of which would eventually become various communities, including Hilton Head Plantation, Palmetto Dunes, and Spanish Wells. The general bought another 1,200 acres, which his son, Charles, used to develop Sea Pines. The first bridge to the island was built in 1956, and modern-day Hilton Head was born.

What makes Hilton Head so special now? Charles Fraser and his business associates focused on development while preserving the environment. And that is what tourists will see today: an island that values its history and its natural beauty.

GETTING HERE AND AROUND

Hilton Head Island is 19 miles east of Interstate 95. Take Exit 8 off Interstate 95 and then U.S. 278 east, directly to the bridges. If you're heading to the southern end of the island, your best bet to save time and avoid traffic is the Cross Island Parkway toll road. The cost is $1.25 each way.

EXPLORING

Your impression of Hilton Head depends on which of the island's developments you make your temporary home. The oldest and best known of Hilton Head's developments, Sea Pines occupies 4,500 thickly wooded acres. It's not wilderness, however; among the trees are three golf courses, tennis clubs, riding stables, and shopping plazas. A free trolley shuttles visitors around the resort. Other well-known communities are Palmetto Dunes and Port Royal Plantation.

TOP ATTRACTIONS

★ Fodor'sChoice **Coastal Discovery Museum.** This wonderful FAMILY museum tells about the history of the Lowcountry. For instance, you'll learn about the early development of Hilton Head as an island resort from the Civil War to the 1930s. There is also a butterfly enclosure, various hands-on programs for children, guided walks, and much more. Take a walk around the grounds to see marshes, open fields, live oaks dripping with Spanish moss, as well as South Carolina's largest Southern red cedar tree, which dates back to 1595. Admission is free, but lectures and tours on various subjects cost between $5 and $10. Although the museum is just off the Cross Island Parkway, the peaceful grounds make it feel miles away. ⊠ *70 Honey Horn Dr., off Hwy. 278, North End* ☎ *843/689–6767* ⊕ *www.coastaldiscovery. org* ⊠ *Free* ☉ *Closed Sun.*

★ Fodor'sChoice **Old Town Bluffton.** Tucked away from the resort areas, charming Old Town Bluffton has several historic homes and churches on oak-lined streets dripping with Spanish moss. The Promenade was built recently and includes several new bars and restaurants. There are also new additions to Old Town, including a microbrewery. At the end of Wharf Street in this artsy community is the Bluffton Oyster Company (*63 Wharf Street*), a place to buy fresh raw local shrimp, fish, and oysters. Grab some picnic fixings from the Downtown Deli (*27 Mellichamp Drive*) and head to the boat dock at the end of Pritchard Street for a meal with a view. Another incredibly beautiful spot for a picnic is the grounds of the Church of the Cross. ⊠ *May River Rd. and Calhoun St., Bluffton* ⊕ *www. oldtownbluffton.com.*

FAMILY **Sea Pines Forest Preserve.** Walking and biking trails take you past a stocked fishing pond, a waterfowl pond, and a 3,400-year-old Native American shell ring at this 605-acre public wilderness tract. Pick up the extensive activity guide at the Sea Pines Welcome Center to take advantage of goings-on—moonlight hayrides, storytelling around campfires, and alligator- and bird-watching boat tours. The preserve is part of the grounds at Sea Pines Resort. Overlooking a small lake, the outdoor chapel has five wooden pews and a wooden lectern engraved with the Prayer of St. Francis. ✉ *Sea Pines Resort, 32 Greenwood Dr., South End* ☎ *843/363–4530, 866/561–8802* 🌐 *www.seapines.com* 🎫 *$6 per car.*

WORTH NOTING

FAMILY **Audubon-Newhall Preserve.** There are hiking trails, a self-guided tour, and seasonal walks on this 50-acre preserve. Native plant life is tagged and identified in this pristine forest. ✉ *Palmetto Bay Rd., off the Cross Island Pkwy., South End* ☎ *843/842–9246* 🌐 *www.hiltonheadaudubon.org* 🎫 *Free.*

★ Fodor's Choice FAMILY **Harbour Town.** The closest thing the Sea Pines development has to a downtown is Harbour Town, a charming area centered on a circular marina that's filled with interesting shops and restaurants. Rising above it all is the landmark candy-cane-stripe Hilton Head Lighthouse, which you can climb to enjoy a view of Calibogue Sound. ✉ *Lighthouse Rd., South End* ☎ *866/561–8802* 🌐 *www.seapines.com.*

Stoney-Baynard Ruins. Check out the Stoney-Baynard Ruins, the remnants of a plantation home and slave quarters built in the 1700s by Captain John "Saucy Jack" Stoney. A cotton planter named William Edings Baynard bought the place in 1840. On the National Register of Historic Sites, only parts of the walls are still standing. The ruins are not easy to find, so ask for directions at the Sea Pines Welcome Center at the Greenwood Drive gate. ✉ *Plantation Dr., near Baynard Cove Rd., South End* 🎫 *Free.*

8

WHERE TO EAT

$$$ 🍴 **Black Marlin Bayside Grill.** *Seafood.* If you want to dine with a view of the "blue," then head to this seafood eatery in Palmetto Bay Marina. The place draws a steady stream of customers most days, but Saturday and Sunday brunch are the highlights for eggs Benedict and live entertainment. **Known for:** a hopping happy hour; an outdoor Hurricane Bar with a Key West vibe. [$] *Average main: $23* ✉ *Palmetto Bay Marina, 86 Helmsman Way, South End* ☎ *843/785–4950* 🌐 *www.blackmarlinhhi.com.*

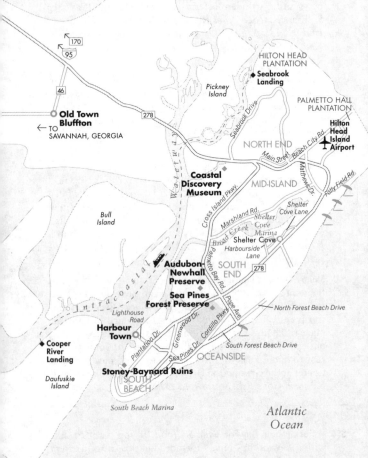

Hilton Head Island

Port Royal Sound

HILTON HEAD PLANTATION

◆ Seabrook Landing

PALMETTO HALL PLANTATION

170
95

46

○ **Old Town Bluffton**

← TO SAVANNAH, GEORGIA

Pickney Island

278

Seabrook Drive

NORTH END

Main Street

Beach City Rd.

✈ **Hilton Head Island Airport**

Matthews Dr.

Folly Field Rd.

Coastal Discovery Museum

MID-ISLAND

Cross Island Pkwy.

Marshland Rd.

Shelter Cove Lane

Broad Creek

Shelter Cove Marina

Shelter Cove

Bull Island

Harbourside Lane

SOUTH END

278

Pope Ave.

Audubon-Newhall Preserve

Sea Pines Forest Preserve

Palmetto Bay Rd.

North Forest Beach Drive

Lighthouse Road

Harbour Town ○

Greenwood Dr.

Sea Pines Dr.

Cordillo Pkwy.

South Forest Beach Drive

OCEANSIDE

Plantation Dr.

◆ **Cooper River Landing**

Daufuskie Island

Stoney-Baynard Ruins

SOUTH BEACH

South Beach Marina

Atlantic Ocean

Intracoastal Waterway

0   1/2 mi

0   1/2 km

KEY
🏖 *Beach*
⛴ *Ferry*

Shrimp Boats Forever

Watching shrimp trawlers coming into their home port at sunset, with mighty nets raised and an entourage of hungry seagulls, is a cherished Lowcountry tradition. The shrimping industry has been an integral staple of the South Carolina economy for nearly a century. (Remember Bubba Gump?) It was booming in the 1980s. But alas, cheap, farm-raised shrimp from foreign markets and now the cost of diesel fuel are deci-mating the shrimpers' numbers. The season for fresh-caught shrimp is May to December. Lowcountry residents support the freelance fishermen by buying only certified, local wild shrimp in restaurants and in area fish markets and supermarkets. Visitors can follow suit by patronizing local restaurants and markets that display the logo that reads "Certified Wild American Shrimp." Or you can simply ask before you eat.

$$$ × **Captain Woody's.** *Seafood.* If you're looking for a fun,
FAMILY casual, kid-friendly seafood restaurant, Captain Woody's is the place to go. Start with the creamy crab bisque, oysters on the half shell, or the sampler platter, which includes crab legs, shrimp, and oysters. **Known for:** grouper sandwiches, including the buffalo grouper, grouper melt, and grouper Reuben; a lively atmosphere. Ⓢ *Average main: $22* ✉ *6 Target Rd., South End* ☎ *843/785–2400* ⊕ *www.captainwoodys.com.*

$$$$ × **Frankie Bones.** *Italian.* This restaurant, which is dedicated to Frank Sinatra, appeals to an older crowd that likes the traditional Italian dishes on the early dining menu. But during happy hour, the bar and the surrounding cocktail tables are populated with younger patrons who order flatbread pizzas and small plates. **Known for:** cool twists on traditional dishes; drinks for dessert (the tiramisu martini is to die for). Ⓢ *Average main: $26* ✉ *1301 Main St., North End* ☎ *843/682–4455* ⊕ *www.frankieboneshhi.com.*

$ × **Harold's Country Club & Grill.** *American.* Not the "country club" you might expect, Harold's Country Club & Grill is a remodeled gas station in the little town of Yemassee, just east of Interstate 95, south of Charleston. There's a buffet every Thursday, wings and things like seafood baskets and hamburgers on Friday, and steak or chicken with a variety of sides on Saturday. **Known for:** cheerful ladies slapping meat on your plate cafeteria-style; great music; kitschy dining rooms. Ⓢ *Average main: $13* ✉ *97 U.S. 17A, Yemassee* ☎ *843/589–4360* ⊕ *www.haroldscountryclub.com* ☉ *Closed Sun.–Wed.*

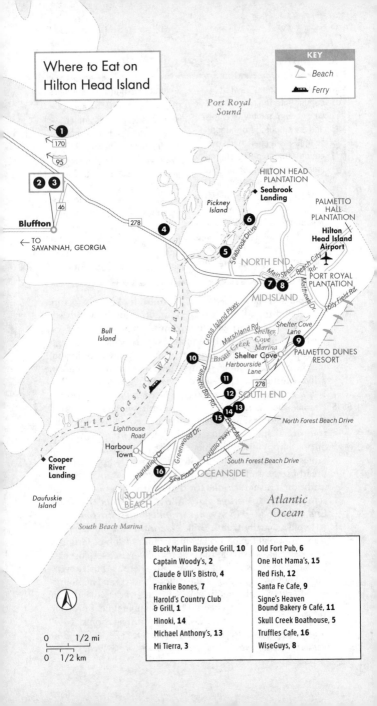

Where to Eat on Hilton Head Island

KEY
≥ Beach
⛴ Ferry

Port Royal Sound

Bluffton

← TO SAVANNAH, GEORGIA

HILTON HEAD PLANTATION

◆ Seabrook Landing

PALMETTO HALL PLANTATION

Hilton Head Island Airport

Pickney Island

NORTH END

MID-ISLAND

PORT ROYAL PLANTATION

Bull Island

Intracoastal Waterway

Marshland Rd

Shelter Cove Marina

Shelter Cove Lane

PALMETTO DUNES RESORT

Shelter Cove

Harbourside Lane

SOUTH END

Broad Creek

Cross Island Pkwy.

Beach City Rd.

Matthews Dr.

Folly Field Rd.

North Forest Beach Drive

Lighthouse Road

◆ Cooper River Landing

Harbour Town

Daufuskie Island

SOUTH BEACH

Greenwood Dr.

Plantation Dr.

Sea Pines Dr.

Cordillo Pkwy.

South Forest Beach Drive

OCEANSIDE

Atlantic Ocean

South Beach Marina

0   1/2 mi
0   1/2 km

Black Marlin Bayside Grill, **10**	Old Fort Pub, **6**
Captain Woody's, **2**	One Hot Mama's, **15**
Claude & Uli's Bistro, **4**	Red Fish, **12**
Frankie Bones, **7**	Santa Fe Cafe, **9**
Harold's Country Club & Grill, **1**	Signe's Heaven Bound Bakery & Café, **11**
Hinoki, **14**	Skull Creek Boathouse, **5**
Michael Anthony's, **13**	Truffles Cafe, **16**
Mi Tierra, **3**	WiseGuys, **8**

★ $$$ Fodor's Choice 🍴 **Hinoki.** *Japanese.* A peaceful oasis awaits you at Hinoki, which has some of the best sushi on Hilton Head. Try the Hilton Head roll, which is whitefish tempura and avocado, the Hinoki roll with asparagus and spicy fish roe topped with tuna and avocado, or one of the more than 50 sushi and sashimi choices. **Known for:** superfresh sushi; extensive sake menu. [$] *Average main: $23* ✉ *Orleans Plaza, 37 New Orleans Rd., South End* ☎ *843/785–9800* 🌐 *hinokihhi.com* 🕒 *Closed Sun.*

MODERN TAKEOUT. When you just don't feel like going out for a bite, a local delivery service is here to help. Hiltonheaddelivers.com delivers restaurant food to homes, condos, and hotels from 5 to 9:45 pm seven days a week for a $5.50 delivery charge. A variety of restaurants take part, including One Hot Mama's, WiseGuys, and more. Visit 🌐 hiltonheaddelivers.com for more details.

★ $$$$ Fodor's Choice 🍴 **Michael Anthony's.** *Italian.* Owned by a talented, charismatic Philadelphia family, this restaurant has a convivial spirit, and its innovative pairings and plate presentations are au courant. You can expect fresh, top-quality ingredients, simple yet elegant sauces, and waiters who know and care about the food and wine they serve. **Known for:** cooking demonstrations/classes; on-site market with fresh pasta; wine tastings. [$] *Average main: $30* ✉ *Orleans Plaza, 37 New Orleans Rd., Suite L, South End* ☎ *843/785–6272* 🌐 *www.michael-anthonys.com* 🕒 *Closed Sun. No lunch.*

8

COOKING CLASS. Learn to prepare Italian cuisine in a hands-on cooking class at Michael Anthony's. Classes include samples of the dishes and wine. Demonstration classes, wine tastings, and programs for visiting corporate groups are also available. There is a high demand for these classes, so reserve your place as far in advance as possible on Michael Anthony's website (🌐 www.michael-anthonys.com).

$$ 🍴 **Mi Tierra.** *Mexican.* There's nothing fancy here, just great Mexican food and decor that has a Southwestern feel, with tile floors, colorful sombreros, and paintings of chili peppers hanging on the walls. Start with a margarita and the chips and salsa, and don't forget to order the guacamole and bean dip as well. **Known for:** delicious comfort food; authentic Mexican dishes; extensive menu and daily specials. [$] *Average main: $15* ✉ *130 Arrow Rd.,*

South End ☎ *843/342–3409* 🌐 *www.mitierrabluffton.com* ⏲ *No lunch weekends.*

$$$$ 🍴 **Old Fort Pub.** *European.* Overlooking the sweeping marshlands of Skull Creek, this romantic restaurant has almost panoramic views. It offers one of the island's best overall dining experiences: the building is old enough to have some personality, and the professional staffers diligently do their duty. **Known for:** amazing, decadent entrées beautifully presented; a lovely Sunday brunch; gorgeous views; romantic atmosphere. [$] *Average main: $33* ✉ *Hilton Head Plantation, 65 Skull Creek Dr., North End* ☎ *843/681–2386* 🌐 *www.oldfortpub.com* ⏲ *No lunch.*

$$ FAMILY 🍴 **One Hot Mama's.** *Barbecue.* This heavenly barbecue joint is a Hilton Head institution because of its upbeat atmosphere, graffiti-strewn walls, and melt-in-the-mouth pulled pork and fall-off-the-bone ribs. But the place also offers some unusual choices: the wings, which have won multiple awards at Hilton Head's Rib Burnoff and Wing Fest, come with tasty sauces ranging from strawberry-jalapeño to Maui Wowii. **Known for:** lots of fun in the "Barmuda Triangle" (other bars are just steps away). [$] *Average main: $19* ✉ *7A Greenwood Dr., South End* ☎ *843/682–6262* 🌐 *onehotmamas.com.*

★ Fodor's Choice 🍴 **Red Fish.** *American.* This seafood eatery's
$$$$ "naked" catch of the day—seafood grilled with olive oil, lime, and garlic—is a heart-healthy specialty that many diners say is the best thing on the menu. The restaurant's wine cellar is filled with some 1,000 bottles, and there's also a retail wineshop so you can take a bottle home. **Known for:** fabulous food; fabulous service; gluten-free selections. [$] *Average main: $30* ✉ *8 Archer Rd., South End* ☎ *843/686–3388* 🌐 *www.redfishofhiltonhead.com* ⏲ *No lunch Sun.*

$$$$ 🍴 **Santa Fe Cafe.** *Southwestern.* Walk through the doors and you're greeted by the sights, sounds, and aromas of New Mexico: Native American rugs, Mexican ballads, steer skulls and horns, and the pungent smells of chilies and mesquite on the grill. The restaurant is perhaps best experienced on a rainy, chilly night when the adobe fireplaces are cranked up. **Known for:** rooftop cantina with fireplace, music; tasty margaritas. [$] *Average main: $28* ✉ *807 William Hilton Pkwy., Mid-Island* ☎ *843/785–3838* 🌐 *santafehhi.com* ⏲ *No lunch weekends.*

★ Fodor's Choice 🍴 **Signe's Heaven Bound Bakery & Café.** *American.*
$ Every morning, locals roll in for the deep-dish French toast, crispy polenta, and whole wheat waffles. Since 1972, European-born Signe has been feeding islanders her delicious

soups and quiches, curried chicken salad, and loaded hot and cold sandwiches. **Known for:** to-die-for baked goods; the "beach bag" (a lunch packed with goodies to take to the beach); cozy, friendly atmosphere. [$] *Average main: $8* ✉ *93 Arrow Rd., South End* ☎ *843/785–9118* 🌐 *www.signesbakery.com* ⏲ *Closed Sun. Dec.–Feb. No dinner.*

★ Fodor'sChoice 🍴 **Skull Creek Boathouse.** *American.* Soak up the salty atmosphere in this pair of dining areas where almost every table has a view of the water. Outside is a third dining area and a bar called the Buoy Bar at Marker 13 where Adirondack chairs invite you to sit back, relax, and catch the sunset. **Known for:** great views; fun atmosphere; seafood from the "Dive Bar"; tasty sandwiches and po'boys with a Southern twist. [$] *Average main: $17* ✉ *397 Squire Pope Rd., North End* ☎ *843/681–3663* 🌐 *www.skullcreekboathouse.com.*
$$
FAMILY

$$$ 🍴 **Truffles Cafe.** *American.* When a restaurant keeps its customers happy for decades, there's a reason: you won't find any of the namesake truffles on the menu, but instead there's grilled salmon with a mango-barbecue glaze and barbecued baby back ribs. There's a second Hilton Head location on Pope Avenue, and a Bluffton branch that has a lovely outdoor seating area. **Known for:** wide-ranging menu; very popular with locals. [$] *Average main: $20* ✉ *Sea Pines Center, 71 Lighthouse Rd., South End* ☎ *843/671–6136* 🌐 *www.trufflescafe.com* ⏲ *Closed Sun. No lunch.*

$$$$ 🍴 **WiseGuys.** *Steakhouse.* The red-and-black decor is modern and sophisticated at this restaurant—it's a little art deco, a little contemporary. The food is a spin on the classics, starting with seared tuna sliders and an incredible beef tenderloin carpaccio topped with baby arugula and horseradish cream. **Known for:** cool urban atmosphere; mouthwatering steaks. [$] *Average main: $32* ✉ *1513 Main St., North End* ☎ *843/842–8866* 🌐 *wiseguyshhi.com* ⏲ *No lunch.*

BLUFFTON

★ Fodor'sChoice 🍴 **Claude & Uli's Bistro.** *European.* It's hard to go wrong with a chef who has cooked at Maxim's in Paris, the Connaught Hotel in London, and Ernie's in San Francisco. Chef Claude Melchiorri, who grew up in Normandy, France, and his wife, Uli, offer divine food at this atmospheric restaurant tucked away in a strip mall right before the bridges to Hilton Head. **Known for:** intimate ambience; French-bistro feel. [$] *Average main: $28* ✉ *Moss Creek Village, 1533 Fording Island Rd., Bluffton* ☎ *843/837–3336* 🌐 *claudebistro.com* ⏲ *No lunch Sun.–Tues. or in summer.*
$$$$

WHERE TO STAY

★ Fodor's Choice 🏨 **Beach House Hilton Head Island.** *Resort.* On one
$$$ FAMILY of the island's most popular stretches of sand, the Beach House Hilton Head Island is within walking distance of lots of shops and restaurants. **Pros:** the location cannot be beat; renovations have made this a very desirable destination; professional staff. **Cons:** in summer the number of kids raises the noise volume; small front desk can get backed up. [$] *Rooms from: $249* ✉ *1 S. Forest Beach Dr., South End* ☎ *843/785–5126* 🌐 *www.beachhousehhi.com* 🛏 *202 rooms* 🍴 *No meals.*

$$$$ FAMILY 🏨 **Disney's Hilton Head Island Resort.** *Resort.* The typical cheery colors and whimsical designs at Disney's Hilton Head Island Resort create a look that's part Southern beach resort, part Adirondack hideaway. **Pros:** family-friendly vibe; young and friendly staffers; plenty of space to spread out. **Cons:** it's a time-share property; expensive rates. [$] *Rooms from: $414* ✉ *22 Harbourside La., Mid-Island* ☎ *843/341–4100* 🌐 *hiltonhead.disney.go.com* 🛏 *123 units* 🍴 *No meals.*

$$$ FAMILY 🏨 **Hampton Inn on Hilton Head Island.** *Hotel.* Although it's not on the beach, this attractive hotel is a good choice for budget travelers. **Pros:** good customer service; moderate prices; more amenities than you might expect. **Cons:** not on a beach; parking lot views. [$] *Rooms from: $219* ✉ *1 Dillon Rd., Mid-Island* ☎ *843/681–7900* 🌐 *www.hamptoninn.com* 🛏 *103 rooms, 12 studios* 🍴 *Breakfast.*

★ Fodor's Choice 🏨 **Hilton Head Marriott Resort & Spa.** *Hotel.* Private
$$$$ FAMILY balconies with views of the palm-shaded grounds are the best reason to stay at this resort facing the Atlantic Ocean. **Pros:** steps from the beach; lots of amenities; one of the best-run operations on the island. **Cons:** rooms could be larger; in summer kids are everywhere. [$] *Rooms from: $359* ✉ *1 Hotel Circle, Palmetto Dunes, Mid-Island* ☎ *843/686–8400* 🌐 *www.marriott.com/hotels/travel/hhhgr-hilton-head-marriott-resort-and-spa* 🛏 *513 rooms* 🍴 *No meals.*

★ Fodor's Choice 🏨 **The Inn at Harbour Town.** *Hotel.* The most buzz-
$$$$ worthy of Hilton Head's properties, this European-style boutique hotel has a proper staff clad in kilts that pampers you with British service and a dose of Southern charm. **Pros:** a service-oriented property; central location; three golf courses: Heron Point; Atlantic Dunes, and Harbour Town Golf Links; complimentary parking. **Cons:** no water views; two-day minimum on most weekends. [$] *Rooms from: $309* ✉ *Sea Pines, 7 Lighthouse La., South End* ☎ *843/785–3333* 🌐 *www.seapines.com* 🛏 *60 rooms* 🍴 *No meals.*

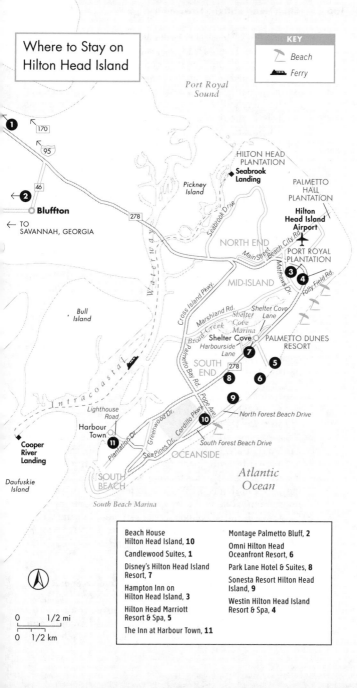

Where to Stay on Hilton Head Island

KEY

Beach

Ferry

Port Royal Sound

HILTON HEAD PLANTATION

Seabrook Landing

PALMETTO HALL PLANTATION

Pickney Island

Hilton Head Island Airport

170

95

46

Bluffton

← TO
SAVANNAH, GEORGIA

278

Seabrook Drive

NORTH END

Main Street

Beach City Rd.

Matthews Dr.

PORT ROYAL PLANTATION

Folly Field Rd.

MID-ISLAND

Cross Island Pkwy.

Marshland Rd.

Shelter Cove Lane

Shelter Cove Marina

Bull Island

Broad Creek

Shelter Cove

PALMETTO DUNES RESORT

Harbourside Lane

Palmetto Bay Rd.

SOUTH END

278

Intracoastal Waterway

Lighthouse Road

Harbour Town

North Forest Beach Drive

Pope Ave.

Cordillo Pkwy.

South Forest Beach Drive

Greenwood Dr.

OCEANSIDE

Cooper River Landing

Plantation Dr.

Sea Pines Dr.

SOUTH BEACH

Atlantic Ocean

Daufuskie Island

South Beach Marina

0   1/2 mi
0   1/2 km

Beach House
Hilton Head Island, **10**

Candlewood Suites, **1**

Disney's Hilton Head Island
Resort, **7**

Hampton Inn on
Hilton Head Island, **3**

Hilton Head Marriott
Resort & Spa, **5**

The Inn at Harbour Town, **11**

Montage Palmetto Bluff, **2**

Omni Hilton Head
Oceanfront Resort, **6**

Park Lane Hotel & Suites, **8**

Sonesta Resort Hilton Head
Island, **9**

Westin Hilton Head Island
Resort & Spa, **4**

★ Fodor'sChoice **Montage Palmetto Bluff.** *B&B/Inn.* About 15
$$$$ minutes from Hilton Head, the Lowcountry's most luxurious resort sits on 20,000 acres that have been transformed into a perfect replica of a small island town, complete with its own clapboard church. **Pros:** 18-hole May River Golf Club on-site; tennis/bocce/croquet complex has an impressive retail shop; the river adds both ambience and boat excursions. **Cons:** the mock Southern town is not the real thing; not that close to the amenities of Hilton Head. $ *Rooms from: $580* ✉ *1 Village Park Sq., Bluffton* ☎ *843/706–6500, 866/706–6565* 🌐 *www.montagehotels.com/palmettobluff* ⇨ *50 cottages, 75 inn rooms* 🍴 *No meals.*

$$$$ FAMILY **Omni Hilton Head Oceanfront Resort.** *Resort.* At this beachfront hotel with a Caribbean sensibility, the spacious accommodations range from studios to two-bedroom suites. **Pros:** competes more with condos than hotels because of the size of its accommodations; lots of outdoor dining options. **Cons:** wedding parties can be noisy; cell phone service is spotty. $ *Rooms from: $349* ✉ *23 Ocean La., Palmetto Dunes, Mid-Island* ☎ *843/842–8000* 🌐 *www.omnihiltonhead.com* ⇨ *323 rooms* 🍴 *No meals.*

$$ **Park Lane Hotel & Suites.** *Hotel.* The island's only all-suites property has a friendly feel, which is probably why many guests settle in for weeks. **Pros:** one of the island's most reasonably priced lodgings; parking and Wi-Fi are free; playground for the kids. **Cons:** doesn't have an upscale feel; more kids means more noise, especially around the pool area. $ *Rooms from: $176* ✉ *12 Park La., South End* ☎ *843/686–5700* 🌐 *www.hiltonheadparklanehotel.com* ⇨ *156 suites* 🍴 *No meals.*

$$$$ FAMILY **Sonesta Resort Hilton Head Island.** *Resort.* Set in a luxuriant garden that always seems to be in full bloom, the Sonesta Resort is the centerpiece of Shipyard Plantation, which means you'll have access to all its various amenities, including golf and tennis. **Pros:** close to all the restaurants and nightlife in Coligny Plaza; spacious rooms; free parking. **Cons:** Wi-Fi and cell phone service can be a problem; service is sometimes impersonal. $ *Rooms from: $299* ✉ *Shipyard Plantation, 130 Shipyard Dr., South End* ☎ *843/842–2400, 800/334–1881* 🌐 *www.sonesta.com/hiltonheadisland* ⇨ *340 rooms* 🍴 *No meals.*

★ Fodor'sChoice **Westin Hilton Head Island Resort & Spa.** *Resort.*
$$$$ FAMILY A circular drive winds around a sculpture of long-legged marsh birds as you approach this beachfront resort, whose lush landscape lies on the island's quietest stretch of sand. **Pros:** great for destination weddings; the beach here is

absolutely gorgeous; pampering spa; guests have access to the Port Royal Golf & Racquet Club. **Cons:** lots of groups in the off-season. [$] *Rooms from: $314* ✉ *2 Grass Lawn Ave., Port Royal Plantation, North End* ☎ *800/933–3102, 843/681–4000* 🌐 *www.westinhiltonheadisland.com* 🛏 *416 rooms* 🍴 *No meals.*

BLUFFTON

$ 🏨 **Candlewood Suites.** *Hotel.* At this suites-only hotel, the guest rooms are comfortable and tastefully decorated in muted browns and beiges. **Pros:** location makes it convenient to Hilton Head, Beaufort, and Savannah; every room has a full kitchen; free guest laundry. **Cons:** cell phone service is hit-or-miss; set back from road, it can be difficult to find. [$] *Rooms from: $129* ✉ *5 Young Clyde Court, Bluffton* ☎ *843/705–9600* 🌐 *www.candlewoodsuites.com/blufftonsc* 🛏 *124 suites* 🍴 *No meals.*

PRIVATE VILLA RENTALS

Hilton Head has some 6,000 villas, condos, and private homes for rent, almost double the number of the island's hotel rooms. Villas and condos seem to work particularly well for families with children, especially if they want to avoid the extra costs of staying in a resort. Often these vacation homes cost less per diem than hotels of the same quality. Guests on a budget can further economize by cooking some of their own meals.

Villas and condos are primarily rented by the week, Saturday to Saturday. It pays to make sure you understand exactly what you're getting before making a deposit or signing a contract. For example, a property owner in the Hilton Head Beach & Tennis Club advertised that his villa sleeps six. That villa had one small bedroom, a foldout couch, and a hall closet with two very narrow bunk beds. That's a far cry from the three-bedroom villa you might have expected. TIP→ **Before calling a vacation rental company, make a list of the amenities you want.** Ask for pictures of each room and ask when the photos were taken. If you're looking for a beachfront property, ask exactly how far it is to the beach. Make sure to ask for a list of all fees, including those for parking, cleaning, pets, security deposits, and utility costs. Finally, get a written contract and a copy of the refund policy.

RENTAL AGENTS

Hilton Head Vacation Rentals. Representing more than 250 vacation rentals ranging in size from one to seven bedrooms, Hilton Head Vacation Rentals has villas, condos, and homes with oceanfront views. It offers various packages that include golf and other activities. Rentals are generally for three to seven days. ⊠ *578 William Hilton Pkwy.* ☎ *843/785–8687* ⊕ *www.hiltonheadvacation.com.*

Resort Rentals of Hilton Head Island. This company represents some 275 homes and villas, including many located inside the gated communities of Sea Pines, Palmetto Dunes, and Shipyard Plantation. Others are in North and South Forest Beach and the Folly Field area. Stays are generally Saturday to Saturday during the peak summer season; three- or four-night stays may be possible off-season. Most of the properties are privately owned, so decor and amenities can vary. ⊠ *32 Palmetto Bay Rd., Suite 1B, Mid-Island* ☎ *800/845–7017* ⊕ *www.hhivacations.com.*

Sea Pines Resort. The vast majority of the overnight guests at Sea Pines Resort rent one of the 500 suites, villas, and beach houses. One- and two-bedroom villas have a minimum stay of four nights. For stays of four or more nights, you must arrive on Saturday, Sunday, Monday, or Tuesday. Three- and four-bedrooms villas have a minimum stay of seven nights, and you've got to check in on Saturday. All houses have Internet access, and most have Wi-Fi. Housekeeping is usually an additional charge. ⊠ *32 Greenwood Dr., South End* ☎ *843/785–3333, 866/561–8802* ⊕ *www.seapines.com/vacation-rentals.*

NIGHTLIFE AND PERFORMING ARTS

NIGHTLIFE

Bars, like everything else on Hilton Head, are often in gate communities or shopping centers. Some are hangouts frequented by locals, and others get a good mix of both locals and visitors. There are a fair number of clubs, many of them restaurants that crank up the music after diners depart.

Big Bamboo. Decked out like a World War II–era officers' club, this South Pacific–themed bar and restaurant features live music most nights of the week. ⊠ *Coligny Plaza, 1 N. Forest Beach Dr., South End* ☎ *843/686–3443* ⊕ *www.bigbamboocafe.com.*

Comedy Magic Cabaret. Several nights a week this lounge brings top-flight comedic talent to Hilton Head. Start off with dinner and drinks downstairs at Pelican's Point Seafood & Steakhouse, then head upstairs for the comedy. Tickets are $22 to $26 per person. ■TIP➜ **Book ahead, because the shows sell out fairly quickly.** ✉ *South Island Square, 843 William Hilton Pkwy., South End* ☎ *843/681–7757* ⊕ *www. comedymagiccabaret.com.*

★ Fodor'sChoice **The Jazz Corner.** The elegant supper-club atmosphere at this popular spot makes it a wonderful setting in which to enjoy an evening of jazz, swing, or blues. There's a special martini menu, an extensive wine list, and a late-night menu. ■TIP➜ **The club fills up quickly, so make reservations.** ✉ *The Village at Wexford, 1000 William Hilton Pkwy., Suite C-1, South End* ☎ *843/842–8620* ⊕ *www. thejazzcorner.com.*

Reilley's Plaza. Dubbed the "Barmuda Triangle" by locals, the bars at this plaza include One Hot Mama's, Reilley's, the Lodge Martini, and Jump & Phil's Bar & Grill. It's the closest thing Hilton Head Island has to a raging club scene. ✉ *Hilton Head Plaza, Greenwood Dr., right before gate to Sea Pines, South End.*

★ Fodor'sChoice **The Salty Dog Cafe.** If there's one thing you
FAMILY shouldn't miss on Hilton Head Island, it's the iconic Salty Dog Cafe. It's the ideal place to escape, sit back, and enjoy the warm nights and ocean breezes in a tropical setting at the outdoor bar. There's live music (think Jimmy Buffett) seven nights a week during high season. Bring the family along for kid-friendly entertainment, including music, magic, and face painting at 7 pm throughout the summer. ✉ *South Beach Marina, 224 S. Sea Pines Dr., South End* ☎ *843/671–5199* ⊕ *www.saltydog.com.*

Santa Fe Cafe. A sophisticated spot for cocktails in the early evening, the Santa Fe Cafe is also a great place to lounge in front of the fireplace or sip top-shelf margaritas at the rooftop cantina. ✉ *807 William Hilton Pkwy., Mid-Island* ☎ *843/785–3838* ⊕ *www.santafehhi.com.*

PERFORMING ARTS

★ Fodor'sChoice **Arts Center of Coastal Carolina.** Locals love the exhibits at the Walter Greer Gallery and the theater productions at the Arts Center of Coastal Carolina. Programs for children are also popular. ✉ *14 Shelter Cove La., Mid-Island* ☎ *843/686–3945* ⊕ *www.artshhi.com.*

FAMILY **Hilton Head Island Gullah Celebration.** This showcase of Gullah life through arts, music, and theater is held at a variety of sites throughout the Lowcountry in February. ☎ *843/255–7304* ⊕ *www.gullahcelebration.com.*

★ Fodor'sChoice **Hilton Head Symphony Orchestra.** A selection of summer concerts—including the popular Symphony Under The Stars—are among the year-round performances by the symphony. Most events are at the First Presbyterian Church. ✉ *First Presbyterian Church, 540 William Hilton Pkwy., Mid-Island* ☎ *843/842–2055* ⊕ *www.hhso.org.*

FAMILY **Main Street Youth Theatre.** A variety of performances showcasing young local talent are presented by Main Street Youth Theatre. ✉ *25 New Orleans Rd., Mid-Island* ☎ *843/689–6246* ⊕ *www.msyt.org.*

SPORTS AND THE OUTDOORS

Hilton Head Island is a mecca for the sports enthusiast and for those who just want a relaxing walk or bike ride on the beach. There are 12 miles of beaches, 24 public golf courses, more than 50 miles of public bike paths, and more than 300 tennis courts. There's also tons of water sports, including kayaking and canoeing, parasailing, fishing, sailing, and much more.

BEACHES

A delightful stroll on the beach can end with an unpleasant surprise if you don't put your towels, shoes, and other earthly possessions way up on the sand. Tides here can fluctuate as much as 7 feet. Check the tide chart at your hotel.

FAMILY **Alder Lane Beach Park.** A great place for solitude even during the busy summer season, this beach has hard-packed sand at low tide, making it great for walking. It's accessible from the Marriott Grand Ocean Resort. **Amenities:** lifeguards; showers; toilets. **Best for:** solitude; swimming; walking. ✉ *Alder La., off South Forest Beach Rd., South End.*

BEACH RULES. **Animals are not permitted on Hilton Head beaches between 10 and 5 from Memorial Day through Labor Day. Animals must be on leash. No alcohol, glass, littering, indecent exposure, unauthorized vehicles, fires and fireworks, shark fishing, removal of any live beach fauna, sleeping between midnight and 6 am, and kites not under manual control.**

Island Gators

The most famous photo of Hilton Head's brilliant developer, Charles Fraser, ran in the *Saturday Evening Post* in the late 1950s. It shows him dressed as a dandy, outfitted with a cane and straw hat, with an alligator on a leash.

These prehistoric creatures are indeed indigenous to this subtropical island. What you will learn if you visit the Coastal Discovery Museum, where the old photograph is blown up for an interpretive board on the island's early history, is that someone else had the gator by the tail (not shown) so that it would not harm Fraser or the photographer.

Nowadays, in Sea Pines Center, there is a life-size, metal sculpture of an alligator that all the tourists, and especially their kids, climb on to have their pictures taken. And should you happen to see a live gator while exploring the island or playing a round of golf, please don't feed it. Although, if you have the courage, you might want to take a snapshot.

Burkes Beach. This beach is usually not crowded, mostly because it is a bit hard to find and there are no lifeguards on duty. **Amenities:** none. **Best for:** solitude; sunrise; swimming; windsurfing. ✉ *60 Burkes Beach Rd., at William Hilton Pkwy., Mid-Island.*

★ Fodor'sChoice **Coligny Beach.** The island's most popular beach is
FAMILY a lot of fun, but during high season it can get very crowded. Accessible from the Beach House Hilton Head Island and several other hotels, it has choreographed fountains that delight little children, bench swings, and beach umbrellas and chaise longues for rent. If you have to go online, there's also Wi-Fi access. **Amenities:** food and drink; lifeguards; parking (no fee); showers; toilets. **Best for:** swimming; windsurfing. ✉ *1 Coligny Circle, at Pope Ave. and South Forest Beach Dr., South End.*

FAMILY **Driessen Beach.** A good destination for families, Driessen Beach is peppered with people flying kites, making it colorful and fun. There's a long boardwalk to the beach. **Amenities:** lifeguards; parking; showers; toilets. **Best for:** sunrise; swimming; walking. ✉ *43 Bradley Beach Rd., at William Hilton Pkwy., Mid-Island.*

8

SAND DOLLARS. Hilton Head Island's beaches hold many treasures, including starfish, sea sponges, and sand dollars. Note that it is strictly forbidden to pick up any live creatures on the beach, especially live sand dollars. How can you tell if they are alive? Live sand dollars are brown and fuzzy and will turn your fingers yellow and brown. You can take sand dollars home only if they're white. Soak them in a mixture of bleach and water to remove the scent once you get home.

Folly Field Beach Park. Next to Driessen Beach, Folly Field is a treat for families. It can get crowded in high season, but even so it's a wonderful spot for a day of sunbathing and swimming. The first beach cottages on Hilton Head Island were built here in the 1950s. **Amenities:** lifeguards; parking; showers; toilets. **Best for:** sunrise; swimming; walking. ✉ *55 Starfish Dr., off Folly Field Rd., North End.*

Mitchelville Beach Park. Not ideal for swimming because of the many sharp shells on the sand and in the water, Mitchelville Beach Park is a terrific spot for a walk or beachcombing. It is not on the Atlantic Ocean, but rather on Port Royal Sound. **Amenities:** parking; toilets. **Best for:** solitude; walking. ✉ *124 Mitchelville Rd., Hilton Head Plantation, North End.*

MAY RIVER SANDBAR. Known as the "Redneck Riviera," the May River Sandbar is pure party. Basically, the sandbar is just that: a small island of sand on the May River in Bluffton, which is the town that vacationers must go through on U.S. 278 to get to Hilton Head. The sandbar is accessible only by boat and only at low tide. Locals will plan their weekends around the time of low tide to head out to the sandbar. Boaters drop anchor and the party begins. Horseshoe and cornhole games are set up, picnic baskets unpacked, and cold drinks poured. To get there, go north by boat on Calibogue Sound and turn left west at the May River. The sandbar is at Red Marker 6.

BIKING

More than 50 miles of public paths crisscross Hilton Head Island, and pedaling is popular along the firmly packed beach. The island keeps adding more to the boardwalk network as visitors are using it and because it's such a safe alternative for kids. Bikes with wide tires are a must if you want to ride on the beach. They can save you a spill should you hit loose sand on the trails. Keep in mind when crossing streets that, in South Carolina, vehicles have the right-of-way. ■TIP→ **For a map of trails, visit www.hiltonhead-islandsc.gov.**

Bicycles from beach cruisers to mountain bikes to tandem bikes can be rented either at bike stores or at most hotels and resorts. Many can be delivered to your hotel, along with helmets, baskets, locks, child carriers, and whatever else you might need.

FAMILY **Hilton Head Bicycle Company.** You can rent bicycles, helmets, and adult tricycles from the Hilton Head Bicycle Company. ✉ *112 Arrow Rd., South End* ☎ *843/686–6888, 800/995–4319* ⊕ *www.hiltonheadbicycle.com.*

FAMILY **Pedals Bicycles.** Rent beach bikes for adults and children, kiddy karts, jogging strollers, and mountain bikes at Pedals. ✉ *71A Pope Ave., South End* ☎ *843/842–5522, 888/699–1039* ⊕ *www.pedalsbicycles.com.*

FAMILY **South Beach Bike Rentals.** Rent bikes, helmets, tandems, and adult tricycles at this spot in Sea Pines. ✉ *230 S. Sea Pines Dr., Sea Pines, South End* ☎ *843/671–2453* ⊕ *www.south-beach-cycles.com.*

CANOEING AND KAYAKING
This is one of the most delightful ways to commune with nature on this commercial but physically beautiful island. Paddle through the creeks and estuaries and try to keep up with the dolphins.

★ Fodor'sChoice **Outside Hilton Head.** Boats, canoes, kayaks,
FAMILY and paddleboards are available for rent. The company also offers nature tours and dolphin-watching excursions. ✉ *Shelter Cove Marina, 1 Shelter Cove La., Mid-Island* ☎ *843/686–6996, 800/686–6996* ⊕ *www.outsidehilton-head.com.*

FISHING
Although anglers can fish in these waters year-round, in April things start to crank up and in May most boats are heavily booked. May is the season for cobia, especially in Port Royal Sound. In the Gulf Stream you can hook king mackerel, tuna, wahoo, and mahimahi. ■TIP→ **A fishing license is necessary if you are fishing from a beach, dock, or pier. They are $11 for 14 days.** Licenses aren't necessary on charter fishing boats because they already have their licenses.

FAMILY **Bay Runner Fishing Charters.** With more than four decades of experience fishing these waters, Captain Miles Altman takes anglers out for trips lasting three to eight hours. Evening shark trips are offered May to August. ⊠ *Shelter Cove Marina, 1 Shelter Cove La., Mid-Island* ☎ *843/290–6955* ⊕ *www.bayrunnerfishinghiltonhead.com.*

FAMILY **Bulldog Fishing Charters.** Captain Christian offers his guests 4-, 6-, 8-, and 10-hour fishing tours on his 32-foot boat. ⊠ *1 Hudson Rd., departs from docks at Hudson's Seafood House on the Docks, Mid-Island* ☎ *843/422–0887* ⊕ *bulldogfishingcharters.com.*

★ Fodor's Choice **Capt. Hook Party Boat.** Deep-sea fishing tours are
FAMILY available on this large party boat, which sells concessions as well. The friendly crew teaches children how to bait hooks and reel in fish. ⊠ *Shelter Cove Marina, 1 Shelter Cove La., Mid-Island* ☎ *843/785–1700* ⊕ *www.captain-hookhiltonhead.com.*

FAMILY **Fishin' Coach.** Captain Dan Utley offers a variety of fishing tours on his 22-foot boat to catch redfish and other species year-round. ⊠ *2 William Hilton Pkwy., North End* ☎ *843/368–2126* ⊕ *www.fishincoach.com.*

FAMILY **Gullah Gal Sport Fishing.** Fishing trips are available on a pair of 34-foot boats, the *Gullah Gal* and *True Grits.* ⊠ *Shelter Cove Marina, 1 Shelter Cove La., Mid-Island* ☎ *843/842–7002* ⊕ *www.hiltonheadislandcharterfishing.com.*

FAMILY *Integrity.* The 38-foot charter boat *Integrity* offers offshore and near-shore fishing. ⊠ *Harbour Town Yacht Basin, Mariners Way, Sea Pines, South End* ☎ *843/671–2704, 843/422–1221* ⊕ *www.integritycharterfishing.com.*

FAMILY **Palmetto Lagoon Charters.** Captain Trent Malphrus takes groups for half- or full-day excursions to the region's placid saltwater lagoons. Redfish, bluefish, flounder, and black drum are some of the most common trophy fish. ⊠ *Shelter Cove Marina, 1 Shelter Cove La., Mid-Island* ☎ *866/301–4634* ⊕ *www.palmettolagooncharters.com.*

FAMILY **The Stray Cat.** The Stray Cat will help you decide whether you want to fish "in-shore" or go offshore into the deep blue. ⊠ *2 Hudson Rd., North End* ☎ *843/683–5427* ⊕ *www.straycatcharter.com.*

GOLF

Hilton Head is nicknamed "Golf Island" for good reason: the island itself has 24 championship courses (public, semi-private, and private), and the outlying area has 16 more. Each offers its own packages, some of which are great deals. Almost all charge the highest green fees in the morning and lower fees as the day goes on. Lower rates can also be found in the hot summer months. It's essential to book tee times in advance, especially in the busy spring and fall months; resort guests and club members get first choices. Most courses can be described as casual-classy, so you will have to adhere to certain rules of the greens. ■TIP→ **The dress code on island golf courses does not permit blue jeans, gym shorts, or jogging shorts. Men's shirts must have collars.**

★ Fodor's Choice **The Heritage PGA Tour Golf Tournament.** The most internationally famed golf event in Hilton Head is the annual RBC Heritage PGA Tour Golf Tournament, held mid-April. There are a wide range of ticket packages available. Tickets are also available at the gate. ⊠ *Sea Pines Resort, 2 Lighthouse La., South End* ⊕ *www.rbcheritage.com.*

TEE OFF ON A BUDGET. Golfing on Hilton Head can be very expensive after you tally up the green fee, cart fee, rental clubs, gratuities, and so on. But there are ways to save money. There are several courses in Bluffton that are very popular with the locals, and some are cheaper to play than the courses on Hilton Head Island. Another way to save money is to play late in the day. At some courses, a round in the morning is more expensive than 18 holes in the late afternoon.

GOLF COURSES

Arthur Hills and Robert Cupp at Palmetto Hall. There are two prestigious courses at Palmetto Hall Plantation: Arthur Hills and Robert Cupp. Arthur Hills is a player favorite, with its trademark undulating fairways punctuated with lagoons and lined with moss-draped oaks and towering pines. Robert Cupp is a very challenging course, but is great for the higher handicappers as well. ⊠ *Palmetto Hall, 108 Fort Howell Dr., North End* ☎ *843/689–9205* ⊕ *www. palmettodunes.com* ⊠ *$109* ⚲ *Arthur Hills: 18 holes, 6257 yards, par 72. Robert Cupp: 18 holes, 6025 yards, par 72* ⚲ *Reservations essential.*

Country Club of Hilton Head. Although it's part of a country club, the course is open for public play. A well-kept secret, it's rarely too crowded. This 18-hole Rees Jones–designed course is a more casual environment than many of the other golf courses on Hilton Head. ⊠ *Hilton Head Plantation, 70 Skull Creek Dr., North End* ☏ *843/681–4653, 866/835–0093* ⊕ *www.clubcorp.com/Clubs/Country-Club-of-Hilton-Head* ⌨ *$105* ⚑ *18 holes, 6543 yards, par 72.*

Golden Bear Golf Club at Indigo Run. Located in the upscale Indigo Run community, Golden Bear Golf Club was designed by golf legend Jack Nicklaus. The course's natural woodlands setting offers easygoing rounds. It requires more thought than muscle, yet you will have to earn every par you make. Though fairways are generous, you may end up with a lagoon looming smack ahead of the green on the approach shot. And there are the fine points—the color GPS monitor on every cart and women-friendly tees. After an honest, traditional test of golf, most golfers finish up at the plush clubhouse with some food and drink at Just Jack's Grille. ⊠ *Indigo Run, 100 Indigo Run Dr., North End* ☏ *843/689–2200* ⊕ *www.goldenbear-indigorun.com* ⌨ *$109* ⚑ *18 holes, 6643 yards, par 72.*

★ FodorsChoice **Harbour Town Golf Links.** Considered by many golfers to be one of those must-play-before-you-die courses, Harbour Town Golf Links is extremely well known because it has hosted the RBC Heritage Golf Tournament every spring for the last four decades. Designed by Pete Dye, the layout is reminiscent of Scottish courses of old. The Golf Academy at the Sea Pines Resort is ranked among the top 10 in the country. ⊠ *Sea Pines Resort, 11 Lighthouse La., South End* ☏ *843/842–8484, 800/732–7463* ⊕ *www. seapines.com/golf* ⌨ *$350* ⚑ *18 holes, 7099 yards, par 71* ⚐ *Reservations essential.*

Robert Trent Jones at Palmetto Dunes. One of the island's most popular layouts, this course's beauty and character are accentuated by the 10th hole, a par 5 that offers a panoramic view of the ocean (one of only two on the entire island). It's among the most beautiful courses in the Southeast, with glittering lagoons punctuating 11 of the 18 holes. ⊠ *Palmetto Dunes, 7 Robert Trent Jones La., North End* ☏ *843/785–1138* ⊕ *www.palmettodunes.com* ⌨ *$95* ⚑ *18 holes, 6570 yards, par 72* ⚐ *Reservations essential.*

GOLF SCHOOLS

Golf Learning Center at Sea Pines Resort. The well-regarded golf academy offers hourly private lessons by PGA-trained professionals and one- to three-day clinics to help you perfect your game. ⊠ *Sea Pines, 100 N. Sea Pines Dr., South End* ☎ *843/785–4540* ⊕ *www.golfacademy.net.*

Palmetto Dunes Golf Academy. There's something for golfers of all ages at this academy: instructional videos, daily clinics, and multiday schools. Lessons are offered for ages three and up, and there are special programs for women. Free demonstrations are held with Doug Weaver, former PGA Tour pro and director of instruction for the academy. Take advantage of the free swing evaluation and club-fitting. ⊠ *Palmetto Dunes Oceanfront Resort, 7 Trent Jones La., Mid-Island* ☎ *843/785–1138* ⊕ *www.palmettodunes.com.*

BLUFFTON GOLF COURSES

There are several beautiful golf courses in Bluffton, which is just on the other side of the bridges to Hilton Head Island. These courses are very popular with locals and can often be cheaper to play than the courses on Hilton Head Island.

Crescent Pointe. An Arnold Palmer Signature Course, Crescent Pointe is fairly tough, with somewhat narrow fairways and rolling terrain. There are numerous sand traps, ponds, and lagoons, making for some demanding yet fun holes. Some of the par 3s are particularly challenging. The scenery is magnificent, with large live oaks, pine-tree stands, and rolling fairways. Additionally, several holes have spectacular marsh views. ⊠ *Crescent Pointe, 1 Crescent Pointe, Bluffton* ☎ *843/706–2600* ⊕ *www.crescentpointegolf.com* ⌑ *$52–$63* ⚐ *18 holes, 6447 yards, par 71.*

Eagle's Pointe. This Davis Love III–designed course—located in the Eagle's Pointe community in Bluffton—is one of the area's most playable. Eagle's Pointe attracts many women golfers because of its women-friendly tees, spacious fairways, and large greens. There are quite a few bunkers and lagoons throughout the course, which winds through a natural woodlands setting that attracts an abundance of wildlife. ⊠ *Eagle's Pointe, 1 Eagle's Pointe Dr., Bluffton* ☎ *843/757–5900* ⊕ *www.eaglespointegolf.com* ⌑ *$35–$55* ⚐ *18 holes, 6399 yards, par 72.*

Island West Golf Club. Fuzzy Zoeller and golf course designer Clyde Johnston designed this stunningly beautiful course set amid the natural surroundings at Island West. There are majestic live oaks, plenty of wildlife, and expansive marsh views on several holes. Golfers of all skill levels can find success on this succession of undulating fairways. There are

8

several holes where the fairways are rather generous, while others can be demanding. This is a fun and challenging course for golfers of all handicaps. ☒ *Island West, 40 Island West Dr., Bluffton* ☎ *843/689–6660* ⊕ *www.islandwestgolf. net* ☒ *$35–$45* ⚑ *18 holes, 6208 yards, par 72.*

★ Fodor'sChoice **The May River Golf Club.** An 18-hole Jack Nicklaus course, this has several holes along the banks of the scenic May River and will challenge all skill levels. The greens are Champion Bermuda grass and the fairways are covered by Paspalum, the latest eco-friendly turf. Caddy service is always required. No carts are allowed earlier than 9 am to encourage walking. ☒ *Palmetto Bluff, 476 Mount Pelia Rd., Bluffton* ☎ *843/706–6500* ⊕ *www.palmettobluff.com* ☒ *$315* ⚑ *18 holes, 7171 yards, par 72* ⚐ *Reservations essential.*

Old South Golf Links. There are many scenic holes overlooking marshes and the intracoastal waterway at this Clyde Johnson–designed course. It's a public course, but that hasn't stopped it from winning awards. It's reasonably priced, and reservations are recommended. ☒ *50 Buckingham Plantation Dr., Bluffton* ☎ *843/785–5353* ⊕ *www.oldsouthgolf. com* ☒ *$60–$75* ⚑ *18 holes, 6772 yards, par 72.*

PARASAILING

For those looking for a bird's-eye view of Hilton Head, it doesn't get better than parasailing. Newcomers will get a lesson in safety before taking off. Parasailers are then strapped into a harness, and as the boat takes off, the parasailer is lifted about 500 feet into the sky.

FAMILY **H2O Sports.** You can soar above Hilton Head and can check out the views up to 25 miles in all directions with this popular company located in Sea Pines. ☒ *149 Lighthouse Rd., Sea Pines, South End* ☎ *843/671–4386, 877/290–4386* ⊕ *www.h2osports.com.*

★ Fodor'sChoice **Sky Pirate Parasail.** You can glide 500 feet in the
FAMILY air over Palmetto Bay Marina and Broad Creek on a trip with this company. ☒ *Broad Creek Marina, 18 Simmons Rd., Mid-Island* ☎ *843/842–2566* ⊕ *www.skypirateparasail.com.*

TENNIS

There are more than 300 courts on Hilton Head. Tennis comes in at a close second as the island's premier sport after golf. It is recognized as one of the nation's best tennis destinations. Hilton Head has a large international organization of coaches. ▪TIP→ **Spring and fall are the peak seasons for cooler play, with numerous tennis packages available at the resorts and through the schools.**

★ Fodor'sChoice **Palmetto Dunes Tennis & Pickleball Center.** Ranked
FAMILY among the best in the world, this facility at the Palmetto Dunes Oceanfront Resort has 26 clay tennis courts (6 of which are lighted for night play) and eight pickleball courts. There are lessons geared to players of every skill level given by enthusiastic staffers. Daily round-robin tournaments add to the festive atmosphere. ⊠ *Palmetto Dunes Oceanfront Resort, 6 Trent Jones La., Mid-Island* ☎ *843/785–1152* ⊕ *www.palmettodunes.com.*

FAMILY **Port Royal Racquet Club.** The occasional magnolia tree dots the grounds of the Port Royal Racquet Club, which has 10 clay and 4 hard courts. The professional staff, stadium seating, and frequent tournaments are why it is ranked among the best in the world. ⊠ *Port Royal Plantation, 15 Wimbledon Court, Mid-Island* ☎ *843/686–8803* ⊕ *www. portroyalgolfclub.com.*

FAMILY **Sea Pines Racquet Club.** The highly rated club has 21 clay courts, as well as instructional programs and a pro shop. There are special deals for guests of Sea Pines. ⊠ *5 Lighthouse La., Sea Pines Resort, South End* ☎ *843/363–4495* ⊕ *www.seapines.com/tennis.*

★ Fodor'sChoice **Van der Meer Tennis Center.** Recognized for its tennis instruction for players of all ages and skill levels, this highly rated club in Shipyard Plantation has 17 hard courts, 4 of which are covered and lighted for night play. The Van der Meer Tennis Center also offers courts at the Shipyard Racquet Club, which has 20 courts. ⊠ *19 DeAllyon Ave., Shipyard Plantation, South End* ☎ *800/845–6138* ⊕ *www. vandermeertennis.com.*

ZIP LINE TOURS

★ Fodor'sChoice **ZipLine Hilton Head.** Take a thrilling tour of Hil-
FAMILY ton Head on a zipline over ponds and marshes and past towering oaks and pines. This company offers eight ziplines, two suspended sky bridges, and a dual-cable racing zipline. Guests are harnessed and helmeted, and must be at least 10 years old and weigh between 80 and 250 pounds. ⊠ *33 Broad Creek Marina Way, Mid-Island* ☎ *843/682–6000* ⊕ *ziplinehiltonhead.com.*

SHOPPING

Hilton Head is a great destination for those who love shopping, starting with the Tanger outlet malls. Although they're officially in Bluffton, visitors drive by the outlets on U.S. 278 to get to Hilton Head Island. Tanger Outlet I has been completely renovated and reopened with many high-end stores, including Saks OFF 5th, DKNY, Michael Kors, and more.

ART GALLERIES

★ Fodor'sChoice **Ben Ham Images.** The extraordinary photography of Ben Ham focuses on Lowcountry landscapes. ✉ *90 Capital Dr., Suite 104, Mid-Island* ☎ *843/842–4163* ⊕ *www. benhamimages.com.*

Red Piano Gallery. Original art by contemporary artists can be found at this upscale gallery. ✉ *220 Cordillo Pkwy., Mid-Island* ☎ *843/842–4433* ⊕ *redpianoartgallery.com.*

Walter Greer Gallery. Part of the Arts Center of Coastal Carolina, this modern gallery showcases local artists. ✉ *Arts Center of Coastal Carolina, 14 Shelter Cove La., Mid-Island* ☎ *843/681–5060* ⊕ *www.artshhi.com/greer-gallery.*

GIFTS

★ Fodor'sChoice **Markel's.** The very helpful and friendly staff at Markel's is known for wrapping gifts with giant bows. You'll find unique Lowcountry gifts, including hand-painted wineglasses and beer mugs, lawn ornaments, baby gifts, greeting cards, and more. ✉ *1008 Fording Island Rd., Bluffton* ☎ *843/815–9500* ⊕ *www.markelsgifts.com.*

Pretty Papers. Fine stationery and gifts are available at Pretty Papers. ✉ *The Village at Wexford, 1000 William Hilton Pkwy., Suite E7, Mid-Island* ☎ *843/341–5116* ☉ *Closed Sun.*

★ Fodor'sChoice **Salty Dog T-Shirt Factory.** You can't leave Hilton Head without a Salty Dog T-shirt, so hit this factory store for the best deals. The iconic T-shirts are hard to resist, and there are lots of choices for kids and adults in various colors and styles. ✉ *69 Arrow Rd., South End* ☎ *843/842–6331* ⊕ *www.saltydog.com.*

FAMILY **The Storybook Shoppe.** Charming, whimsical, and sweet describe this children's bookstore. It has a darling area for little ones to read as well as educational toys for infants to teens. ✉ *41A Calhoun St., Bluffton* ☎ *843/757–2600* ⊕ *www.thestorybookshoppe.com* ☉ *Closed Sun.*

FAMILY **Top of the Lighthouse Shop.** The Hilton Head Lighthouse is the island's iconic symbol, and this shop celebrates the red-and-white-striped landmark. ✉ *149 Lighthouse Rd., Sea Pines, South End* ☎ *866/305–9814* ⊕ *www.harbourtownlighthouse.com/shop.*

JEWELRY

Bird's Nest. Local handmade jewelry, accessories, and island-themed charms are available at this popular spot. ✉ *Coligny Plaza, 1 N. Forest Beach Dr., #21, South End* ☎ *843/785–3737* ⊕ *www.thebirdsnesthiltonhead.com.*

Forsythe Jewelers. This is the island's leading jewelry store, offering pieces by famous designers. ✉ *71 Lighthouse Rd., Sea Pines, South End* ☎ *843/671–7070* ⊕ *www.forsythejewelers.biz* ⊙ *Closed Sun.*

Goldsmith Shop. Classic jewelry, much of it with island themes, is on sale at the Goldsmith Shop. ✉ *3 Lagoon Rd., South End* ☎ *843/785–2538* ⊕ *www.thegoldsmithshop.com.*

MALLS AND SHOPPING CENTERS

Coligny Plaza. Things are always humming at this shopping center, which is within walking distance of the most popular beach on Hilton Head. Coligny Plaza has more than 60 shops and restaurants, including unique clothing boutiques, souvenir shops, and the expansive Piggly Wiggly grocery store. There are also bike rentals and free family entertainment throughout summer. ✉ *Coligny Circle, 1 N. Forest Beach Dr., South End* ☎ *843/842–6050.*

FAMILY **Harbour Town.** Distinguished by a candy-striped lighthouse, Harbour Town wraps around a marina and has plenty of shops selling colorful T-shirts, casual resort wear, and beach-themed souvenirs. ✉ *Sea Pines, 32 Greenwood Dr., South End* ☎ *866/561–8802* ⊕ *www.seapines.com/recreation/harbour-town.*

Shops at Sea Pines Center. Clothing for men and women, the best local crafts, and fine antiques are the draw at this outdoor shopping center. You can even get a massage at the on-site day spa. ✉ *71 Lighthouse Rd., South End* ☎ *843/363–6800* ⊕ *www.theshopsatseapinescenter.com.*

South Beach Marina. Looking like a New England fishing village, South Beach Marina is the place for beach-friendly fashions. ✉ *232 S. Sea Pines Dr., South End.*

8

KID STUFF. Free outdoor children's concerts are held at Harbour Town in Sea Pines and Shelter Cove Harbor throughout the summer months. Guitarist Gregg Russell has been playing for children under Harbour Town's mighty Liberty Oak tree for decades. He begins strumming nightly at 8 in the summer, except on Saturday. It's also tradition for kids to get their pictures taken at the statue of Neptune at Harbour Town. At Shelter Cove, longtime island favorite Shannon Tanner performs a fun, family show at 6:30 pm and 8 pm weekdays from Memorial Day through Labor Day.

FAMILY **Old Town Bluffton.** A charming area, Old Town features local artist galleries, antiques, and restaurants. ⊠ *Downtown Bluffton, May River Rd. and Calhoun St., Bluffton* ☎ *843/706–4500* ⊕ *www.oldtownbluffton.com.*

★ Fodor'sChoice **Tanger Outlets.** There are two halves to this popular shopping center: Tanger Outlet I has more than 40 upscale stores, as well as popular eateries like Olive Garden, Panera Bread, and Longhorn Steakhouse. Tanger Outlet II has Abercrombie & Fitch, Banana Republic, the Gap, and Nike, along with 60 others stores. There are also several children's stores, including Gymboree and Carter's. ⊠ *1414 Fording Island Rd., Bluffton* ☎ *843/837–5410, 866/665–8679* ⊕ *www.tangeroutlet.com/hiltonhead.*

The Village at Wexford. Upscale shops, including Lilly Pulitzer and Le Cookery, as well as several fine-dining restaurants can be found in this shopping area. There are also some unique gift shops and luxe clothing stores. ⊠ *1000 William Hilton Pkwy.* ⊕ *www.villageatwexford.com.*

SPAS

Spa visits have become a recognized activity on the island, and for some people they are as popular as golf and tennis. In fact, spas have become one of the top leisure-time destinations, particularly for golf "widows." And this popularity extends to the men as well; previously spa-shy guys have come around, enticed by couples massage, deep-tissue sports massage, and even the pleasures of the manicure and pedicure.

There are East Indian–influenced therapies, hot-stone massage, Hungarian organic facials—the treatments span the globe. Do your research, go online, and call or stop by the various spas and ask the locals their favorites. The quality of therapists island-wide is noteworthy for their training, certifications, and expertise.

Faces. This place has been pampering loyal clients for more than three decades, thanks to body therapists, stylists, and cosmetologists who really know their stuff. Choose from the line of fine cosmetics, enjoy a manicure and pedicure, or have a professional do your evening makeup for that special occasion. ⊠ *The Village at Wexford, 1000 William Hilton Pkwy., South End* ☎ *843/785–3075* ⊕ *www.facesdayspa.com.*

★ Fodors Choice **Heavenly Spa by Westin.** This is the quintessential spa experience on Hilton Head. Known internationally for its innovative treatments, the Heavenly Spa incorporates local traditions. Prior to a treatment, clients are told to put their worries in a basket woven from local sweetgrass; de-stressing is a major component of the therapies here. The relaxation room with its teas and healthy snacks and the adjacent retail area with products like sweetgrass scents are heavenly, too. In-room spa services are available, as are romance packages. ⊠ *Westin Resort Hilton Head Island, 2 Grasslawn Ave., Port Royal Plantation, North End* ☎ *843/681–1019* ⊕ *www.westinhiltonheadisland.com.*

Spa Montage Palmetto Bluff. Dubbed the "celebrity spa" by locals, this two-story facility is the ultimate pamper palace. The names of the treatments, which often have a Southern accent, are almost as creative as the treatments themselves. There are Amazing Grace and The Deep South body therapies, and sensual soaks and couples massage. The spa also offers a variety of other services, including pedicures and manicures, facials and other skin treatments, and a hair salon. ⊠ *Palmetto Bluff, 1 Village Park Sq., Bluffton* ☎ *843/706–6270* ⊕ *spamontage.com.*

Spa Soleil. A wide variety of massages and other treatments are offered at Spa Soleil. The tantalizing teas and snacks make your time here a soothing, therapeutic experience. This is an amazing island treasure. ⊠ *Hilton Head Marriott Resort & Spa, 1 Hotel Circle, Palmetto Dunes, Mid-Island* ☎ *843/686–8420* ⊕ *www.marriott.com/hotels/travel/hhhgr-hilton-head-marriott-resort-and-spa.*

BEAUFORT

*38 miles north of Hilton Head via U.S. 278 and Rte. 170;
70 miles southwest of Charleston via U.S. 17 and U.S. 21.*

Charming homes and churches grace this old town on Port Royal Island. Come here on a day trip from Hilton Head,

Savannah, or Charleston, or to spend a quiet weekend at a B&B while you shop and stroll through the historic district. Beaufort continues to gain recognition as an art town and supports a large number of galleries for its diminutive size. Visitors are drawn equally to the town's artsy scene and to the area's water-sports possibilities. The annual Beaufort Water Festival, which takes place over 10 days in July, is the premier event. For a calendar of Beaufort's annual events, check out ⊕ *www.beaufortsc.org*.

More and more transplants have decided to spend the rest of their lives here, drawn to Beaufort's small-town charms, and the area is burgeoning. A truly Southern town, its picturesque backdrops have lured filmmakers here to shoot *The Big Chill, The Prince of Tides,* and *The Great Santini,* the last two being Hollywood adaptations of best-selling books by the late author Pat Conroy. Conroy had waxed poetic about the Lowcountry and called the Beaufort area home.

To support Beaufort's growing status as a tourist destination, it has doubled the number of hotels in recent years. Military events like the frequent graduations (traditionally Wednesday and Thursday) at the marine base on Parris Island tie up rooms.

GETTING HERE AND AROUND

Beaufort is 25 miles east of Interstate 95, on U.S. 21. The only way to get here is by private car or Greyhound bus.

ESSENTIALS

Well-maintained public restrooms are available at the Beaufort Visitors Center. You can't miss this former arsenal; a crenellated, fortlike structure, it is now beautifully restored and painted ocher.

The Beaufort County Black Chamber of Commerce (⊕ *www.bcbcc.org*) puts out an African American visitor's guide, which takes in the surrounding Lowcountry. The Beaufort Visitors Center gives out copies.

Visitor Information Beaufort Regional Chamber of Commerce. ✉ *1106 Carteret St.* ☎ *843/525–8500* ⊕ *www.beaufortchamber. org.* **Beaufort Visitors Center.** ✉ *713 Craven St.* ☎ *843/525–8500* ⊕ *www.beaufortsc.org.*

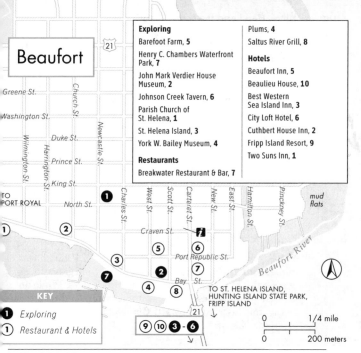

TO
PORT ROYAL

Exploring

Barefoot Farm, **5**

Henry C. Chambers Waterfront Park, **7**

John Mark Verdier House Museum, **2**

Johnson Creek Tavern, **6**

Parish Church of St. Helena, **1**

St. Helena Island, **3**

York W. Bailey Museum, **4**

Restaurants

Breakwater Restaurant & Bar, **7**

Plums, **4**

Saltus River Grill, **8**

Hotels

Beaufort Inn, **5**

Beaulieu House, **10**

Best Western Sea Island Inn, **3**

City Loft Hotel, **6**

Cuthbert House Inn, **2**

Fripp Island Resort, **9**

Two Suns Inn, **1**

KEY

Exploring

Restaurant & Hotels

TO ST. HELENA ISLAND, HUNTING ISLAND STATE PARK, FRIPP ISLAND

EXPLORING

TOP ATTRACTIONS

Barefoot Farm. Check out this farm stand for perfect watermelons, rhubarb, and strawberry jam. ⊠ *939 Sea Island Pkwy., St. Helena Island* ☎ *843/838–7421.*

★ Fodor'sChoice **Henry C. Chambers Waterfront Park.** Off Bay Street, FAMILY this park is a great place to survey the scene. Trendy restaurants and bars overlook these 7 beautifully landscaped acres along the Beaufort River. At night everyone strolls along the river walk. ⊠ *1006 Bay St.* ☎ *843/525–7000* ⊕ *www.cityofbeaufort.org.*

St. Helena Island. About 9 miles southeast of Beaufort, St. Helena Island is a stronghold of the Gullah culture. Several African American–owned businesses in its tight-knit community of Frogmore make this quite the tourist magnet. ⊠ *Rte. 21, St. Helena Island* ⊕ *www.beaufortsc.org/area/st.-helena-island.*

FAMILY **York W. Bailey Museum.** The museum at the Penn Center has displays on the heritage of Sea Island African Americans; it also has pleasant grounds shaded by live oaks. Dating from 1862, Penn Center was the first school for the newly emancipated slaves. These islands are where Gullah, a musical language that combines English and African languages, developed. This museum and the surrounding community of St. Helena Island are a major stop for anyone interested in the Gullah history and culture of the Lowcountry. ✉ *16 Penn Center Circle W, St. Helena Island* ☎ *843/838–2432* 🌐 *www.penncenter.com* 🎟 *$5.*

WORTH NOTING

John Mark Verdier House Museum. Built in the Federal style, this 1804 house has been restored and furnished as it would have been prior to a visit by Marquis de Lafayette in 1825. It was the headquarters for Union forces during the Civil War. ✉ *801 Bay St., Downtown Historic District* ☎ *843/379–6335* 🌐 *historicbeaufort.org* 🎟 *$10* ⏲ *Closed Sun.*

★ Fodor's Choice **Parish Church of St. Helena.** The 1724 church was turned into a hospital during the Civil War, and gravestones were brought inside to serve as operating tables. While on church grounds stroll the peaceful cemetery and read the fascinating inscriptions. ✉ *505 Church St.* ☎ *843/522–1712* 🌐 *www.sthelenas1712.org.*

WHERE TO EAT

★ Fodor's Choice 🍴 **Breakwater Restaurant & Bar.** *Eclectic.* This downtown restaurant offers small tasting plates such as tuna tartare and fried shrimp, but if you prefer not to share there are main dishes like lamb meat loaf and filet mignon with a truffle demi-glace. The presentation is as contemporary as the decor. **Known for:** contemporary approach to Lowcountry cuisine; elegant atmosphere. [$] *Average main: $30* ✉ *203 Carteret St., Downtown Historic District* ☎ *843/379–0052* 🌐 *www.breakwatersc.com* ⏲ *Closed Sun. No lunch.*
$$$$

$$ 🍴 **Johnson Creek Tavern.** *American.* There are times when you just want a cold one accompanied by some raw oysters. Head to Johnson Creek Tavern and sit outside to take advantage of the marsh views. **Known for:** decorated dollar bills stapled to the wall; fresh seafood; $1 happy hour beers. [$] *Average main: $19* ✉ *2141 Sea Island Pkwy., Harbor Island* ☎ *843/838–4166* 🌐 *www.johnsoncreektavern.com.*

$$$ 🍴 **Plums.** *American.* This hip restaurant began its life in 1986 in a homey frame house with plum-color awnings shading the front porch. An oyster bar that looks out to Bay Street, Plums still uses old family recipes for its soups, crab-cake

CLOSE UP

Writer Pat Conroy on Beaufort

Many fans of best-selling author, the late Pat Conroy, consider Beaufort *his* town because of his autobiographical novel *The Great Santini*, which was set here. He, too, considered it home base: "We moved to Beaufort when I was 15. We had moved 23 times. (My father was in the Marines.) I told my mother, 'I need a home.' Her wise reply was: 'Well, maybe it will be Beaufort.' And so it has been. I have stuck to this poor town like an old barnacle. I moved away, but I came running back in 1993."

A number of Hollywood films have been shot here, not just Conroy's. "The beautiful white house on the Point was called the 'Big Santini House' until the next movie was shot and now it is known as 'The Big Chill House.' If a third movie was made there, it would have a new name.

"One of the great glories of Beaufort is found on St. Helena Island," he said. "You get on Martin Luther King Jr. Boulevard and take a right at the Red Piano Too Art Gallery to the Penn Center. Before making the right turn, on the left, in what was the Bishop family's general store, is Gullah Grub, one of the few restaurants that serve legitimate Gullah food."

He continued: "At the end of St. Helena, toward the beach, take Seaside Road. You will be in the midst of the Gullah culture. You end up driving down a dirt road and then an extraordinary avenue of oaks that leads to the Coffin Point Plantation, which was the house where Sally Field raised Forrest Gump as a boy."

sandwiches, and curried chicken salad. **Known for:** raw bar; inventive burgers, sandwiches for lunch; sophisticated dinner menu. $ *Average main: $22* ✉ *904 Bay St., Downtown Historic District* ☎ *843/525–1946* 🌐 *www.plumsrestaurant.com.*

★ Fodor's Choice ✕ **Saltus River Grill.** *American.* The hippest eatery in Beaufort, Saltus River Grill wins over diners with its sailing motifs, breezy patio, and modern Southern menu. The bar opens at 4 pm, as does the raw bar with its tempting array of oysters and sushi specials. **Known for:** signature she-crab soup; steaks, seafood, and sushi; breathtaking views. $ *Average main: $32* ✉ *802 Bay St., Downtown Historic District* ☎ *843/379–3474* 🌐 *www.saltusrivergrill.com* ⏲ *No lunch.*

$$$$

Even though accommodations in Beaufort have increased in number, prime lodgings can fill up fast, so do call ahead.

$$$ ⊠ **Beaufort Inn.** *B&B/Inn.* This 1890s Victorian inn charms you with its handsome gables and wraparound verandas. **Pros:** in the heart of the historic district; beautifully landscaped space. **Cons:** atmosphere in the main building may feel too dated for those seeking a more contemporary hotel; no water views. Ⓢ *Rooms from: $209 ⊠ 809 Port Republic St., Downtown Historic District ☎ 843/379–4667 ⊕ www. beaufortinn.com ⤙ 32 rooms, 4 apartments ⦿ Breakfast.*

$$$ ⊠ **Beaulieu House.** *B&B/Inn.* From the French for "beautiful place," Beaulieu House is the only waterfront bed-and-breakfast in Beaufort on Cat Island—it's a quiet, relaxing inn with airy rooms decorated in Caribbean colors. **Pros:** great views; scrumptious gourmet hot breakfast; short drive to Beaufort historic district. **Cons:** thin walls; hot water can be a problem; a bit off the beaten path. Ⓢ *Rooms from: $205 ⊠ 3 Sheffield Ct. ☎ 843/770–0303 ⊕ beaulieuhouse. com ⤙ 5 rooms ⦿ Breakfast.*

$$ ⊠ **Best Western Sea Island Inn.** *Hotel.* This well-maintained motel in the heart of the Historic District puts you within walking distance of many shops and restaurants. **Pros:** only swimming pool in downtown Beaufort; directly across from marina and an easy walk to art galleries and restaurants; breakfast included. **Cons:** air-conditioning is loud in some rooms; breakfast room can be noisy. Ⓢ *Rooms from: $179 ⊠ 1015 Bay St. ☎ 843/522–2090 ⊕ www.sea-island-inn.com ⤙ 43 rooms ⦿ Breakfast.*

$$ ⊠ **City Loft Hotel.** *Hotel.* This 1960s-era motel was cleverly transformed by its hip, young owners to reflect their high-tech, minimalist style. **Pros:** stylish decor; use of the adjacent gym; very accommodating staff. **Cons:** the sliding Asian screen that separates the bathroom doesn't offer full privacy; no lobby or public spaces. Ⓢ *Rooms from: $189 ⊠ 301 Carteret St., Downtown Historic District ☎ 843/379–5638 ⊕ www.citylofthotel.com ⤙ 22 rooms ⦿ No meals.*

$$$ ⊠ **Cuthbert House Inn.** *B&B/Inn.* Named after the original Scottish owners, who made their money in cotton and indigo, this 1790 home is filled with 18th- and 19th-century heirlooms and retains the original Federal fireplaces and crown and rope molding. **Pros:** owners are accommodating; complimentary wine and hors d'oeuvres service; great walk-about location. **Cons:** some furnishings are a bit busy; some artificial flower arrangements; stairs creak. Ⓢ *Rooms*

The World of Gullah

In the Lowcountry, Gullah refers to several things: a language, a people, and a culture. Gullah (the word itself is believed to be derived from *Angola*), an English-based dialect rooted in African languages, is the unique language, more than 300 years old, of the African Americans of the Sea Islands of South Carolina and Georgia. Most locally born African Americans of the area can understand, if not speak, Gullah.

Descended from thousands of slaves who were imported by planters in the Carolinas during the 18th century, the Gullah people have maintained not only their dialect but also their heritage. Much of Gullah culture traces back to the African rice-coast culture and survives today in the art forms and skills, including sweetgrass basket making, of Sea Islanders. During the colonial period, when rice was king, Africans from the West African rice kingdoms drew high premiums as slaves. Those with basket-making skills were extremely valuable because baskets were needed for agricultural and household use. Made by hand, sweetgrass baskets are intricate coils of marsh grass with a sweet, haylike aroma.

Nowhere is Gullah culture more evident than in the foods of the region. Rice appears at nearly every meal—Africans taught planters how to grow rice and how to cook and serve it as well. Lowcountry dishes use okra, peanuts, *benne* (a word of African origin for sesame seeds), field peas, and hot peppers. Gullah food reflects the bounty of the islands: shrimp, crabs, oysters, fish, and such vegetables as greens, tomatoes, and corn. Many dishes are prepared in one pot, a method similar to the stewpot cooking of West Africa.

On St. Helena Island, near Beaufort, Penn Center is the unofficial Gullah headquarters, preserving the culture and developing opportunities for Gullahs. In 1852 the first school for freed slaves was established at Penn Center. You can delve into the culture further at the York W. Bailey Museum.

On St. Helena, many Gullahs still go shrimping with hand-tied nets, harvest oysters, and grow their own vegetables. Nearby on Daufuskie Island, as well as on Edisto, Wadmalaw, and John's islands near Charleston, you can find Gullah communities. A famous Gullah proverb says, *If oonuh ent kno weh oonuh dah gwine, oonuh should kno weh oonuh come f'um.* Translation: If you don't know where you're going, you should know where you've come from.

8

CONROY'S FRIPP ISLAND

"What has Fripp Island meant to me?" Pat Conroy, one of the Lowcountry's famous writers, answered: "The year was 1964. I was living in Beaufort. And when the bridge to Fripp Island was built, I was a senior in high school. My English teacher *and* my chemistry teacher moonlighted as the island's first security guards. It was a pristine island; there were no houses on it yet, and it was as beautiful as any desert island.

"In 1978, my mother moved over there, and all our summers were spent on the island. It was to be her last home. That sealed the island in our family's history. In 1989, I bought a house there, both because it is a private island and thus good for a writer, but also so that our family—my brothers and sisters—could always have a home on Fripp to come to."

from: $225 ⊠ *1203 Bay St., Downtown Historic District* ☎ *843/521–1315* ⊕ *www.cuthberthouseinn.com* ⇨ *7 rooms, 3 suites* ♦O♦ *Breakfast.*

$$ ▢ **Two Suns Inn.** *B&B/Inn.* With its unobstructed bay views and wraparound veranda complete with porch swing, this historic home—built in 1917 by an immigrant Lithuanian merchant—offers a distinctive Beaufort experience. **Pros:** most appealing is the Charleston room, with its own screened-porch and water views; it's truly peaceful. **Cons:** decor is unsophisticated; although on Bay Street it's a bike ride or short drive downtown; third-floor skylight room is cheapest but least desirable. ⓢ *Rooms from: $169* ⊠ *1705 Bay St., Downtown Historic District* ☎ *843/522–1122, 800/532–4244* ⊕ *www.twosunsinn.com* ⇨ *6 rooms* ♦O♦ *Breakfast.*

FRIPP ISLAND

$$$$ ▢ **Fripp Island Resort.** *Resort.* On the island made famous in
FAMILY *Prince of Tides,* with 3½ miles of broad, white beach and unspoiled scenery, this resort has long been known as one of the more affordable and casual on the island. **Pros:** fun for all ages; the beach bar has great frozen drinks and live music; two golf courses: Ocean Creek and Ocean Point. **Cons:** far from Beaufort; some dated decor; could use another restaurant with contemporary cuisine. ⓢ *Rooms from: $374* ⊠ *1 Tarpon Blvd., Fripp Island* ✢ *19 miles south of Beaufort* ☎ *855/602–5893* ⊕ *www.frippislandresort.com* ⇨ *210 units* ♦O♦ *No meals.*

PRIVATE VILLAS ON FRIPP ISLAND

There are more than 200 private villas for rent on Fripp Island (but no hotels). Fripp Island Golf & Beach Resort (⊕ *www.frippislandresort.com*) offers a range of rental options, including homes, villas, and golf cottages, many with oceanfront or golf views.

NIGHTLIFE AND PERFORMING ARTS

Emily's. This fun hangout is populated with locals who graze on tapas while eyeing one of the four wide-screen TVs. The piano sits idle until a random patron sits down and impresses the crowd. The bar is full of local characters. There is a separate dining room. ⊠ *906 Port Republic St., Downtown Historic District* ☎ *843/522–1866* ⊕ *www. emilysrestaurantandtapasbar.com.*

Luther's. A late-night waterfront hangout, Luther's is casual and fun, with a young crowd watching the big-screen TVs or dancing to rock music live bands on Thursday, Friday, and Saturday nights. Luther's also has a terrific late-night menu. The decor features exposed brick, pine paneling, and old-fashioned posters on the walls. ⊠ *910 Bay St., Downtown Historic District* ☎ *843/521–1888.*

SPORTS AND THE OUTDOORS

BEACHES

★ FodorsChoice **Hunting Island State Park.** This secluded park 18 FAMILY miles southeast of Beaufort has 4 miles of public beaches— some dramatically eroding. The light sand beach decorated with driftwood and the subtropical vegetation is breathtaking. The state park was founded in 1938 to preserve and promote the area's natural wonders, and it harbors 5,000 acres of rare maritime forests. You can kayak in the tranquil lagoon; stroll the 1,300-foot-long fishing pier (among the longest on the East Coast); and go fishing or crabbing. For sweeping views, climb the 167 steps of the 1859 **Hunting Island Lighthouse.** Bikers and hikers can enjoy 8 miles of trails. The nature center has exhibits, an aquarium, and lots of turtles; there is a resident alligator in the pond. **Amenities:** none. **Best for:** solitude; sunrise; swimming; walking. ⊠ *2555 Sea Island Pkwy., St. Helena Island* ☎ *866/345–7275* ⊕ *www.southcarolinaparks.com* ☞ *$5.*

8

BIKING

Beaufort looks different from two wheels. In town, traffic is moderate, and you can cruise along the waterfront and through the historic district. However, if you ride on the sidewalks or after dark without a headlight and a rear red reflector, you run the risk of a city fine of nearly $150. If you stopped for happy hour and come out as the light is fading, walk your bike back "home." Some inns lend or rent out bikes to guests, but alas, they may not be in great shape and usually were not the best even when new.

FAMILY **Lowcountry Bicycles.** If you want a decent set of wheels, contact Lowcountry Bicycles. Bikes are $8 an hour or $25 a day. ⊠ *102 Sea Island Pkwy.* ☎ *843/524–9585* ⊕ *www. lowcountrybicycles.com.*

BOATING

Beaufort is where the Ashepoo, Combahee, and Edisto rivers form the A.C.E. Basin, a vast wilderness of marshes and tidal estuaries loaded with history. For sea kayaking, tourists meet at the designated launching areas for fully guided, two-hour tours.

FAMILY **Barefoot Bubba's.** Less than 1 mile from Hunting Island, Barefoot Bubba's rents bikes and kayaks and will deliver them to the park or anywhere in the area. ⊠ *2135 Sea Island Pkwy., St. Helena Island* ☎ *843/838–9222* ⊕ *barefootbubbasurfshop.com.*

★ Fodor'sChoice **Beaufort Kayak Tours.** Owner-operators Kim and
FAMILY David Gundler of Beaufort Kayak Tours are degreed naturalists and certified historical guides. The large cockpits in the kayaks make for easy accessibility and the tours go with the tides, not against them, so paddling isn't strenuous. The tours meet at various public landings throughout Beaufort County. ☎ *843/525–0810* ⊕ *www.beaufortkayaktours.com* ⊡ *$50.*

GOLF

Most golf courses are about a 10- to 20-minute scenic drive from Beaufort.

Dataw Island. This upscale island community is home to Tom Fazio's Cotton Dike golf course, with spectacular marsh views, and Arthur Hill's Morgan River golf course, with ponds, marshes, and wide-open fairways. The lovely 14th hole of the latter overlooks the river. To play you must be accompanied by a member or belong to another private club. ⊠ *100 Dataw Club Rd., Dataw Island* ✛ *6*

Sea Monkeys

There is a colony of monkeys living on Morgan Island, a little isle near Fripp Island. If you are in a boat cruising or on a fishing charter and think you might be seeing monkeys running on the beach, you are not hallucinating from sun exposure. The state of South Carolina leases one of these tiny islands to raise monkeys, both those that are used for medical research and also rare golden rhesus monkeys sold as exotic pets. This deserted island and the subtropical climate and vegetation have proved ideal for their breeding. But you can't land on the island or feed the monkeys, so bring binoculars or a long-lens camera.

miles east of Beaufort ☎ 843/838–8250 ⊕ www.dataw.org ⚲ $69–$120 ⚘ Cotton Dike: 18 holes, 6787 yards, par 72. Morgan River: 18 holes, 6657 yards, par 72.

Fripp Island Golf & Beach Resort. This resort has a pair of championship courses. Ocean Creek Golf Course, designed by Davis Love, has sweeping views of saltwater marshes. Designed by George Cobb, Ocean Point Golf Links runs alongside the ocean the entire way. This is a wildlife refuge, so you'll see plenty of animals, particularly the graceful marsh deer. In fact, the wildlife and ocean views may make it difficult for you to keep your eyes on the ball. To play, nonguests must belong to a private golf club. ⊠ 2119 Sea Island Pkwy., Fripp Island ☎ 843/838–3535, 843/838–1576 ⊕ www.frippislandresort.com ⚲ $75–$99 ⚘ Ocean Creek: 18 holes, 6613 yards, par 71. Ocean Point: 18 holes, 6556 yards, par 72.

Sanctuary Golf Club at Cat Island. This is a semiprivate club, so members get priority. Its scenic course is considered tight with plenty of water hazards. ⊠ Cat Island, 8 Waveland Ave. ☎ 843/524–0300 ⊕ catislandssanctuarygolf.com ⚲ $40–$80 ⚘ 18 holes, 6673 yards, par 72.

SHOPPING

ART GALLERIES

★ Fodor'sChoice **Red Piano Too Gallery.** More than 150 Lowcountry artists are represented at the Red Piano Too Gallery, considered one of the area's best (if not the best) art spaces. It carries folk art, books, fine art, and much more.

8

Much of the art at the gallery represents the Gullah culture. ✉ *870 Sea Island Pkwy., St. Helena Island* ☎ *843/838–2241* ⊕ *redpianotoo.com.*

Rhett Gallery. The Rhett Gallery sells Lowcountry art by four generations of the Rhett family, including remarkable wood carvings. There are also antique maps, books, Civil War memorabilia, and Audubon prints. ✉ *901 Bay St., Downtown Historic District* ☎ *843/524–3339* ⊕ *rhettgallery.com.*

DAUFUSKIE ISLAND

13 miles (approximately 45 minutes) from Hilton Head via ferry.

From Hilton Head you can take a 45-minute ferry ride to nearby Daufuskie Island, the setting for Pat Conroy's novel *The Water Is Wide,* which was made into the movie *Conrack.* The boat ride may very well be one of the highlights of your vacation. The Lowcountry beauty unfolds before you, as pristine and unspoiled as you can imagine. The island is in the Atlantic, nestled between Hilton Head and Savannah. Many visitors do come just for the day, to play golf and have lunch or dinner; kids might enjoy biking or horseback riding. On weekends, the tiki hut at Freeport Marina whirrs out frozen concoctions as a vocalist sings or a band plays blues and rock and roll. The island also has acres of unspoiled beauty. On a bike, in a golf cart, on horseback, you can easily explore the island. You will find remnants of churches, homes, and schools—some reminders of antebellum times. Guided tours include such sights as an 18th-century cemetery, former slave quarters, a "praise house," an 1886 African Baptist church, the schoolhouse where Pat Conroy taught, and the Haig Point Lighthouse. There are a number of small, artsy shops like the Iron Fish Gallery.

GETTING HERE AND AROUND

The only way to get to Daufuskie is by boat, as it is a bridgeless island. The public ferry departs from Broad Creek Marina on Hilton Head Island several times a day. On arrival to Daufuskie you can rent a golf cart (not a car) or bicycle or take a tour. Golf carts are the best way to get around the island. Enjoy Daufuskie (⊕ *enjoydaufuskie.com*) offers golf cart rentals to tourists when they come to visit. If you are coming to Daufuskie Island for a multiday stay with luggage and/or groceries, and perhaps a dog, be absolutely certain that you allow a full hour to park and check in for the ferry, particularly on a busy summer weekend. Whether you are staying on island or just day-tripping, the ferry costs $34 round-trip. Usually the first two pieces of luggage are free, and then it is $10 apiece.

TOURS

Freeport Marina, where the public ferry disembarks on Daufuskie Island, includes the Freeport General Store, a restaurant, overnight cabins, and more. A two-hour bus tour of the island by local historians will become a true travel memory. The ferry returns to Hilton Head Island on Tuesday night in time to watch the fireworks at Shelter Cove at sundown.

Live Oac, based on Hilton Head, is an owner-operated company that offers Lowcountry water adventures such as nature tours, fishing excursions, and dolphin cruises. On its first-class hurricane-deck boats you are sheltered from sun and rain; tours, usually private charters, are limited to six people. Captains are interpretive naturalist educators and U.S. Coast Guard licensed.

Take a narrated horse-drawn carriage tour of historic Beaufort with Southurn Rose Buggy Tours and learn about the city's fascinating history and its antebellum and Victorian architecture.

Tour Contacts **Live Oac.** ✉ *43 Jenkins Rd., North End* ☎ *888/254–8362* 🌐 *www.liveoac.com.* **Southurn Rose Buggy Tours.** ✉ *1002 Bay St., Downtown Historic District* ☎ *843/524–2900* 🌐 *www.southurnrose.com.*

8

WHERE TO EAT

$$ FAMILY ✕ **Old Daufuskie Crab Company Restaurant.** *Seafood.* This outpost, with its rough-hewn tables facing the water, serves up surprisingly good fare. The specialties are deviled crab and chicken salad on buttery grilled rolls; many diners also enjoy the Lowcountry buffet with its pulled pork and sides like butter beans and potato salad. **Known for:** incredible sunsets; colorful bar; reggae and rock music. [$] *Average main: $17* ✉ *Freeport Marina, 1 Cooper River Landing Rd.* ☎ *843/342–8687* 🌐 *www.enjoydaufuskie.com/daufuskie-crab-company.*

WHERE TO STAY

$$$$ **Sandy Lane Villas.** *Rental.* A luxurious, oceanfront low-rise condominium complex, the twin Sandy Lane Villas buildings look out to the simple boardwalk that leads directly to a nearly deserted beach. **Pros:** spacious and private; unobstructed ocean views. **Cons:** not a homey beach cottage; 20 minutes from Freeport Marina. [$] *Rooms from: $475* ✉ *Sandy Lane Villas, 2302 Sandy La.* ☎ *843/785–8021* 🌐 *www.daufuskieislandrentals.com* 🛏 *32 villas* 🍴 *No meals.*

TRAVEL SMART
CHARLESTON

GETTING HERE AND AROUND

When you're headed to Charleston, you can fly into Charleston International Airport or one of the nearby private airports. The city is reachable by train or bus as well, but you'll certainly need a car if you want to explore beyond the historic downtown, where it's more convenient to get around on foot. Taxis or pedicabs can take you around the city and may be more convenient than driving, especially if your lodging offers free parking.

If Hilton Head is your destination, choose between the Savannah/Hilton Head Island International Airport or the smaller Hilton Head Island Airport. You'll need a car to get around if you want to explore more of the island.

▌ AIR TRAVEL

Charleston International Airport is served by Alaska, Allegiant, American Airlines, Delta, Frontier, Jet-Blue, Southwest, and United. You'll find more frequent flights in high season.

Airlines and Airports Airline and Airport Links.com. ⊕ *www.airline-andairportlinks.com.*

Airline-Security Issues Transportation Security Administration. ☎ *866/289–9673* ⊕ *www.tsa.gov.*

AIRPORTS

Charleston International Airport is about 12 miles west of downtown. Charleston Executive Airport on John's Island is used by noncommercial aircraft, as is Mount Pleasant Regional Airport.

Airport Information Charleston Executive Airport. ⊠ *2742 Fort Trenholm Rd., Johns Island* ☎ *843/559–2401, 843/746–7600* ⊕ *www.atlanticaviation.com.* **Charleston International Airport.** ⊠ *5500 International Blvd., North Charleston* ☎ *843/767–7000* ⊕ *www.iflychs.com.* **Mount Pleasant Regional Airport.** ⊠ *700 Faison Rd., Mount Pleasant* ☎ *843/884–8837.*

GROUND TRANSPORTATION

Several cab companies serve the airport. Most companies, including Yellow Cab, average $25. Green Taxi, which offers hybrid vehicles, charges a minimum of $45 for an airport run. To ride in style, book a limo or other luxury vehicle through Charleston Black Cab Company or Charleston Downtown Limo.

Charleston International Airport Ground Transportation arranges shuttles for $14 per person to downtown. You can arrange to be picked up by the same service when returning to the airport by making a reservation with the driver.

Airport Transfers Charleston Black Cab Company. ☎ *843/216–2627* ⊕ *charlestonblackcabcompany.com.* **Charleston Downtown Limo.** ☎ *843/723–1111, 843/973–0990* ⊕ *charlestondowntownlimo.com.* **Charleston International Airport Ground Transportation.** ⊠ *5500*

International Blvd., North Charleston
☎ 843/767–7026 ⊕ www.chs-air-
port.com.

▌ BOAT AND FERRY TRAVEL

Boaters—many traveling the intracoastal waterway—dock at Ashley Marina and City Marina, in
Charleston Harbor. The Charleston Water Taxi is a delightful way
to travel between Charleston and
Mount Pleasant. Some people take
the $12 round-trip journey just for
fun. It departs from the Charleston
Maritime Center. Do not confuse
its address at 10 Wharfside as being
near the area of Adger's Wharf,
which is on the lower peninsula.
The water taxi departs daily every
hour from 9 am to 8 pm daily from
mid-March to mid-November; 10
am to 6 pm Saturday only from
mid-November to December 26;
10 am to 6 pm December 26–31;
and 10 am to 6 pm Saturday only
from January 1 to mid-March. It
also offers dolphin cruises and harbor boat rides.

**Boat and Ferry Contacts Ashley
Marina.** ✉ 33 Lockwood Dr., Medical University of South Carolina
☎ 843/722–1996 ⊕ www.theharbor-
ageatashleymarina.com. **Charleston
City Marina.** ✉ 17 Lockwood Dr.,
Medical University of South Carolina
☎ 843/723–5098 ⊕ www.charleston-
citymarina.com. **Charleston Water
Taxi.** ✉ Charleston Maritime Center,
10 Wharfside St., Ansonborough
☎ 843/330–2989 ⊕ www.charleston-
watertaxi.com.

▌ CAR TRAVEL

You'll probably need a car in
Charleston if you plan on visiting
destinations outside the city's Historic District or have your heart
set on trips to Walterboro, Edisto
Island, Beaufort, Bluffton, or Hilton Head.

Although you'll make the best
time traveling along the inter-
states, keep in mind that smaller
highways offer some delightful
scenery and the opportunity to
stumble upon funky roadside diners, leafy state parks, and historic
town squares. The area is rural, but
it's still populated, so you'll rarely
drive for more than 20 or 30 miles
without passing roadside services,
such as gas stations, restaurants,
and ATMs.

GASOLINE

Gas stations are not hard to find,
either in the city limits or in the
outlying areas. Prices are charac-
teristically less expensive than up
north. Similarly, outside Charleston, in North Charleston and the
suburbs, gas is usually cheaper than
at the few gas stations downtown.

PARKING

Parking within Charleston's Historic District can be difficult. Street
parking can be aggravating, as
meter readers are among the city's
most efficient public servants. Public parking garages are $1 per hour,
with a $16 maximum per day.
Some private parking garages and
lots charge around $2 for the first
hour and then $1 for each addi-
tional hour; the less expensive
ones charge a maximum of $10 to

$12 a day if you park overnight. Some private lots charge a flat rate of around $10 per day, so it's the same price whether you're there 45 minutes or six hours. Most of the hotels charge a valet-parking fee.

RENTAL CARS

All of the major car-rental companies are represented in Charleston, either at the airport or in town. Enterprise has both an airport and a downtown location, good prices, and will pick you up.

RENTAL CAR INSURANCE

Everyone who rents a car wonders whether the insurance that the rental companies offer is worth the expense. No one—including us—has a simple answer. If you own a car, your personal auto insurance may cover a rental to some degree; always read your policy's fine print. If you don't have auto insurance, then seriously consider buying the collision- or loss-damage waiver (CDW or LDW) from the car-rental company, which eliminates your liability for damage to the car. Some credit cards offer CDW coverage, but it's usually supplemental to your own insurance and rarely covers SUVs, minivans, luxury models, and the like. If your coverage is secondary, you may still be liable for loss-of-use costs from the car-rental company. But no credit-card insurance is valid unless you use that card for *all* transactions, from reserving to paying the final bill. It's sometimes cheaper to buy insurance as part of your general travel insurance policy.

ROADSIDE EMERGENCIES

Discuss with the rental agency what to do in the case of an emergency, as this sometimes differs between companies, and make sure you understand what your insurance covers. It's a good rule of thumb to let someone at your accommodation know where you are heading and when you plan to return. Keep emergency numbers with you, just in case.

ROADS

Interstate 26 traverses the state from northwest to southeast and terminates at Charleston. U.S. 17, the coastal road, also passes through Charleston. Interstate 526, also called the Mark Clark Expressway, runs primarily east–west, connecting the West Ashley area, North Charleston, Daniel Island, and Mount Pleasant.

▮ CRUISE SHIP TRAVEL

Cruise ships sailing from Charleston depart from the Union Pier Terminal, which is in Charleston's historic district. If you are driving, however, and need to leave your car for the duration of your cruise, take the East Bay Street exit off the new, majestic Ravenel Bridge on Interstate 17 and follow the "Cruise Ship" signs. On ship embarkation days police officers will direct you to the ship terminal from the intersection of East Bay and Chapel streets. Cruise parking is located adjacent to Union Pier.

Information Port of Charleston.
✉ *Union Pier, 280 Concord St., Market* ☎ *843/958–8298 for cruise*

information ⊕ www.port-of-charles-ton.com.

AIRPORT TRANSFERS
Several cab companies service the airport; expect to pay between $25 and $35 for a trip downtown. Airport Ground Transportation arranges shuttles, which cost $12 to $15 per person to the downtown area, double for a return trip to the airport. CARTA's bus No. 11, a public bus, now goes to the airport for a mere $1.75; it leaves downtown from the Meeting/Mary Street parking garage every 50 minutes, from 5:45 am until 11:09 pm.

PARKING
Parking costs $17 per day ($119 per week) for regular vehicles, $40 per day ($280 per week) for RVs or other vehicles more than 20 feet long. A free shuttle bus takes you to the cruise-passenger terminal. Be sure to drop your large luggage off at Union Pier before you park your car; only carry-on-size luggage is allowed on the shuttle bus, so if you have any bags larger than 22 inches by 14 inches, they will have to be checked before you park. Also, you'll need your cruise tickets to board the shuttle bus.

▌ PUBLIC TRANSPORTATION

The Charleston Area Regional Transportation Authority, the city's public bus system, takes passengers around the city and to the suburbs. Bus 11, which goes to the airport, is convenient for travelers. CARTA buses go to James Island, West Ash-ley, and Mount Pleasant. From Mount Pleasant you can catch CARTA's Flex Service to the beach at Sullivan's Island for $3.

CARTA operates DASH, which runs free buses that look like vintage trolleys along three downtown routes that crisscross at Marion Square.

Contacts Charleston Area Regional Transportation Authority (*CARTA*). ✉ *Downtown Historic District* ☎ *843/724–7420* ⊕ *www. ridecarta.com.*

▌ TAXI AND PEDICAB TRAVEL

Circling the Historic District, pedicabs are a fun way to get around in the evening, especially if you are barhopping. Three can squeeze into one pedicab; the average cost is $5 per person for a 10-minute ride.

Contacts Bike Taxi. ☎ *843/532–8663* ⊕ *www.biketaxi.net.* **Charleston Green Taxi.** ☎ *843/819–0846* ⊕ *www.charlestongreentaxi.com.* **Charleston Pedicab.** ✉ *Market* ☎ *843/577–7088* ⊕ *pedicabcharleston.com.* **Charleston Rickshaw Company.** ☎ *843/723–5685* ⊕ *www. charlestonrickshaw.com.* **Metro Limo-Taxi.** ✉ *1949 Ivy Hall Rd., North Charleston* ☎ *843/572–5083.* **Yellow Cab of Charleston.** ☎ *843/577–6565* ⊕ *www.yellowcabofcharleston. com.*

▮ TRAIN TRAVEL

Amtrak has service from such major cities as New York, Philadelphia, Washington, Richmond, Savannah, and Miami. Taxis meet every train; a ride to downtown averages $35.

Contacts **Charleston Amtrak Station.** ✉ *4565 Gaynor Ave., North Charleston* ☎ *843/744–8264, 800/872–7245* ⊕ *www.amtrak.com.*

ESSENTIALS

▎ COMMUNICATIONS

INTERNET

Most area lodgings have in-room Wi-Fi for their guests. Internet cafés are rare, but many coffee shops have Wi-Fi available for free or a minimal fee.

Contacts Cybercafes. ⊕ *www.cybercafes.com.*

▎ EMERGENCIES

The Medical University of South Carolina Hospital and Roper Hospital have 24-hour emergency rooms. Rite Aid Pharmacy, across from MUSC, closes at 10 pm daily; on weekends the pharmacy counter closes at 8 pm.

Hospitals Medical University of South Carolina Hospital. ⊠ *171 Ashley Ave., Medical University of South Carolina* ☎ *843/792–2300* ⊕ *www.muschealth.com.* **Roper Hospital.** ⊠ *316 Calhoun St., Upper King* ☎ *843/724–2000* ⊕ *www.rsfh.com.*

Late-Night Pharmacy Rite Aid Pharmacy. ⊠ *261 Calhoun St., Upper King* ☎ *843/805–6022* ⊕ *www.riteaid.com.*

▎ HOURS OF OPERATION

Like most American cities, Charleston businesses generally operate on a 9-to-5 schedule. Shops downtown will often open at 10 am and close at 6 pm, with some conveniently staying open until 7.

Around the Market area, clothing stores stay open as late as 9, and candy shops and souvenir stores may remain open even later.

▎ MAIL

The main post office is downtown on Broad Street, and there is a major branch in West Ashley. For overnight shipping, FedEx and the UPS Store have downtown branches.

Post Offices Downtown Station. ⊠ *83 Broad St., South of Broad* ☎ *803/926–6354* ⊕ *www.usps.com.* **West Ashley Station.** ⊠ *78 Sycamore St., West Ashley* ☎ *803/926– 6354* ⊕ *www.usps.com.*

Parcel Shipping FedEx. ⊠ *73 St. Philip St., Upper King* ☎ *843/723– 5130* ⊕ *www.fedex.com.* **UPS Store Downtown Charleston.** ⊠ *164 Market St., Mount Pleasant* ☎ *843/723– 1220* ⊕ *charleston-sc-2386. theupsstorelocal.com.* **UPS Store Mount Pleasant.** ⊠ *1000 Johnnie Dodds Blvd., Suite 103, Mount Pleasant* ☎ *843/856–9099* ⊕ *www. theupsstorelocal.com/2130* ⊠ *1643 Savannah Hwy., Suite B, West Ashley* ☎ *843/763–6894* ⊕ *www.theupsstorelocal.com/2114.*

▎ MONEY

As in most cities, banks are open weekdays 9 to 5. There are countless branches in the downtown area, all with ATMs.

CREDIT CARDS

Reporting Lost Cards American Express. ☎ *800/528–4800* ⊕ *www. americanexpress.com.* **MasterCard.** ☎ *800/627–8372* ⊕ *www.mastercard. com.* **Visa.** ☎ *800/847–2911* ⊕ *www. visa.com.*

▌ SAFETY

Downtown Charleston is considered a very safe area. Historic District (from Broad Street, to Upper King Street, Mary Street, and slightly beyond) is bustling until midnight during the week and later on weekends. A lot of late-night crime is directed at those who drink too much, so if you'd had a few you might consider taking a taxi to your hotel. Lock your car doors, and don't leave valuables in sight.

▌TIP→ **Distribute your cash, credit cards, IDs, and other valuables between a deep front pocket, an inside jacket or vest pocket, and a hidden money pouch. Don't reach for the money pouch once you're in public.**

▌ TAXES

In Charleston, sales tax on most purchases is 8.5%. Hotels are taxed at 13.5% (12.5% in Mount Pleasant). In Charleston area restaurants, the tax is 10.5% for food, beer, and wine.

▌ TIPPING

In upscale restaurants, tip 15% to 20%. In less expensive family restaurants, 15% is the norm. For taxis, a tip of 10% to 15% is typical. Passengers are often more generous in pedicabs, as the drivers are working up a sweat.

▌ TOURS

In a city known for being pedestrian-friendly, walking tours around Charleston are very popular. Many newcomers opt for horse-and-buggy tours, mostly on large wagons holding a dozen or so people, but private horse-drawn carriage trips by day or night are definitely a romantic option.

BICYCLE TOURS

Charleston has relatively flat terrain—they don't call this the Lowcountry for nothing—so a bicycle is a pleasant way to explore the region. The affable owners of Charleston Bicycle Tours lead a maximum of a dozen people on a variety of trips.

Contacts **Charleston Bicycle Tours.** ⊠ *164 Market St., Suite 104, Downtown Historic District* ☎ *843/881–9878* ⊕ *charlestonbicycletours.com.*

BOAT TOURS

Charleston Harbor Tours offers tours that give the history of the harbor. In business since 1908, the company offers a great overview of the areas. SpiritLine Cruises, which runs the ferry to Fort Sumter, also offers harbor tours and dinner cruises ($50 to $60). The dinner cruises leave from Patriots Point Marina in Mount Pleasant and include a three-course dinner and dancing to music by a local DJ. Sandlapper Tours focuses on regional history, coastal wildlife, and nocturnal ghostly lore. All harbor cruises range between

$20 and $50. On the 84-foot-tall schooner *Pride,* you can enjoy an eco-friendly sail and the natural sounds of Charleston Harbor on a two-hour harbor cruise, a dolphin cruise, a sunset cruise, or romantic full-moon sails. Tours range from $28 to $46.

Contacts Charleston Harbor Tours. ✉ *Charleston Maritime Center, 10 Wharfside St., Ansonborough* ☎ *843/722-1112* ⊕ *www.charlestonharbortours.com.* **Sandlapper Tours.** ✉ *Charleston Maritime Center, 10 Wharfside St., Ansonborough* ☎ *843/849-8687* ⊕ *www.sandlappertours.com.* **Schooner Pride.** ✉ *Aquarium Wharf, 360 Concord St., Ansonborough* ☎ *800/344-4483, 843/722-1112* ⊕ *www.schoonerpride.com.* **SpiritLine Cruises.** ✉ *Aquarium Wharf, 360 Concord St., Ansonborough* ☎ *843/722-2628* ⊕ *www.spiritlinecruises.com.*

BUS TOURS

Adventure Sightseeing leads bus tours of the Historic District. The Historic Charleston Foundation pairs local guides with visiting tour groups. Gullah Tours focuses on sights significant to African American culture. Tour guide Alfonso Brown is fluent in the Gullah language.

Contacts Adventure Sightseeing. ✉ *375 Meeting St., Downtown Historic District* ☎ *800/722-5394, 843/762-0088* ⊕ *www.adventuresightseeing.com.* **Gullah Tours.** ✉ *375 Meeting St., Market* ☎ *843/763-7551* ⊕ *www.gullahtours.com.* **Historic Charleston Foundation.** ✉ *188 Meeting St., Market* ☎ *843/723-1623 main office,*

843/722-3405 ticket office ⊕ *www.historiccharleston.org.* **Sites and Insights.** ☎ *843/552-9995* ⊕ *www.sitesandinsightstours.com.*

CARRIAGE TOURS

Carriage tours are a great way to see Charleston. The going rate is about $26 per person. Carolina Polo and Carriage Company, Old South Carriage Company, and Palmetto Carriage Works run horse-and mule-drawn carriage tours of the Historic District. Each follows one of four routes and lasts about one hour. Most carriages queue up at North Market and Anson streets. Carolina Polo and Carriage, which picks up passengers at the Doubletree Guest Suites Historic Charleston on Church Street, has an authentic carriage that is sought after for private tours and wedding parties. Palmetto Carriage Works offers free parking if you book ahead online.

Contacts Carolina Polo and Carriage Company. ✉ *DoubleTree by Hilton Historic District, 181 Church St., Market* ☎ *843/577-6767* ⊕ *www.cpcc.com.* **Old South Carriage Company.** ✉ *14 Anson St., Market* ☎ *843/723-9712* ⊕ *www.oldsouthcarriage.com.* **Palmetto Carriage Works.** ✉ *8 Guignard St., Market* ☎ *843/853-6125* ⊕ *www.palmettocarriage.com.*

ECOTOURS

Barrier Island Ecotours, at the Isle of Palms Marina, runs three-hour pontoon-boat tours to a barrier island. Coastal Expeditions has half-day and full-day naturalist-led kayak tours on local rivers.

Contacts Barrier Island Eco Tours. ✉ *Isle of Palms Marina, 50 41st Ave., Isle of Palms* ☎ *843/886–5000* ⊕ *www.nature-tours.com.* Fodor'sChoice **Coastal Expeditions.** ✉ *514-B Mill St., Mount Pleasant* ☎ *843/884–7684* ⊕ *www.coastalexpeditions.com.*

HELICOPTER TOURS

You can also fly high with helicopters, which offers exquisite views of the city. Tours with Fly In Helicopters start at $35 per person.

Contacts Fly In Helicopters. ✉ *40 Patriots Point Rd., Mount Pleasant* ☎ *843/373–8011* ⊕ *www.flyinhelicopters.com.*

PRIVATE GUIDES

The Charleston Convention & Visitors Bureau has a lengthy list of Charleston's best private tour guides. Charleston's Footprints tour routes can vary, but will wend approximately 16–18 blocks through the French Quarter, South of Broad, White Point Garden, and The Battery.

Contacts Charleston Footprints. ✉ *At Meeting and Chalmers Sts., Downtown Historic District* ☎ *843/478–4718* ⊕ *www.charleston-footprints.com.*

WALKING TOURS

Walking tours on various topics—horticulture, slavery, or women's history—are given by Bulldog Tours, which also has walks that explore the city's supernatural side. Listen to tales of lost souls with Ghosts of Charleston, which travel to historic graveyards.

Let Mary Coy, a fourth-generation Charlestonian and former teacher, bring the history and architecture of Charleston's back alleys and noble streets to life on her two-hour Charleston 101 Tour. Pay attention—there may be a quiz at the end.

Charleston Culinary Tours is a foodie adventure that stops at a variety of restaurants in the Historic District, where you'll experience the area's rich culinary history and Southern hospitality.

Contacts Bulldog Tours. ✉ *18 Anson St., Market* ☎ *843/722–8687* ⊕ *www.bulldogtours.com.* **Charleston Culinary Tours.** ☎ *843/259–2966* ⊕ *charlestonculinarytours.com.* **Charleston 101 Tours.** ✉ *Powder Magazine, 79 Cumberland St., Market* ✛ *1 block from City Market* ☎ *843/556–4753* ⊕ *www.charleston101tours.com.* **Tour Charleston.** ✉ *2A Cumberland St., Market* ☎ *843/723–1670* ⊕ *www.tourcharleston.com.*

▎ TRIP INSURANCE

Comprehensive travel policies let you cancel or cut your trip short because of a personal emergency or illness. Such policies also cover evacuation and medical care in case you are injured or become ill on your trip. Some also cover you for trip delays because of bad weather or mechanical problems as well as for lost or delayed baggage. Another type of coverage to look for is financial default—that is, when your trip is disrupted because a tour operator, airline, or cruise line goes out of business. Generally you must buy this when you book your trip or shortly thereafter.

Expect comprehensive travel insurance policies to cost about 4% to 7% or 8% of the total price of your trip (it's closer to 8% to 12% if you're over age 70). Always read the fine print of your policy to make sure that you are covered for the risks that are of most concern to you. Compare several policies to make sure you're getting the best price and range of coverage available.

■TIP→ When traveling to the Carolina Lowcountry during hurricane season, there's a chance that a severe storm will disrupt your plans. The solution? Look for hotels and resorts that let you rebook if a storm strikes.

Comprehensive Travel Insurers **Allianz Travel Insurance.** ☎ 866/884–3556 ⊕ www.allianz-travelinsurance.com. **CSA Travel Protection.** ☎ 800/873–9855 ⊕ www.csatravelprotection.com. **HTH Worldwide.** ☎ 610/254–8700 ⊕ hthworldwide.net. **Travel Guard.** ☎ 800/826–4919 ⊕ www.travel-guard.com. **Travel Insured International.** ☎ 800/243–3174 ⊕ www.travelinsured.com.

Insurance Comparison Sites **Insure My Trip.com.** ☎ 800/487–4722 ⊕ www.insuremytrip.com. **Square Mouth.com.** ☎ 800/240–0369 ⊕ www.squaremouth.com.

▌ VISITOR INFORMATION

The Charleston Area Convention & Visitors Bureau runs the Charleston Visitor Center, which has information about the city as well as Kiawah Island, Seabrook Island, Mount Pleasant, North Charleston, Edisto Island, Summerville, and the Isle of Palms. The Preservation Society of Charleston has information on house tours.

Contacts **Charleston Visitor Center.** ⊠ 375 Meeting St., Upper King ☎ 800/774–0006 ⊕ www.charlestoncvb.com. **Preservation Society of Charleston.** ⊠ 147 King St., Lower King ☎ 843/722–4630 ⊕ www.preservationsociety.org.

INDEX

PHOTO CREDITS

Fodor's InFocus CHARLESTON

Editorial: Douglas Stallings, *Editorial Director*; Margaret Kelly, Jacinta O'Halloran, *Senior Editors*; Kayla Becker, Alexis Kelly, Amanda Sadlowski, *Editors*; Teddy Minford, *Content Editor*; Rachael Roth, *Content Manager*

Design: Tina Malaney, *Design and Production Director*; Jessica Gonzalez, *Production Designer*

Photography: Jennifer Arnow, *Senior Photo Editor*

Maps: Rebecca Baer, *Senior Map Editor*; Mark Stroud (Moon Street Cartography), Ed Jacobus, and David Lindroth, *Cartographers*

Production: Jennifer DePrima, *Editorial Production Manager*; Carrie Parker, *Senior Production Editor*; Elyse Rozelle, *Production Editor*

Business & Operations: Chuck Hoover, *Chief Marketing Officer*; Joy Lai, *Vice President and General Manager*; Stephen Horowitz, *Director of Business Development and Revenue Operations*; Tara McCrillis, *Director of Publishing Operations*; Eliza D. Aceves, *Content Operations Manager and Strategist*

Public Relations and Marketing: Joe Ewaskiw, *Manager*; Esther Su, *Marketing Manager*

Writers: Stratton Lawrence, Sally Mahan

Editor: Rachael Roth

Production Editor: Carrie Parker

5th Edition

ISBN 978-1-64097-088-5

ISSN 1943–0167

SPECIAL SALES

This book is available at special discounts for bulk purchases for sales promotions or premiums. For more information, e-mail SpecialMarkets@fodors.com.

PRINTED IN THE UNITED STATES OF AMERICA

10 9 8 7 6 5 4 3 2 1

ABOUT OUR WRITERS

Stratton Lawrence settled in Charleston in 2003 after the rambling childhood of a Navy brat and a degree in history from Davidson College. A former staff writer at *Charleston City Paper*, he's a frequent contributor to *Charleston Magazine* and managing editor of the content marketing firm, Stone Temple. He lives with his family on Folly Beach, where he drew inspiration for his first book, *Images of America: Folly Beach*, released in 2013 by Arcadia Publishing. For this edition he updated the Where to Stay, Nightlife and the Arts, Where to Eat, Sports and the Outdoors, and Shopping chapters.

Sally Mahan is originally from Detroit. She fell in love with the Lowcountry several years ago when she moved to Savannah to work at *The Savannah Morning News*. She left the Lowcountry to work as an editor in Key West, and then went back to Michigan to work at *The Detroit Free Press*. However, her heart remained in the Lowcountry. In 2004, she settled in her adopted hometown of Bluffton, just minutes from Hilton Head Island. She updated the Hilton Head chapter and Travel Smart for this edition.

EUGENE FODOR

Hungarian-born Eugene Fodor (1905–91) began his travel career as an interpreter on a French cruise ship. The experience inspired him to write *On the Continent* (1936), the first guidebook to receive annual updates and discuss a country's way of life as well as its sights. Fodor later joined the U.S. Army and worked for the OSS in World War II. After the war, he kept up his intelligence work while expanding his guidebook series. During the Cold War, many guides were written by fellow agents who understood the value of insider information. Today's guides continue Fodor's legacy by providing travelers with timely coverage, insider tips, and cultural context.